PRAISE FOR

The Kneeling Man

A *Ms.* Most Anticipated Title of the Year
A *Library Journal* Best Book of the Year

"This untidy, honest, fascinating account compels the reader to reflect on profound questions of loyalty and race . . . All of us want to see our parents as heroes. It is to Ms. Seletzky's great credit that she explores the depths of her father's story with love, hope and critical realism."
—JOHNATHAN EIG, *The Wall Street Journal*

"*The Kneeling Man* is an impressive account of a man who began life in poverty, played a unique role in civil rights history, overcame precedent and prejudice in the Memphis Police Department, had a remarkable CIA career, and retired with dignity." —HAYDEN PEAKE, *Studies in Intelligence*

"*The Kneeling Man* portrays the legacy of a troubled time, at once an intimate family history and a chronicle of how race remains a sharp dividing line in American society." —DALE SINGER, *St. Louis Post-Dispatch*

"[Leta McCollough Seletzky] digs deep and casts wide. Part history, part memoir, part meditation on race and America, the book is a gripping account of a complicated city in a tumultuous moment, with implications into the present day." —ARAM GOUDSOUZIAN, *Chapter 16*

"An absorbing memoir . . . Seletzky's detailed yet fluid prose shapes her father's story into a compelling narrative arc—beginning with his birth in Mississippi and ending with his 1999 retirement from the CIA—while holding space for her to grapple with Mac's history as a Black man spying on Black Power activists for the police . . . *The Kneeling Man* will enlighten generations to come about a pivotal, disturbing moment in our nation's history."
—ALICE CARY, *BookPage* (starred review)

"Marrell 'Mac' McCollough, who had infiltrated a militant Black Power group, went on to become a CIA agent. He was allowed to tell his daughter who employed him, but not what his mission was. She saw him intermittently and only pieced together the story of his life in fits and starts over several years. Sometimes she was reluctant to know the full truth, but in the end she felt compelled to write an engrossing narrative that adumbrates the story of a life that becomes her own."

—CARL ROLLYSON, *The New York Sun*

"Powerful, well-organized, and fast-moving . . . Seletzky's compelling account of the story of the sanitation workers' strike, the Reverend King's profound leadership, and efforts to overcome racism in Memphis are richly enlightening and may help illuminate the underlying causes of the January 2023 Memphis police murder of Tyre Nichols." —*Booklist* (starred review)

"Get comfortable, because once you start reading you will not be able to put this book down. *The Kneeling Man* is a spellbinding account of a daughter piecing together her father's mysterious role witnessing the assassination of Martin Luther King Jr. With gorgeous prose and emotional honesty, Leta McCollough Seletzky brings us on her journey to uncover deeply hidden family secrets and to better understand our own."

—JENNIFER TAUB, author of *Big Dirty Money* and *Other People's Houses*

"*The Kneeling Man* is the heretofore unknown story of a chapter of United States history. It tells the life story of the author's father, Marrell 'Mac' McCollough, a witness to the assassination of Rev. Dr. Martin Luther King Jr. In the iconic photo of Dr. King lying on the balcony of the Lorraine Motel in a pool of his blood, the man kneeling beside him is Marrell McCollough. The backstory to this historical image is that Mr. McCollough was an undercover Memphis police officer working on a local Black militant group known as the Invaders. Mr. McCollough is one of those unsung American heroes whom history either ignores or has inadvertently forgotten. The telling of his unique story is inspiring and revelatory, from Mississippi childhood to the U.S. Army to the Memphis Police Department to the CIA. Mr. McCollough has lived the quintessential American life, not as a Black man but as an American. He is a true American hero! I wholeheartedly recommend Ms. Seletzky's wonderful, thought-provoking memoir of her father."

—RON STALLWORTH, author of *Black Klansman*

"*The Kneeling Man*, the captivating true story of Leta McCollough Seletzky's father, a Memphis police officer who witnessed the assassination of Rev. Dr. Martin Luther King Jr., is a spy thriller and an intimate family portrait set deep in the Jim Crow South and an extraordinary inquiry of the civil rights movement in Memphis. Seletzky's power is telling those details that bring the past into resonance, causing us to think and to feel in equal measure. Painstakingly researched and absolutely riveting, *The Kneeling Man* is one of those rare books that feels electric before you read the first page and long after you set it down. We'll be talking about this book for a long time."

—LAUREN HOUGH, author of *Leaving Isn't the Hardest Thing*

"Millions of people recognize the photo, but until now hardly anyone has known the incredibly fascinating life story of the man at the center of it: undercover cop and future CIA agent Marrell McCollough. His daughter Leta captures the complexity and humanity of her father's life in this deeply engrossing narrative, which is both an important work of history and an unforgettable family story."

—DAVID J. GARROW, Pulitzer Prize–winning author of *Bearing the Cross* and *The F.B.I. and Martin Luther King, Jr.*

"An important and moving book that everyone should read. Leta is a talent."

—MOLLY JONG-FAST, author of *The Social Climber's Handbook*

"In *The Kneeling Man*, Leta McCollough Seletzky mixes reportage with personal reflection, helping readers understand a famous photograph of the assassination of Martin Luther King by deftly exploring what exists outside the frame of the image. Through her deep dive into her father's connection to that photograph—and by engaging with the harsh realities of the Southern past and civil rights era—Seletzky links her present with her father's past by seeking to learn the truth about both, no matter how untidy or unpleasant that might be. This is a brave book."

—W. RALPH EUBANKS, author of *A Place Like Mississippi* and *Ever Is a Long Time*

"A searing portrait of a man divided between his country and his identity. At once historical and timely, Seletzky gifts us a captivating, charged, and wholly nuanced narrative that grips you from the first page and does not let go."

—MARGARET WILKERSON SEXTON, author of *A Kind of Freedom* and *On the Rooftop*

The Kneeling Man

My Father's Life as a Black Spy Who Witnessed the Assassination of Martin Luther King Jr.

Leta McCollough Seletzky

Counterpoint
Berkeley, California

This is a work of nonfiction. However, some correspondences and documents have been shortened for clarity, and some dialogue has been reconstructed from memory.

First Counterpoint edition: 2023
First paperback edition: 2024

The Library of Congress has cataloged the hardcover edition as follows:
Names: Seletzky, Leta McCollough, author.
Title: The kneeling man : my father's life as a Black spy who witnessed the assassination of Martin Luther King Jr. / Leta McCollough Seletzky.
Other titles: My father's life as a Black spy who witnessed the assassination of Martin Luther King Jr.
Description: First Counterpoint edition. | Berkeley : Counterpoint, 2023.
Identifiers: LCCN 2022047271 | ISBN 9781640094727 (hardcover) | ISBN 9781640094734 (ebook)
Subjects: LCSH: McCollough, Marrell, 1944– | Invaders (Black Power Group)—History. | Police—Tennessee—Memphis—Biography. | Undercover operations—Tennessee—Memphis. | King, Martin Luther, Jr., 1929-1968—Assassination. | United States. Central Intelligence Agency—Officials and employees—Biography. | African Americans—Tennessee—Memphis—Social conditions—20th century. | Memphis (Tenn.)—Race relations—History—20th century. | Seletzky, Leta McCollough. | Memphis (Tenn.)—Biography.
Classification: LCC F444.M553 M336 2023 | DDC 976.8/19092 [B]—dc23/eng/20221005
LC record available at https://lccn.loc.gov/2022047271

Paperback ISBN: 978-1-64009-641-7

Cover design by Steve Leard
Cover photograph © Joseph Louw
Book design by Jordan Koluch

COUNTERPOINT
2560 Ninth Street, Suite 318
Berkeley, CA 94710
www.counterpointpress.com

Printed in the United States of America
10 9 8 7 6 5 4 3 2 1

This project is supported in part by an award from the National Endowment for the Arts.

For Dad, Ma, Grandma, and Granddaddy

And on Dad's behalf, for his children and grandchildren,
and his siblings, and his first cousin Jesse McCullar

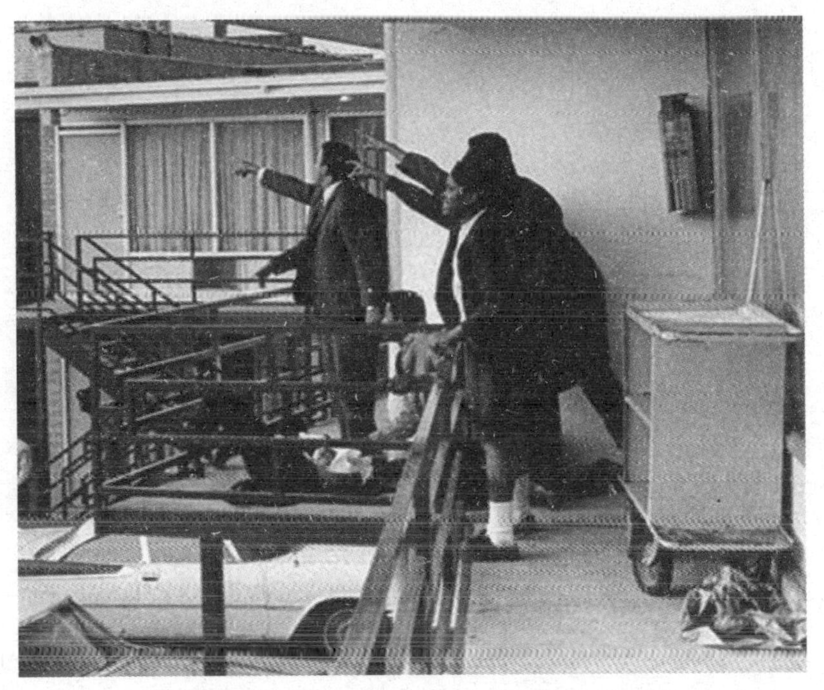

Reproduced with permission from Joseph Louw/
The LIFE Images Collection/Getty Images

He who learns must suffer. And even in our sleep, pain that cannot forget falls drop by drop upon the heart, and in our own despair, against our will, comes wisdom to us by the awful grace of God.

—AESCHYLUS

Contents

The Kneeling Man

1.

Explosion

On Thursday, April 4, 1968, just before six in the evening, five people stepped into the parking lot of the Lorraine Motel in Memphis and beheld a spectacle. No more than ten yards away, the Reverend Dr. Martin Luther King Jr. was leaning on the teal railing of the motel's second-floor balcony, talking to a small crowd below. He and the crowd were laughing, their words just beyond hearing range, as the last rays of sunlight glinted off the motel's rectangular picture windows.

The group of five had been split between two cars, a cobalt blue Volkswagen Fastback and a white Pontiac Tempest, having just come from Clayborn Temple, where they were helping with grassroots efforts to support the city's striking sanitation workers.

Their work wove an easy kinship between them, though one, the Volkswagen's driver, seemed a little quieter than the rest when conversation got going. They knew him as Marrell, the twenty-three-year-old minister of transportation for a Black militant group called the Invaders. Others called him Mac.

Just before noon that day, Mac had encountered three of them deep in conversation at the church.

"Hey, let's see if Marrell will take us," said Clara, a brown-skinned student activist in bobby socks, as she gestured toward him. Standing beside her was Mary, another student activist, also in bobby socks.

"Take you where?" he asked.

"Shopping for four-button overalls," Baby Jesus said. "I need 'em for the march."

Baby Jesus was what they called James Orange, aide to King and project coordinator for his Southern Christian Leadership Conference (SCLC). The nickname was ironic, given the man's six-foot-three, three-hundred-pound frame; he towered over Mac, himself not a small man at a muscular six feet tall plus a two-inch afro. But Baby Jesus's long goatee sprouted from a cherubic ebony face with gentle eyes framed by horn-rimmed glasses. He'd been in town all week with colleagues from the SCLC, preparing for King's next big march for the sanitation workers.

Mac nodded. Four-button overalls were part of that peasant farmer vibe, the de rigueur look for a poor people's demonstration. Clara had a car and could've taken Baby Jesus shopping herself, but why not let the Invaders' transportation minister do the driving?

They piled into Mac's car, first stopping at the shops along Main Street. Finding nothing, they checked the venerable old Goldsmith's department store downtown, which carried a variety of menswear but not the overalls. Someone recommended checking the new Sears out east on Poplar Avenue. No luck. The pattern repeated itself all over town as they combed store after store without success. Finally, they returned to Clayborn Temple, where they ran into the fiery and slightly built James Bevel, who managed the SCLC's direct action and nonviolent education programs.

By now, it was getting close to dinnertime. Baby Jesus invited the college students to share a meal at the Lorraine, the SCLC's base of operations in Memphis. Bevel was planning to head there, too, and it made sense for Mac to come along. The SCLC had rented the Invaders a couple of rooms while the two groups were in talks about the role the Invaders might play in the upcoming march. The five of them decided to carpool over, with Mac driving Baby Jesus and Bevel while Clara drove Mary.

Dressed in jeans and a lightweight pullover jacket, Mac walked toward Clara's car, parked behind his. He recognized a few people in the crowd near King's balcony, members of a gospel group called the Operation Breadbasket Band. Orange and Bevel walked in their direction.

Mac exchanged a few words with Clara and Mary. Just then, a

thunderous boom echoed through the air. Mac looked up and saw King fall backward to the balcony floor.

"Dr. King has been shot!" screamed someone in the crowd.

Mac looked out in the direction opposite where King had been standing, toward a couple of ramshackle buildings across Mulberry Street. He saw no one, either in the buildings or on the ground. His eyes swept the parking lot, the street, the sidewalks. No one running, no one with a gun.

Then he spotted a cluster of movement across Mulberry Street. People were running out of the rear door of the fire station just opposite the motel.

He looked at the balcony again. One of King's aides, Rev. Jesse Jackson, peered out from behind an adjacent doorway toward King's fallen body.

The next thing Mac knew, his legs were carrying him toward King, sprinting up an external staircase and onto the second-floor balcony. Had he stopped to consider a course of action and the possible consequences, he probably would've melted into the crowd, but something automatic propelled him.

As he reached the balcony, it occurred to him that the shooter might not be finished. He dropped to a crawl and made his way to King, grabbing a white towel from a cleaning cart along the way.

Mac's eyes locked on the gaping hole in the right side of King's head and neck as it gushed blood onto the gray concrete. The wound began around his cheekbone, traveling down under his Adam's apple. It looked strange, the way the flesh erupted outward, torn back. Droplets of blood speckled the front of King's shirt, from the collar to the middle of his torso.

Mac's mind searched for methods to stop the bleeding. There were only two: a tourniquet—which obviously wouldn't work here—and pressure. He pressed the towel into the wound.

Who did this? he wondered. *Where did the shot come from?*

He remembered basic training in the army, where he learned a technique for figuring out a trajectory or navigating from a fixed point back to where you'd come from. They called it shooting a back azimuth. He looked at King's position on the balcony floor. When King was talking to the people below, he was standing parallel to the balcony, leaning over the railing. He fell at an angle, about 45 degrees to the left, relative to the railing. The shot must have come from his right side, pushing him back and to the left. And the wound looked like it had a downward trajectory. Putting it all together, the shot came from above and to the right, from the back of one of those old buildings across the street. The top floor. Mac counted one, two, three windows over—a little window about half the height of the other two. Right there. Had to be.

Down in the courtyard, throngs of people milled about, sobbing and wailing. Sirens shrieked in every direction, red and blue lights glinting on the motel windowpanes. Help was coming. *One of them needs to get over there to where the shot came from*, he thought.

Clara and Mary now stood feet away from him on the balcony, screaming and pointing across the street. Potent, suffocating odors closed in—burning gunpowder and a sweet cologne overlying sulfurous notes from King's facial hair depilatory. Mac felt a surge of nausea.

Why was the gunpowder odor so intense? The gun had been fired all the way across the street, most likely from inside a building. It didn't make any sense—until you put it together with the extruded flesh of the wound, the shot's thunderous sound, the spray of blood on King's shirt. Even if the shot's sound, and the wound, and the blood spatter could be explained away, what about the concentrated gunpowder smell? Taken together, the details painted a picture he could scarcely believe: the bullet that hit King exploded on impact, as if it contained some kind of incendiary charge.

But how could that be? He'd never heard of such a thing, even in the army. A bullet like that wouldn't be sold in a gun shop. It had to be advanced technology.

People gathered around Mac and King on the balcony, and soon Rev. Ralph Abernathy, King's chief aide, knelt next to King. He placed his hand on the towel, taking over from Mac.

Mac rose, bloodstains making his jacket cling to the left side of his chest. He spotted a police officer nearby, a white man, and the white color of his shirt indicated he was a lieutenant. Mac pulled him to the side.

"I'm an undercover police officer," he said, speaking close to the man's ear. "The shot came from that building across the street, from that window." He pointed to the half-size window. "I heard the shot and saw him fall. I saw how it hit him, the way his body was lying. If you line him up from his head to his feet and add an elevation, that's the trajectory."

As the lieutenant looked across the courtyard at the window, Mac walked away. Seeing Mary and Clara sobbing and keening nearby, he knew he needed to get them away from the scene. He led them down an external staircase and into the parking lot, which swarmed with police. One of the officers told everyone to remain in the area, so the three of them stood around, waiting.

Mary and Clara left after a while, and Mac decided to go to the motel lobby. He found a chair and sat in it. A few people sat nearby while others meandered through, the mood funereal and hushed.

He couldn't believe what he just saw. Didn't want to believe it. What would happen in the city tonight? Would it burn? Grief welled in his chest but found no exit. Tears would not come.

Before he knew it, an hour or more had slipped by. Nobody came to interview him or seemed to care if he remained or not, so he left.

Night had descended by the time Mac pulled into the small carport of his red-brick, ranch-style home. It was in a new housing development south of Midtown, and the neighbors were mostly childless, older Black professionals—postal workers and schoolteachers and such. His soon-to-be wife, Linda, had bought the place with her teaching salary shortly before they met, bringing her elderly mother, Miss Elizabeth, up from Natchez, Mississippi, to live there with her.

Linda rushed to the door as he entered, her face puffy and tear streaked. "Did you hear what happened to Dr. King?"

A radio news program droned in the background. Linda took a step back when she saw the blood on his jacket.

"What happened to you?"

"I was at the Lorraine. I was trying to help him."

He went to their bedroom and stripped off his jacket, folding it and setting it on a high shelf in the closet. After putting on a fresh shirt, he picked up the beige rotary telephone by the bed and called Jerry Davis, a detective in the Memphis Police Department's Domestic Intelligence Bureau.

"Hey, Mac. How you doing?" Davis asked.

"It's been a long day. And you saw what happened to Dr. King. I was there."

"Really?"

Mac described everything that happened.

"We need to know what the Invaders are getting up to tonight," Davis said.

"I'm heading over there shortly."

When Mac emerged from the bedroom, Linda was standing at the stove fixing him a dinner plate, her black hair spilling across the shoulders of her housecoat. Miss Elizabeth, who usually spent the evening in her room praying and reading the Bible, sat in a living room chair close to the kitchen.

Between bites of food, he told Linda what had happened at the Lorraine. She sat across from him, the table before her bare, as she'd already eaten by the time he got home. Miss Elizabeth listened in silence from the living room.

"Baby, I've got to work tonight," he said, pushing away from the table. "I don't know what time I'm going to be back."

Linda nodded. If she was scared, she didn't say so.

This day, April 4, marked his 120th day on the Memphis police force. In his brief and bewildering tenure, seventeen weeks and one day, he could scarcely grasp how he'd gone from a police academy classroom to what he'd just seen and experienced.

The Invaders' base of operations—the crib, as they called it—was a one-bedroom apartment in an oblong, one-story building on Hanauer Street in South Memphis, about a twenty-minute drive from Mac's house. This was where the group socialized, rapped about daily events, hatched their plans. There wasn't much inside, just a few cast-off pieces of furniture, but no television or radio. Drapes, or fabric functioning as drapes, covered the windows. The place was leased to John Burl Smith, one of the group's founders, but neither he nor any of the other leaders were there when Mac arrived. Instead, he found several low-level guys, no more than high school age, sitting there seething. Several Molotov cocktails were at their feet.

"We need to go up to North Memphis," one of them said when Mac walked in. "It's time to burn this shit *down*. But if we do it around here, the roaches'll be all over us."

Everyone knew South Memphis was the Invaders' turf, while North Memphis was the territory of a rival group, the Black Knights.

The guys grabbed the bottles, piled into Mac's car, and headed up to the Black working-class neighborhood of New Chicago. Their conversation on the way was bitter and sharp.

"After what they did to Dr. King, they deserve what we gone do," one said.

"We'll make 'em pay," said another. "We got to do something."

Pulsating with grief, Mac didn't say much beyond a quiet "mmm-hmm" from time to time. Unlike them, he wasn't angry, and he didn't want revenge—not that he thought it was possible anyway. Revenge against who, the mayor? The city? White folks? To him, justice would be catching the killer or killers and dealing with them through the criminal justice system. But the Invaders in his car had a different kind of justice in mind, something more visceral, even cosmic. On some level, they probably knew that the fires they were planning to set would only highlight their powerlessness. Perhaps that deepened their despair.

In the roughly four weeks since Mac had invaded the Invaders, they'd been saying nonviolent protests wouldn't do anything but get Black people hurt. He disagreed, but they hadn't been completely wrong. After nearly two months of marching and picketing, the sanitation workers didn't seem any closer to decent pay, union recognition, or respect from the city's power structure. And on top of that, King was now dead.

But Mac still didn't believe violence was the answer. If anything, aggression toward the authorities was a suicide mission, like facing off against the U.S. military armed with sticks and rocks. They didn't stand a chance. They'd be wiped out, and society would keep on humming along.

In Mississippi where he grew up, white folks could kill you for any reason or no reason at all. While Black people had devised certain methods of self-defense, or at least self-preservation, these almost never involved head-on confrontation. And even then, they never knew when they'd be met with breathtaking violence.

He could never forget what a racist sheriff did to a family friend, though he was a child when it happened. This was in 1955—scarcely thirteen years earlier—in Tate County near Strayhorn, Mississippi, less than eighty-five miles from the site of Emmett Till's murder in Money. Alonzo, a Black truck driver in his twenties, had a wreck one night, running off the very road Mac and his little brother Floyd walked to school. Alonzo crawled out of the truck's cab and into the woods, but somebody saw the accident and called Sheriff Joe Taylor, who had a reputation for killing and torturing Black people. Sheriff Taylor found Alonzo and gunned him down. For nothing. It hurt Mac to his core, and every time he and Floyd walked to school and back, five days a week, they had to walk by the site where it happened.

Mac found Memphis to be far different from Tate County. It seemed like a promising place to lay down roots. For one thing, the city had a professionally trained police department that had hired him even though he was Black. There was racism, of course—neighborhoods where he couldn't live and places he couldn't go—but that way of doing things was slowly coming to an end, he thought. Wasn't his hiring proof of that?

The entire drive to New Chicago, the streets were empty. He'd expected to see law enforcement everywhere, but there was none—no patrol cars, no roadblocks, nothing. He'd noticed this on the way from his house to the crib, too. Where were they? The whole city, especially Black folks, would be on edge this night, of all nights. This was far more serious than the chaotic night of King's march exactly one week earlier, when the governor had deployed the National Guard and tactical units patrolled three and four cars deep. Could it be that police were concentrated in white neighborhoods, keeping the peace there? One thing was clear: the Black neighborhoods Mac was cruising through had been left to their own devices.

And where were the Invaders' leaders, who'd been staying at the Lorraine courtesy of the SCLC? It bothered Mac that he didn't know. He hadn't seen a single one of them at the motel that evening. For all their talk about revolution and killing oppressors, they sure were quiet. Were they off wreaking havoc somewhere? Were they hiding and letting the little guys do the dirty work?

Dark stretches of city blocks flicked past. Soon they were in New Chicago. Mac slowed down, creeping by a row of dilapidated, vacant-looking storefronts.

"Right here, right here," one of the guys said.

Mac pulled next to the curb, keeping the engine running. The others got out and slunk up to the buildings, silhouettes approaching silhouettes under dim streetlamps. Breaking glass shattered the silence. They ran back to the car, backlit by a burst of flames.

A week later, on the morning of April 11, Mac's doorbell rang. Standing on his doorstep were two fastidiously groomed white men in dark suits and starched white shirts. They displayed their badges and introduced themselves as Special Agents Bill Lawrence and Howell Lowe of the FBI. Lawrence, his tall body slightly stooped, looked to be in his midfifties, while Lowe, with his headful of dark hair and ramrod posture, appeared a decade younger.

"Would y'all like some coffee?" Mac asked as they settled onto his mother-in-law's davenport.

They said yes, so Mac brought them cups of instant coffee from the kitchen. The house was empty, except for Miss Elizabeth behind her closed bedroom door. Linda had left a couple of hours earlier for her teaching job.

"So what did you see, Mac?" one of the special agents asked.

Mac gave a chronological account of April 4, starting with meeting

Baby Jesus and the student activists at Clayborn Temple. Lawrence and Lowe took notes.

"I took a towel off the cleaning cart and crawled over to Dr. King," he said. "And when I got there, I smelled a concentrated gunpowder odor. I looked at the wound, and it was blown outward, and there were little spots of blood on his shirt. The bullet exploded."

"I've never heard of an exploding bullet," said one agent.

"Neither have I," said the other.

"That just doesn't exist," the first one continued. "We don't even have anything like that in *our* arsenal."

"Whether you've heard of it or not, that's what happened," Mac said. "Let me give you the jacket I was wearing. His blood's on it."

He excused himself and went to retrieve it from his bedroom. Then he finished giving his account.

They thanked him as they rose to leave. They had what they needed, they said.

2.

The Photograph

You've seen the photo: April 4, 1968, the exterior of Memphis's Lorraine Motel. A mortally wounded Dr. Martin Luther King Jr. lies on a second-floor balcony as blood pools around him on the gray concrete. The toes of his polished dress shoes stick out past the edge of the railing, over the cars in the lot below. Standing above him, three people frantically point to a rooming house across the street. A fourth person's gaze is fixed on the same spot, but with his right hand, he holds a white towel to King's shattered jaw. It's this man I found myself unable to look away from when I first saw the photo at the age of four, maybe five. He's alert and seemingly ready to leap to his feet, his precise reasons for being on that balcony long touched by mystery—even to me. And I'm his daughter.

I have a flickering reel of early memories of my father, Marrell, or "Mac," as he's called by those who know him best: his bare ankles as I play on the floor while he watches football and drinks beer; a flash of straight, white teeth; him cooing words in a singsong voice. These are sparkling, sun-dappled late-1970s scenes. But there are darker ones: Dad and my mother, Peggy, shouting behind a closed bedroom door about his drinking, his affairs. Her tearful calls to her mother on an avocado-green rotary phone: "I want to come home." My own helplessness and fear as our family's foundation crumbled beneath our feet.

In 1977, before my brother Micah was born, Ma, Dad, and I took a family portrait at an Olan Mills in Northern Virginia. In it, Dad stands behind Ma as she holds me. He's wearing a taupe suit and sporting a dark brown afro and goatee. Dressed in a colorful caftan, Ma also has an afro, though hers is auburn. Freckles dot her face, and a slick of light blue eye shadow glazes her lids. I'm fluffy and smiling in my blue, ruffled dress. At the sides of my head sit two sandy-colored afro puffs.

A year after we took that photo, Ma and Dad separated, and Ma took Micah and me from our anodyne Northern Virginia townhouse to her soulful home city of Memphis to stay with her parents. She and Dad briefly reunited a month or so later, Dad loading our delicately reassembled family into his brown Dodge van, which he called "Big Choc," for a long drive to Virginia. But I'd scarcely reacquainted myself with the toys I'd left behind when we packed up and headed back to Memphis a few weeks later, this time for good. It was 1979. I was three, and Micah was almost one. Ma took a full-time job as a reporter for Memphis's *Commercial Appeal*, the larger of the two local newspapers, and Grandma and Grandaddy took care of Micah and me while she was at work. Nobody talked about Dad much.

"You heard from Mac?" Grandma asked Ma from time to time. Ma would affirm succinctly, looking away. Conversation over.

I recall the move to Memphis as a sudden but organic change, as though it would've been impossible for our lives not to have unfolded thus. But Ma would later tell me I'd cried for Dad after we left. She said I once fixated on a man I saw when we were out shopping, convinced that he was Dad by the sight of his legs and shoes. "Daddy!" I screamed over and over.

In Memphis, a host of welcoming faces greeted us. Aside from Grandma and Granddaddy, there were two elegant aunts and four uncles who seemed almost as tall as the ceiling. For a while, we lived in Grandma and Granddaddy's neat white bungalow. It had the air of a cabin in the country: long clotheslines swaying with billowing fabrics and tidy rows of vegetables bursting through the backyard's dark, turned earth.

Micah and I were too young to understand the significance of Dad's presence at King's assassination when Ma showed us *that* photo in *The Commercial Appeal.* We knew only what she told us: "That's your dad. He was a policeman." Conversation over.

Years passed, but Dad never discussed that day. The rest of the family followed suit. A while back, I mentioned to a friend that Dad and I had never broached the topic, and she laughed incredulously.

"Are you serious? I'm all up in my parents' business!"

I laughed too, but my stomach clenched as I thought about how Dad and I had been maneuvering around a gulf of silence for as long as I could remember.

Though the assassination occurred eight years before I was born, that photograph has loomed large in my consciousness for just about as long as I can remember. Dad came and went, but the black-and-white image of horror remained, unalterable and mute. The photo, like my interactions with Dad, hinted at a mystery, something unspoken and perhaps unspeakable. From childhood on, my mind teemed with questions about him—his work, his allegiances, who he really was. It would be decades before I could bring myself to seek the answers.

Once or twice a year from the early to the mid-1980s, Big Choc would materialize next to the curb in front of Grandma and Granddaddy's house. Straight-backed and ebullient, Dad would stride up the walkway, an exotic visitor bearing curious gifts, like a straw mask with cowrie shell eyes or a foot-tall Japanese geisha doll.

As I opened the door, he'd let out a full-throated laugh, addressing me then as he still does today. "Miss Leta!"

I'd approach warily.

"Look at you, girl! Wow, you're getting tall!"

After some coaxing from Grandma or Grandaddy, I'd accept the gift I never wanted. He'd kiss my cheek, his stubble scratching my skin, then turn to Micah with a "Hey, man!"

Looking back, I can see how loving and eager he was, but back then, his presence felt like a threat to my now stable existence. I didn't know him anymore, and I didn't want anything from him. What I wanted was my same old toys and dolls and the same grownups that I saw every day, not unfamiliar trinkets from a less and less familiar Dad.

He'd whisk Micah and me into Big Choc's shag-carpeted belly, taking us on whirlwind rides around town. I didn't want to go, preferring the security of Grandma and Grandaddy's cozy bungalow to these impromptu van rides with a virtual stranger, but I wasn't about to kick up a fuss. I could see he loved us, and I didn't want to act ugly. Plus, even if I did, Grandma and Grandaddy and Ma would have made me go anyway.

So we'd ride all over the city, tasting bony slabs of fried buffalo fish and taking in humid days at Liberty Land amusement park. We'd appear at Aunt Pirl and Uncle Sonny's house in South Memphis. Aunt Pirl, a short, plump woman with a profusion of copper curls, would tease me about my sun-streaked hair, asking in a singsong voice, "Do blondes have more fun?"

We'd swing by Aunt Joyce and Cousin Mickey's stout brick home in South Memphis. Mickey, who was between Micah and me in age, would welcome us to an afternoon of play with a huge grin. There were other relatives, too: Uncle Buck—who was actually Dad's cousin Eugene—and Uncle Floyd and at least two Rickys.

We'd listen to rap and R&B hits on K97 FM, exulting in Dad's shock at the lyrics. The only time I can remember Dad scolding one of us was when Micah, then eleven, rapped along with Kool Moe Dee's "Let's Go":

Jack the Ripper

Down with my ZIPPER!

But we were in for a shock ourselves one night when Dad revealed that he was a country music fan and played a few wailing Charley Pride tunes from a cassette tape.

What kind of Black man listens to country music? I thought.

But I knew that wasn't entirely fair. Micah and I enjoyed plenty of episodes of *The Grand Ole Opry* and *Hee Haw* at Grandma and Grandaddy's house, enough to know that Charley Pride was in fact a brother. So the music was barely acceptable.

According to Ma, Dad worked "for the government," and her demeanor told us not to ask anything more about it. He'd left the Memphis Police Department two years before I was born, and I knew nothing about his current job, only that it that took him to foreign countries for long stretches. Every few months, we'd get a fat envelope bearing strange stamps and stuffed with photos, along with a letter in his long, loopy script: *How are you? I'm doing fine. Your mom told me you're in kindergarten now! I hope to see you soon.*

In some of the photos, he wore a khaki military uniform. In others, he stood next to a jeep. He was large-framed and commanding, his brown skin glistening in the Central African heat. He still visited Memphis sporadically, swooping into town, always a surprise. In between these visits and missives, Micah and I had no idea where he was.

When I was eleven, Dad moved back to the United States and settled in Northern Virginia. He had a new bride, Mary, plus a daughter named Kelly and Mary's aging poodle, Concho. Micah and I visited them for Thanksgiving in their spacious, colonial-style home, where African carvings and tapestries filled the airy rooms.

Over the weekend, Dad took Micah and me to a boxy, featureless low-rise office building we'd never seen before. He flashed an ID badge and breezed through security. We crossed a vast cubicle-filled room to get to Dad's office, where he closed the door. He asked if we knew what he did for a living.

"You work for the government," we said.

"I work for the CIA," he said matter-of-factly, looking us square in the eye. He didn't elaborate beyond directing us to keep that information to ourselves.

In that moment, I became the keeper of a secret. Now I was part of something—one could even say *involved.* But what exactly was I involved in? I didn't know, though I did know the CIA was a spy agency that carried out missions doing who-knows-what across the globe. It seemed both cool and sinister, honorable and questionable.

Does Dad have a gun? I wondered. *What does he do for them?*

True to our word, Micah and I didn't discuss it with anyone, not even each other. Dad had discretion to reveal his occupation to close family members, and he thought we were mature enough to handle the information. He wanted to share this sliver of his world with us, now that he was safely back in the States and we'd be seeing each other more often. Betraying his trust was unthinkable.

Besides, who knew what the penalties were for leaking classified information? What if the government was watching us and listening in on our conversations?

I need to be on my best behavior, I thought.

By the early 1990s, I was a bookish, surly teenager with a special interest in racial justice, having witnessed, among other things, the election of Memphis's first Black mayor and the naked bigotry his achievement coaxed from its hiding places. I pored over Alex Haley's *Autobiography of Malcolm X* and Frantz Fanon's *The Wretched of the Earth*, as well as a couple of books about the Black Panther Party. One day in seventh grade, an older boy at school I sometimes talked to about social issues called himself a radical, and I liked the way it sounded.

"I'm a radical," I announced to Ma as I hopped in her car after school.

She shot me a look. "Don't you *ever* say that. You aren't any radical."

My face burned. I vowed to keep quiet about my political views from then on.

One afternoon in 1993, when I was a high school junior, I was lazily flipping through *The Commercial Appeal* when I came across an article about King's assassination. As I scanned the stories, my father's name leapt out at me. The article said he'd worked undercover to infiltrate a Black militant group called the Invaders.

Undercover. Infiltrate.

I scrambled to assemble the pieces in my head. The truth was inescapable. Dad wasn't just any police officer at the Lorraine Motel when King was shot—he was a *spy*.

The revelation felt like a body blow. I read the words over and over, struggling to take a full breath.

Instinctively, I sympathized with the Invaders; they sounded kind of like the Black Panthers. From my readings, I knew about FBI director J. Edgar Hoover's dirty tactics: spreading misinformation, harassing militants and their families, maybe even murder. Was that what happened here in Memphis with the Invaders? And was Dad involved in it?

My mind reeled with a host of new questions about him. But I didn't dare ask—not then, not in the eighteen months before I left for college, and not even when, despite my political sympathies directly to the contrary, I wound up living with him while interning at the CIA during the summers following my sophomore and junior years of college.

As ambivalent as I was about working for one of the world's foremost spy agencies, I knew those internships would enhance my résumé in a way that my previous jobs at the Gap and Merry-Go-Round never could. After that, I'd have a much better chance pursuing whatever career I wanted, which I had decided was law.

During those two summers of living with Dad, I grew to like him. I enjoyed the lighthearted banter that deepened the dimple in his right cheek.

"Remember how you used to love French fries when you were little?" he asked one evening in the kitchen. "You'd shout, 'More French fries!'"

I didn't remember. I wished I did.

But I hadn't forgotten what I'd read, and it still scared me. I packed it away deep in my subconscious. By now, I was good at that.

By the summer of 2010, I was thirty-four years old, married, and living in Houston. I was in my eighth year of law practice and had recently given birth to my second child, another boy.

His birth had set a question aflame: *What would I tell the kids about their Granddaddy Mac?* I didn't know.

Dad and I kept in touch, mostly over the phone, but these were cordial exchanges that only skirted around the edges of who he was. Unless I asked what I really wanted to know, that wasn't going to change.

I picked up the phone.

I tried not to plan what I would say. Instead, after the usual polite chit-chat, I pushed out the words. "I've been thinking about how we've never discussed King's assassination. I really want to hear about your experience."

Several beats of silence passed.

"Okay," he finally said.

"And it's not just the assassination," I said, the words now pouring forth. "There's a lot I don't know about your life. Your childhood, your time in the army, the CIA stuff."

He chuckled. "That's a lot. Let me get my thoughts together, and I'll send you some notes. Then we can talk."

He sounded relieved, even happy I'd asked.

About a week later, he emailed me a seventeen-page document. I inhaled sharply as I opened the letter, which began with a formal preamble in boldface type:

"Will be as forthcoming as possible but will not disclose classified information. Will keep my solemn oath to my friends and country."

He launched into an account of his early childhood on a farm in 1940s Mississippi, describing his father ("Friends called him Nap, vanilla brown, cross-eyed—hit in eye with rock as child") and mother ("Prideful, primped in potato field"). Three pages in, I was heaving with tears. These sparse sketches of his earliest memories overwhelmed me.

I put the notes aside. For five years. And because I'd suppressed my curiosity about Dad's story for so long, that seemed like nothing.

We still talked now and then, and I felt guilty each time, thinking he must've been wondering what I made of his account. Neither of us brought it up.

It was during that period, in 2011, that my husband—also a lawyer, but for a multinational corporation—took a job within his company that required us to move from Houston to Kazakhstan. We pulled up stakes completely, selling our house and cars to move into company housing and use company transportation. I threw myself into computerized Russian language lessons, learned about Kazakh food and culture, even attended Russian Orthodox church services from time to time. It felt good to shed one lifestyle and plunge into another. I was living in a new context, and it made me feel new, too.

We lived there from 2011 to 2013, and then my husband moved to a new position that took us to Nigeria—another context change, another chance to be new. As much as I enjoyed that aspect of our international itinerancy, I couldn't shake the feeling that something was missing.

So we bought a 1970s-era vacation home in Nevada near Lake Tahoe. At the time, it made a strange kind of sense: I wanted to feel more grounded, so we bought some ground. I was avoiding the real issue of what was missing, of course, but that matter would rear its head soon enough.

In June 2014, the kids and I left Nigeria to spend summer break in the vacation home, and my husband joined us for the first couple of weeks before returning to Nigeria for work. In late July, between hikes and trips to the beach, I began seeing news reports about a Liberian man who arrived by air at Lagos's Murtala Muhammed airport and collapsed, deathly ill from the Ebola virus. This kicked off a wave of infections across the country, and by August, the government had ordered schools shut until mid-October in an attempt to contain the virus. Watching from Tahoe, there seemed to be only one reasonable choice: Stay put and register the boys for school where we were, though it meant we'd be separated from my husband for a time.

The vacation home was now our full-time home, the clothes we'd brought in our suitcases now our wardrobes. This would be our first winter in the High Sierra, with its seemingly unending snow and parade of wildlife—bears, coyotes, and the occasional bobcat—and we were on our own. Parenting alone left me physically and emotionally exhausted, but also bored and restless.

But there were the notes Dad had sent me four years earlier. In all the travel, the moves, the upheavals, I'd managed to bury them in my mind along with my questions about him, or so I thought. As it turned out, I hadn't quite managed to lay them to rest. The notes and the questions came back to visit from time to time, especially in the dark of night.

It was on one such chilly evening in March 2015 that the stories called to me in the darkness and silence. I opened that old email containing the notes, printed the pages, and held them in my hand, telling myself I couldn't quit this time.

I tried to make things easier by reading them while listening to Prince on streaming internet radio in our tiny dry sauna. I learned that you can read in a dry sauna, but it really burns to cry there.

3.

Blues Highway

When Mac arrived at Memphis Police Department headquarters early on a humid July morning in 1967, the receptionist told him the recruiting officer likely wouldn't be in for a couple of hours; he could come back then. But he didn't have anywhere to go. It seemed like a waste of gas to go all the way back home and get settled only to turn around and come back downtown. He didn't know of any place that was open, not where he'd be welcome to linger. So he thanked the receptionist and sat on a hard bench in the lobby, waiting.

As his cousin Eugene had suggested, he was going to apply for a spot on the police force, even though it was probably pointless.

"You were a military policeman, weren't you?" Eugene asked.

"They aren't going to hire any colored folks," Mac said.

"You don't know that. You oughta try."

The pair had been on their way to their shift at the Memphis Sash & Door warehouse that morning when a recruiting ad for the police department came on the car radio—the sound of sirens, followed by a voice-over intoning, "Be a Memphis Police Officer!" and inviting prospective candidates to apply at the Central Police Station.

Not wanting to disappoint Eugene, Mac decided to take his advice. After all, he'd hired Mac for not one but two jobs working under him—one at Memphis Sash & Door and the other at a motorboat engine repair shop—after Mac's return to the States from Germany.

Freshly discharged from the army five months prior, Mac had chosen to move to Memphis rather than return to the Mississippi Delta where he was born and raised. He'd set his sights on building a life that didn't seem possible in the Delta, a college education through the GI Bill and a successful career. But getting on his feet had been hard. For the first few weeks, he walked the streets day after day, putting in job applications and getting nowhere. Seeing his struggles, Eugene stepped in. The jobs were menial, but they paid just enough to live on and gave him a spark of purpose.

Aside from his initial struggles finding employment, grim reports from the war in Vietnam stalked his thoughts, and he was having trouble sleeping. Another of his cousins had been killed over there, as had some of his army buddies, and he'd narrowly escaped being called up himself. When he graduated from military police school in 1964, a company of MPs had just been overrun by the Vietcong and needed reinforcements, plus the army was building up the newly formed 11th Air Assault Division.

The day after graduation, his sergeant went down the class roster in alphabetical order, announcing each soldier's assignment and getting closer to the Ms with each breath. From A through L, most soldiers were going to the Eleventh Air Assault.

Finally, he reached the Ms.

"Martinez, Eleventh Air Assault."

Mac held his breath. The big moment was coming, the brief pronouncement that would determine the course of his future.

"McCollough, Fort Ritchie, Maryland."

Now he could exhale. His breath escaped in a joyful yell, joining the chorus of cheers that heralded new adventures.

All told, around thirty of the hundred or so graduates went to Vietnam, and many of the remaining assignments were to places like Honolulu and White Sands, New Mexico. Mac was the only Fort Ritchie, but he didn't mind. From there, he went to Germany, and before he knew it, his three years of service were ending—just as the war was really heating up. He couldn't shake a feeling of guilt about being spared combat while his cousin and friends weren't. He couldn't find any sense or meaning in it.

Thank goodness he had family to help him. Eugene had done more than give him work. When he was feeling down, Eugene would sit and talk with him or take him for a long drive. Eugene believed in him, and he wanted to honor that by taking a chance on the police job. Besides, all he had to do was fill out an application. He'd planned to go to his shift at the warehouse after picking up the police department paperwork, so he was dressed in his blue jeans, work shirt, and scarred work boots.

Finally, the receptionist looked at him and nodded her head as a middle-aged officer strode past. Mac followed the man into a room just off the lobby.

"Good morning, sir. I'm here to apply for a position with the police department. I heard an ad on the radio this morning."

"Driver's license."

When Mac handed him his Mississippi driver's license, the man's face reddened.

"This license is expired," the man said. "How'd you get down here? I oughta lock you up, you come in here with an expired driver's license—"

"I'm a veteran, sir, and I just got back from Germany after an honorable army discharge. I have a ninety-day grace period to get my license and everything back in order." Mac's words flowed from his lips, though he had no idea whether there was really a ninety-day grace period.

"Okay, then let me see your birth certificate."

"I don't have my birth certificate."

"You have to be at least twenty-one years old for this position," the man said.

"Sir, I'm twenty-three years old. I was just discharged from the army after three years—"

"Where's your 214?" the man asked, referring to Mac's DD Form 214, his report of separation from the military.

"I don't have it."

"Well, I need proof that you're twenty-one."

Mac was getting the distinct impression that the man was being difficult on purpose. If he'd bothered to look at the driver's license, he'd easily find Mac's date of birth.

"What else would you consider proof, sir?"

"You have anyone who can vouch for your age?"

"My high school principal."

The men reached a compromise: Mac would get a letter from the principal attesting that Mac was at least twenty-one. It was summer, so school might not be in session. But given that the recruiting officer said he'd accept the letter in lieu of a birth certificate, Mac thought he may as well try.

Delta Center High School in Walls, Mississippi, was no more than thirty or forty minutes away, and Mac didn't have to pick up Eugene and head to their second job until 3:30. The challenge of completing the errand invigorated him.

Maybe I do have a chance to get on the force, he thought.

But first, he had to get to Walls.

Known as the Blues Highway, Highway 61 was the main route between Memphis and Walls. Driving Eugene's white Thunderbird, Mac took Third Street to get there, passing a collection of small shops, gas stations, and warehouses. At the state line, the urban landscape gave way to a sea of pasture and soybeans punctuated by farmhouses.

A service station, a cafeteria, and a bank delineated the Walls skyline. The rambling, one-story school lay just east of town. As Mac pulled into the faculty parking lot, he was delighted to see cars parked there. He went to the office and told the secretary he needed to see Mr. Johnson.

He was out on sick leave, she said.

When Mac told her he had an urgent matter to discuss, she gave him Mr. Johnson's home address. It was in Hernando, clear across the county.

To get to Hernando, Mac had to navigate back roads, stretches of which were unpaved, through large tracts of lush pastures. Half-listening to talk radio, he felt his investment in the possibility of getting that job growing. He'd devoted his entire morning to the proof-of-age letter, and maybe it hadn't been a waste of time. He had to do his part to make sure it wasn't.

Finally, he arrived at Mr. Johnson's house. The woman who answered the door told him Mr. Johnson wasn't home—he was in the hospital. It wasn't too far from there.

He found the hospital and, after checking in at the visitors' desk, located Mr. Johnson in a private room. A thin Black man in his forties, he was sitting up in bed when Mac entered. When he saw Mac, his face brightened.

Mac asked how he was doing.

"Fine, except for my leg." He explained that he'd broken it and had just undergone an operation.

Mac told him about his efforts to apply for a job with the Memphis Police Department. "I need a letter from you to prove I'm over twenty-one."

"No problem," Mr. Johnson said, smiling. He picked up a notepad and pen from his bedside table, dashed off a note, and signed it.

By the time Mac left the hospital, it was well into the afternoon. There was no way he'd make it to the warehouse in time to pick up Eugene at 3:30, which meant they'd both be late for their shift at the boat repair shop. Mac took I-55 from Hernando to Memphis, driving as fast as the law would allow. He found a parking spot on North Main Street, around the corner from police headquarters. Bounding up the stately building's steep front staircase and rushing into the recruiter's office, he felt like a pipe bomb packed with possibilities. Maybe he'd be able to leave behind menial jobs. Wouldn't that be something?

He handed his proof-of-age letter to the recruiting officer, who looked it over and slapped the application form in Mac's hand.

As Mac turned to leave, the man said, "Oh, you can't take that with you. This is the last day to turn it in. You've got to turn it in by five, otherwise we won't accept it."

Today is the last day? Mac thought. He thumbed through the application, which was several pages long.

"May I borrow a pen?"

He sat there in the office and completed the forms, scribbling in his biographical information, previous addresses, educational and employment history. He needed personal references. He would've written in Mr. Johnson, but the references had to live in Memphis. Fortunately, one of his high school teachers, Mr. Epps, was now living there and working as a postal clerk, so Mac added his name. He also listed his landlady and his pastor.

"Now you've got to go over and take the test," the man said.

The civil service examination would be starting soon in the federal building across the street.

Boxy and grid-like, the [illegible] building at 167 North Main Street guarded the ultramodern Civic Center Plaza's eastern flank. Mac filed in with the police officers and aspiring recruits trickling into the building. An officer directed the applicants to a vestibule outside the examination room on the building's first floor. There were at least fifty of them, all male and all but four or five white. They all sat in metal folding chairs and waited for the test to begin. The other applicants were dressed in street clothes—button-down shirts and slacks—while Mac was still wearing his work clothes from early that morning. No one spoke.

A few minutes before six, a test proctor summoned them into the examination room, a seminar hall with rows of desks. He gave a brief welcome speech from the front of the room, and another proctor standing in the back passed out exam packets. Despite the day's drama—the expired license, the hunt for Mr. Johnson, poor cousin Eugene who'd waited in vain for Mac to pick him up at the warehouse—Mac felt calm and focused. He was nearing the finish line of the application process. His goal of becoming a police officer, which had been distant and abstract that morning, was now concrete and within reach. The proctor at the front announced that applicants could begin, and Mac set to work.

The exam covered math, reading comprehension, writing, and other core skills. It was mostly multiple choice, with some true or false questions. There was also a facial recognition portion, where a proctor briefly displayed photos of various faces and applicants had to answer questions about them from memory. The exam lasted for ninety minutes, but most of the applicants, including Mac, finished ahead of time. As they turned in their packets, administrators directed them to wait in the vestibule.

Mac thought he'd performed well as he strode from the exam room to the waiting area, but he felt a flutter of intimidation as administrators periodically called the names of waiting applicants, who left the room and didn't return. Time dragged on. The forty-five or so remaining applicants sat like soldiers in their metal chairs. Mac sized up many of them as ex-military. Finally, an officer entered the room and congratulated them for having successfully completed the first phase of the selection process. Individual candidate interviews would now begin.

It was after 10:00 p.m. when an officer summoned him to the interview room adjoining the waiting area. Mac took the lone empty chair facing a panel of at least a half-dozen officers wearing crisp white shirts festooned with brass. They questioned him closely about his background, and he talked about his service as a military policeman.

One of the officers interjected, "But being a military police officer and a civilian officer, they aren't the same."

"I know, but I learned the job as a military police officer, and I can learn the job as a city police officer."

Another panelist spoke up. "What's going to happen when you go out there to make an arrest, and somebody calls you a nigger?"

"When you're out there and you're a police officer, it's not about you personally," Mac said. "Your job is to uphold the law and command respect for your position. Whether he calls me a nigger or whatever, my job is to effect an arrest, and that's exactly what I'm going to do."

After a few more questions, the panel sent him back to the waiting area. Even though he'd been up since before dawn, he was wide awake, still fueled by adrenaline from the day's events. He thought the panel liked his answers. He hoped so. Other applicants took their turns in the interview room, and a few didn't return. Their number dwindled to about forty.

Around 11:30, an officer entered the waiting area and told the remaining applicants they'd been selected for training at the police academy—pending a favorable background investigation and physical exam.

As Mac walked out of the federal building onto a deserted Main Street, the pent-up tension of the day overwhelmed him like a swollen river breaching a dam. Tears streamed down his face. He'd made it, and it seemed like he was meant to make it. He thanked God.

As soon as he got home, he called Eugene to tell him about the day's events.

"I told you," Eugene said, laughing.

Mac tried to apologize for not showing up at the warehouse that afternoon, but Eugene wouldn't hear of it.

4.

Delta

On the night of December 6, 1967, everything was new for Mac: his navy blue dress uniform, his Smith & Wesson Model 10 revolver, his gleaming silver badge, and even Mac himself, as one of the few newly commissioned Black Memphis police officers from the academy's thirty-nine-man class to graduate that evening.

The department required recruits to buy their own uniforms at a cost of $70, plus their service revolvers, which cost $75. Mac was prepared, having saved money for extraordinary expenses like that. For thirty-six months—from the time he'd enlisted in the army until his discharge—he'd sent a savings bond to his father back in Mississippi every month, paying $18.50 of his meager paycheck for each bond. At maturity, each one would be valued at $25.

As graduation day approached, he asked his father to send him some of the money, and he received a money order a few days later. It felt good to be able to rely on family for things like that. It was comforting, like having teammates who were always there to help if you got in a fix. For a twenty-three-year-old, he'd seen a good bit of the world, enough to know it was cold and lonely without people on your side. Of course, he'd understood that since his earliest years, when having people to depend on wasn't just reassuring but necessary for survival.

Mac was born the ninth of twelve McCollough children in Tibbs, Mississippi, in 1944. From eldest to youngest, they were Johnnie, Walter (WT), Pandora (Pan), LaPirl (Pirl), Frederick (Top), May Earle (Shag), Levell (Mr. Mane), Johnetta (Bea), Marrell (Jack to his father and Rell to everyone else), Floyd (Hupp), Joyce (Shy Gal), and Doyce (who didn't live long enough to get a nickname).

Their mother and father, Lucille and Walter, rented a forty-acre parcel of land as flat as paper from a white man named Baker who lived in Memphis. Once a year, he'd come down to check on the place and collect the rent, which the McColloughs paid with their earnings from growing cotton and soybeans, plus Walter's fur trapping during the winter. Their squat little house clad in unpainted, weathered wood sat alongside an unpaved road they shared with several other families, all of them Black except for one family of whites. The homes were about a quarter mile apart, and the land they farmed lay behind.

Lucille was a roundish, brown-skinned woman with bow-shaped lips and dreamy eyes, the outer corners of which turned slightly downward, as did Mac's. She dressed plainly, shunned alcohol, and kept her hair pinned close to her head. Fastidious and always busy, she expected the same of the children, and she and the girls kept their little house scrubbed clean. They'd pour buckets of lye soap and water on the wood plank floors and scour them with scrub brooms until they were sparkling. They called that "scrubbing the house." Lucille made the boys leave while they cleaned and didn't allow them back inside until the floors dried. Decades later, when Mac was an adult with his own apartment, he had a hard time trusting a vacuum cleaner or damp mop to keep his floors clean.

You need to scrub, he thought.

Walter was a short, wiry man with light brown skin and close-cropped, tightly coiled hair, drawing him the nickname "Nap." One of his eyes was crossed from being struck with a rock. He took pride in his family history, tracing his ancestry back to a Scotsman who, as the story went, chose an African bride and established a household with her sometime in the nineteenth century. The tale sounded improbable in the 1940s, given the social climate, but Mac later found census records that seemed to bear it out, showing a white man named Junius McCollah living with a Black wife in Sardis, Mississippi.

Walter didn't have much formal education, though he "went as far as he could" in school, as he put it—probably to the eighth or ninth grade. Still, he read and wrote so well that he handled correspondence for his illiterate neighbors. He did a little drinking, as most country folks did, but only on the weekends. On Saturday nights, some of the men from the community would come over to the house and play cards until all hours. But during the week, he'd come in from the fields with his work boots on and spend a quiet evening with the family, sometimes reading the Bible for hours.

During the wintertime, he'd leave before daybreak to go trapping with a neighbor, a man named Huse, several days a week. They'd spend all day setting traps in various places, returning a couple days later to check them. Minks were the prize quarry, and Walter sent the pelts off to Chicago for a good price. Sometimes they'd find only raccoons in the traps, which Walter hated because there was no money in them. But Mac loved when he brought back raccoons because Lucille made them into a delicious roast dinner.

But the money was in mink. Walter had to handle the pelts with care, stretching and cleaning them just so and hanging them to dry in the barn. Keeping the traps in good repair was a lot of work in itself, and he'd spend hours tinkering with them in front of the wood stove in the living room as the children looked on, fascinated.

Lucille and Walter were pious, churchgoing folks. They loved music, especially gospel, though Lucille sometimes sang a few verses from what she called a love song:

My bonnie lies over the ocean
My bonnie lies over the sea
Oh bring back
Bring back
Bring back my bonnie to me

They were both in the church choir, and on many evenings they'd walk in the door laughing after rehearsal, singing the scales and debating the proper notes. They made a game of it, with Walter croaking, in the lowest bass he could muster, "Do, re, mi, fa, so, la!"

Lucille would interject, in a piercing falsetto, "Ti, do!"

If you stood on the road in front of the McColloughs' house and looked to the right, you'd see the woodpile where they kept and chopped firewood, then the vegetable garden, then the unpainted barn where they kept their two mules, then the pigpens. Between the house and the barn was the pump where they got all the water for the household use and the farm. It spewed forth quintessential Delta water with its lingering, silty undertaste. Mac never noticed it growing up because he didn't know anything different, but after he left home and came back, it tasted like mud to him.

Because collecting and heating water was a huge task, bathing was a weekly event for which they had two metal tubs that did double duty as laundry basins. Everyone except the small children bathed in the large tub, using about five gallons of water. It was big enough for kneeling prayer-style. They'd heat a gallon or so on the stove and add the hot water to the rest to create a warm bath—though it didn't stay warm long. The small basin, also called a foot tub, was for the little ones, who bathed in about a gallon and a half of water. The adults bathed behind a closed bedroom door, while the children washed up in the sitting room.

Behind the McColloughs' house was an outhouse, and behind that and off to the right was the pasture where the mules grazed. On the remaining land, they farmed cotton and soybeans as cash crops, with the aid of an old Farmall F-20 tractor and the two mules. They picked the cotton by hand, but the soybeans had to be harvested by combine, which they didn't have. They paid a white farmer up the road to come do that.

In addition to the cash crops, they raised corn for the animals and to make hominy. They also grew sorghum, which they harvested in August and turned into molasses in their mill. There, a solitary mule pulled a long pole in labored circles, turning a stone disc that pressed the sugary juice out of green sorghum canes. The juice collected in a vat sitting on a wood fire below, where it boiled down to dark syrup. Huse and some of the other neighbors would bring their sorghum over to be milled with the McColloughs', and the families would spend an entire weekend doing all the work that went into making molasses: feeding the cane into the mill, stirring the syrup, tending the fire, and leading the mule around in a circle.

The house had a wide front porch with two windows peering out from under a corrugated tin roof. Jutting up from the roof were two chimneys for the two wood stoves, one to heat the sitting room and another for preparing meals in the kitchen.

Crossing the front porch, you'd step into the sitting room with its four-legged cast iron stove, which looked like a pig to Mac. In addition to a couple of chairs, the sitting room contained a bed, making it functionally a bedroom. Turning right, you'd reach two bedrooms, and turning left, you'd enter the dining room, featuring a long wooden table with bench seating and chairs at each end. Straight through the living room was the kitchen, the heart of the house, with its wood stove. High atop the stove sat a bread-box-sized warmer.

Of the fourteen McColloughs, Mac was most closely associated with the warmer, as that was the first place he slept when he came into this world. He was born two months premature, so tiny that the midwife who delivered him feared he wouldn't survive the night. Lucille had fallen asleep, so the midwife converted the warmer into a makeshift incubator, padding it with blankets. She cradled his tiny, blanket-wrapped body in her hands and placed him inside, leaving the door open a crack.

She also took the liberty of naming him.

"I didn't think he'd live, and no baby should die without a name," she explained to Lucille when she awakened. "So I named him Marthurman."

"*Marthurman?* Oh no, no, no, that won't work." Lucille promptly renamed him Marrell, harmonious with the name of his next oldest brother, Levell. He'd pick up the nickname Mac nearly two decades later, in the army.

The McCollough children began helping around the house and farm almost as soon as they were walking and had some dexterity. At six, Mac was gathering firewood and helping Lucille in the garden, and by eight, he was doing real farm work like picking cotton, but with a half-sack slung across his torso rather than a full-sized one.

There were plenty of jobs to be done, from collecting gallons of water from the pump to chopping wood to plowing the fields. Then there were basic household tasks like making the beds, with their wrought-iron frames and wooden slats. The mattresses were made from sewn-together cotton ticking bags that were stuffed with straw, or sometimes cotton, then buttoned up. When Lucille and Walter told the children to make up their beds, they were asking them to unbutton the mattress casings, replace the contents with fresh stuffing, turn it with their hands to fluff it up, then button up the casings and shake them before putting them back on the beds. This was a weekly chore, and a different one from the daily task of *straightening* up the beds, which entailed pulling the coarse brown blankets and hand-stitched quilts neatly over the sheets.

The family often listened to a battery-powered radio with tubes in the back that Walter had to change from time to time. It had an antenna that went out the window and down to a pole in the ground, picking up nearby stations. Their favorite was WDIA out of Memphis, 50,000 watts of good listening. The station was owned by a white man, Bert Ferguson, but all the programming was Black—shows, blues and gospel music, DJs, everything. They liked to listen to a preacher on there, Brother Theo "Bless My Bones" Wade, who punctuated his sermons with the catchphrase that became his nickname. But they enjoyed listening to other stations, too. Walter sometimes listened to the Grand Ole Opry, and they also tuned in to radio shows, like *Beulah*, about a Black maid caring for a white household, or *The Lone Ranger*.

Lucille charged each of the older girls with caring for a younger sibling. Mac went to Shag, seven years older. She had a kind disposition and showered him with attention, though she suffered from pain spells that left her bedridden from time to time. Looking back, Mac suspected it was sickle cell disease, which was later diagnosed in their sister Joyce.

People often talked about how pretty Shag was, with her dazzling smile and dimpled cheeks like Mac's. Unlike most of the girls who hot-combed their hair straight, she wore hers natural. It formed into waves when she put water in it.

Likewise, Lucille didn't wear elaborate hairstyles. She never wore cosmetics or jewelry, either, though she took more pride in her appearance than she let on. One day she and Mac were out in the garden picking potatoes when he was about five. A man came trucking down the road in a horse-drawn wagon, *tch tch tch tch*. As he passed their house, he tipped his hat.

"Hello, Miss Lucille!"

When she spotted him, her hands flew to her hair and dress, smoothing and primping as the potatoes she held in her apron tumbled to the ground.

Imma tell Daddy she was fixing herself up for that man! Mac thought.

Every morning before dawn, Lucille got up and fixed breakfast for Walter, who'd eat and be gone by the time the children awoke. Then she'd cook for them. The family grew most of what they ate: pinto beans, peas, greens, lettuce, cabbage, tomatoes, okra, hot peppers, watermelon, cantaloupes, peanuts. They got milk from their cow and eggs from their chickens and guinea fowl. They ate every part of the pig, starting with the ham—which didn't last long—and moving on to the shoulders, ribs, belly, fatback, hocks, neck bones, intestines, ears, tail, and finally the feet.

Once the weather turned cold around November, Walter would drive his 1937 Lincoln Zephyr, which had been converted into a pickup truck, over to Helena, Arkansas, to buy food wholesale. He'd return with barrels of flour, huge cans of lard, and long rolls of pork rinds, enough food to last all winter. They didn't need a calendar to know when spring was near; they could tell by their dwindling rations. By the end of winter, they were literally scraping the bottom of the barrel.

Walter supplemented their food supply with game he hunted and trapped: deer, rabbits, raccoons, possums. He also bought a few staples from the store, like cornmeal, canned fish, and cheap cuts of beef.

Breakfast was usually rice, biscuits, and sliced fatback. They had molasses on the side, which they stirred together with butter and sopped up with the biscuits. Their midday meal, which they called dinner, featured buttermilk with cornbread crumbled into it. At supper, their last meal of the day, they often ate biscuits again, plus beans, greens, and cornbread. They also sometimes ate pan-fried patties of canned salmon or mackerel, or small amounts of beef they parceled out between themselves. It wasn't until Mac enlisted in the army that he finally got his very own steak.

Several of Mac's older siblings had moved away by the time he came along, though they visited often. His eldest sister, Pan, had two daughters who were like sisters to him, and he loved playing with them, as well as his younger siblings Floyd and Joyce, plus the neighbor children. They'd run up and down the road, getting into rock fights and running home.

But more often than not, asthma sent Mac home wheezing and kept him there. He couldn't run around with the other kids like he wanted. Lucille and Walter did everything they could to treat it. Nearly every day, Lucille rubbed his chest with a combination of turpentine and a medication called asafetida that made him feel like he had warm coals under his skin. Then she'd dress him in a special undergarment she created to lock in the effect of the treatment, a thick piece of wool blanket with a neck hole cut in it. She'd press it with a hot iron and put it on him while it was still warm. On top of that, he wore his clothes—always long sleeves, because Lucille and Walter thought it was the air that was making him sick.

If Mac had an asthma attack, Lucille would give him a breathing treatment she created, which involved having him sit up in bed under a tent she fashioned around him using an old sheet propped up with a broomstick. Then she'd burn a few cotton seeds in a small metal tray and hold it inside the tent so he could inhale the fumes. Walter had his own preparation for

Mac, a special drink concocted from milk, raw eggs, and whisky that had a slimy texture Mac could hardly stand.

Mac remembered early childhood as a happy time in his life, an idyllic haze of warm memories: Walter and his older brothers harvesting beans and taking them to market in West Helena, Arkansas; riding the tractor in Walter's lap; WT coming back on army furlough from the Philippines and bringing Mac a child-sized soldier's uniform, complete with an Eisenhower jacket and a pocketful of foreign money. These days marked a high point against which he'd measure his family's fall.

Walter made the children feel special for being McColloughs. He talked about it like it was a badge of honor, telling them about his parents, grandparents, and uncles. His father, Willis Eugene, had been a relatively prosperous farmer—so prosperous that in the mid-1920s, he was one of the first people in Mississippi to buy an automobile, a Ford Model T. He bought it for Walter, and when Walter went to the train depot to pick it up, he found it waiting for him wrapped in tar paper.

He and the other grown folks were always emphasizing the importance of reputation, and as far as Mac could tell, his family had a good one. They were respectable, not in the sense of having money but in having a good name. People saw them as upstanding and responsible. They came from people they took pride in, and Mac carried that pride inside himself. Still, he knew there were limits to the respect they got, namely when they encountered white people.

When Mac was four, he and Walter stopped by a general store after a trip to the cotton gin, and several white men were sitting on the store's front porch. He and Walter went on in and bought what they needed. As they were leaving, one of the men offered Mac the cherry soda he'd been drinking.

Mac shook his head no. Grown folks were always saying not to drink after people, so he couldn't understand why his father looked so agitated.

"Go on, son," Walter said.

"I don't want it. They been drinking out of it."

"Take it, boy," Walter snapped.

Mac took it, bewildered. *Why do you tell me not to drink after somebody, and now I got to take this?* he thought.

5.

Black Nights Keep Falling

The calamities arrived in a group of three, as such things often unfold. First, Mac's one-year-old sister, Doyce, got sick in early 1949, when Mac was five. Up until then, she'd been perfectly healthy, but one day she went into convulsions. Walter and Lucille rushed her to the hospital but returned home without her. She'd passed. Many years later, Mac saw stories like Doyce's in a PBS documentary about pesticides, reminding him of how Walter would come home covered in poison after spraying the fields.

At Doyce's viewing, Mac couldn't bear to look at her body in its tiny coffin. He didn't want to be part of what was happening, didn't want the image taking up residence in his mind. If he refused to witness it, he thought, he could distance himself from the reality—and finality—of her death. Later he'd regret that choice, wishing he'd taken that last opportunity to see her face.

Then Lucille got sick. One day, she was walking through the house in her robe when she fainted to the floor. Walter took her to a charity hospital in Mound Bayou, and it seemed like things went from bad to worse overnight. She was back and forth to the hospital for months, her stays growing longer and longer. Her body shrank until she wasn't roundish anymore but thin and frail. Neither Walter nor anyone else told the children what was wrong with her, and maybe they didn't know. Walter made regular treks to see her, never bringing the children, and she returned home for brief visits on occasion.

Mac couldn't understand what was happening, only that things were getting terrible. With Lucille in the hospital, the household now consisted of Walter, Pirl, Shag, Mr. Mane, Bea, Mac, Floyd, and Joyce, plus Pan's two children, though Pan was living somewhere else with her husband, Willie. WT was also living elsewhere with his new wife, and Johnnie was in the veterans' hospital in Memphis on an extended stay, undergoing tuberculosis treatment. Mac wasn't sure where Top was.

Without Lucille to send the children to school or set a rhythm to the day, things descended into disorder. Even if someone had been there to make them go to school, the children had nothing suitable to wear on their backs or feet. For months on end, Floyd and Mac—when he wasn't sick—ran around the yard with no direction, wearing ragged clothes. Walter struggled to pay the mounting medical bills, though Lucille was in a charity hospital. Mac once overheard Walter say he owed $2,000. Walter sold the tractor, then the other farm equipment.

We're poor now, Mac thought.

Unable to afford the rent, Walter loaded all the family's possessions into their wagon in the fall of 1949 and drove their two mules to a new place in Tunica County called Walnut Lake. He took up sharecropping cotton on a ten-acre plot, bringing Shag, Pirl, Bea, Mr. Mane, Mac, and Floyd with him and sending Joyce to live with Lucille's sister Emma, up in what they called the hills of Tate County. Pan and Willie moved into a house on an adjoining five-acre plot.

Their new home was what folks called a shotgun house, three rooms connected end on end such that if you fired a shot through the front door, it would pass through unobstructed out the back. They got water from a pump on the property of white neighbors up the road. That family had two small children, too young for Mac and Floyd to play with, but on warm afternoons, they'd invite the McColloughs over to watch their television set. They'd pull it out onto their porch for the occasion, and the two families would sit in the grass and watch cartoons or *Howdy Doody* or whatever was on and laugh. It was here that Mac saw a television for the first time.

On the other hand, he *had* seen a film before once—at his brother WT's juke house. Walter and Lucille were against his running such an unseemly business, but they couldn't do anything about it—he was grown. He'd found an old abandoned house down the road from their place in Tibbs, located the owner, and arranged to rent it. Then he cleaned it up, set up a kitchen with a fry cook, found somebody to bring in beer and white lightning, and soon the place was jumping. That was all a successful juke joint required. Sometimes a local would come in and sing the blues—it wasn't hard to find somebody who could do that—and folks would sit around tables playing cards, cussing, arguing, and getting drunk. Mac didn't see that part firsthand because children weren't allowed inside, except for one night when somebody brought in a movie projector, and they had a special showing of *Tarzan*. The onscreen action looked terrifying in its realism to Mac, as if the animals were about to pounce through the screen.

The older white couple the McColloughs sharecropped for lived in a house on a noncultivated section of the farm, which spread out over forty acres or so. The husband suffered from some kind of illness and never left the house. Mac never saw him once, though he did meet the wife. Mac and Floyd were walking down the road past her house one evening when she came to her front door with a plate in her hand. She called them over and handed it to them with a smile. It was thick slices of something brown and lumpy.

"Thank you, miss," they said.

When they got down the road a bit, they looked at the plate, then each other. Mac pinched off a chunk with his fingers.

What is it? he wondered. It had the color and fragrance of meat but felt like bread.

Floyd made a face. "You gone eat that?"

Mac put it in his mouth and began to chew. His face brightened. "It's good!"

Floyd dug in, and they soon finished the plate. It wasn't until Mac was in the army that he tried a dish called meatloaf and realized it was what the woman had given them.

Unlike their place in Tibbs, where they rented the house and land but kept all their earnings from their crops, they started off in debt at this place. The white couple provided the furnishing—a monetary advance against expected earnings—at the beginning of the spring growing season. Walter used that money to buy fertilizer, feed, and food. When the crops came in at harvest, Walter went back to the owners to settle the books. He had to pay back the advance, which put him back where he started before: $0. The following spring, he got another advance and went through the cycle again.

The McColloughs were used to being self-sufficient, but now they were barely getting by. Walter couldn't afford to buy several months' worth of food wholesale in Helena anymore. The furnishing money was only enough for smaller amounts of food, which they now bought retail.

The road that went past their house led into a lonely patch of woods a couple of miles away and dead-ended in front of a bootlegger's place. Sometimes they'd see his mule-drawn cart wobbling down the road, filled with corn and bags of sugar. Walter and the boys got invited over once—Mac wasn't sure why—and the bootlegger showed them the pit in the ground where he fermented sour mash. After a while he'd have to replace the sour mash with fresh ingredients, and sometimes he'd give the old mash to Walter. Walter fed it to his pigs, and they ate it until they got stumble-down drunk.

Mr. Mane, who was eleven or so, took a liking to the bootlegger and was soon performing odd jobs for him, like carrying sugar and water. The bootlegger wasn't paying him as far as anybody knew, but things were in such disarray that nobody was keeping up with what the boy was doing. Mac didn't remember him ever attending school, and he'd always tended toward precocious behavior—mannish, as the grown folks called it, hence his nickname.

Then Shag got sick, or at least sicker than normal, and for longer, too. She was fifteen and had been going different places with seventeen-year-old Pirl, typical teenage girl adventures. The next thing Mac knew, Shag was in the hospital giving birth. The baby was stillborn, and a day or so later, Shag died.

Sickness and death seemed to be everywhere, from the air to the dirt. In 1951, with Lucille still hospitalized, Walter got word that the sickly husband of the landowning couple had died. After harvest, Walter moved again, this time to a place near Senatobia in the hills of Tate County. This was where Lucille was from, and she still had family nearby. He took Bea, Mac, and Floyd with him, while Mr. Mane stayed behind in Walnut Lake with the bootlegger. Pan and Willie were living in Strayhorn, while Pirl had gotten married and moved to Memphis, about forty miles from Senatobia.

When Walter, Bea, Mac, and Floyd first arrived in Tate County, they stayed with Lucille's sister George Anne for a few months. She lived at a large farming and ranching community, Double J Ranch, though people commonly called it Cahill Farm after one of the owners. It was known for its Polled Hereford show cattle, naturally hornless beef cows that were docile and put on weight fast.

By November 1951, Walter found work there doing day labor, basic farm jobs like planting, plowing, chopping wood, and feeding cattle. His specialty was driving the tractor, which wasn't something just anyone could do. It required specialized knowledge about how to set the angle of the plow for the job and how close to get to the plants' delicate root systems. An unskilled tractor driver could destroy a field, but Walter was an expert. Still, he was paid almost nothing for the work, around thirty cents an hour, which usually worked out to three dollars a day, though during the fall cotton harvest, he'd be paid based on how much he picked. It was enough to survive, but only just.

Mr. Mane came up from Walnut Lake and took a day labor job feeding and grooming the cattle. It was dirty work, but it put a little money in his pocket for trips to Senatobia, the county seat. He began to take an interest in Mac and Floyd, coming back from town with small treats for them—candy, a toy, or a comic book, often accompanied by a can of Spam they'd fry up and use for sandwiches. The newfound responsibility of a job and the money that came along with it gave Mr. Mane a swell of confidence.

The family's first house there was a tumbledown old place with four or five rooms. It sat on a hilltop a good distance from the six or so other households living on the farm. Like the other houses, it lacked running water, and the McColloughs had to haul water up the hill from the community well, about half a mile away. It was hard to get up to the house when the road was icy. One time Lucille's doctor, a white woman called Dr. Ethel, had to use a jeep to bring Lucille up to the house from the hospital.

The McColloughs were assigned a ten-acre plot of land to sharecrop. While Walter and Mr. Mane did day labor, the rest of the family was expected to work the land.

WT and his wife Mary moved in with them for a while, and with Shag gone, Mary stepped in to help keep an eye on Mac. Mac thought Mary was the prettiest woman he'd ever seen, with her angelic face and flowing hair. Her legs were covered in thick, dark hair, something he knew the men around there liked.

After a few months, they moved into a different house, smaller but better located. Like most of the homes there, it was a tin-roofed shotgun house, three rooms from front to back. The kitchen was in the very back, and they used the front and middle rooms as bedrooms.

Then Lucille died. The last time Mac saw her was when he was seven, on her last visit home for Christmas in 1951. After spending a few days with the family, smiling as they opened gifts, she left on New Year's Day.

As with Doyce, Mac refused to look at her during the viewing. He couldn't do it. But after that, his asthma disappeared, and no one could explain it.

When Lucille died, Walter changed. No longer did he read the Bible when he came home from working. Instead, he drank. On the weekends, he'd go out to juke joints and drink some more. He never stopped providing for the family, never became a brawler or a lawbreaker, but he ceased to be the father Mac had known. He became a different man, a hardened man.

People said he'd cursed God. Mac heard one of his aunts talking about it once, saying Walter told her, "I lived my life serving God. When Doyce got sick, I prayed for him to save her, but she died. I prayed for him to save Lucille, and she died, too. Why would I keep wasting my time with him?"

On a Sunday around noon in spring 1952, Walter walked through the front door with a woman at his side. He'd been gone since Saturday evening—not unusual for him—leaving Mac and Floyd in Mary and Bea's care. But coming home with a woman, that was unusual.

She walked to the middle of the front room and posed in a wide, bow-legged stance. "How ya like-a me?" she asked in a playful tone. "I'm your new mama."

Mac stared at her. She looked like she was dressed for church, with her fancy hat.

Well, you ain't my mama, he thought. *Why should I like you?*

But from the moment she crossed that threshold, she was the woman of the house.

"I know how to raise children," she reminded Mac and Floyd from time to time, brandishing her childrearing résumé so they wouldn't mistake her for someone inexperienced. "You not the first ones I raised."

Miss Ethel was in her forties and had married her first husband young. The man had many children when they met, and she went on to have one with him. When he died, she married another man with several children and raised them, too. Mac and Floyd were her third set. For her, mothering was a fine art, and she considered herself a virtuoso.

Tall and lean, she often struck that wide-legged pose she called "standing back into her legs." She said it was this stance that first attracted Walter to her. "He saw me standing back into my legs."

That was all Mac knew about how they met. He couldn't even say for sure she and Walter were officially married, having seen no evidence of a wedding or visit to the justice of the peace. But he had no reason to doubt it, either. She did mention a proposal, that raising children had been part of Walter's proposal to her.

"He told me he needed someone to be a mother to his children," she said. "And I was born for that."

She had no formal education and could neither read nor write. Walter had tried to teach her a few times, but it never stuck, and she soon gave up. But she was an intelligent woman with plenty of common sense. She knew how to run a household, set routines for meals and chores, keep clothes clean and patched. With her efforts, the family soon began to right itself. Mr. Mane, Mac, and Floyd sensed her devotion to them and gave her theirs in return.

Though Walter and Miss Ethel worked hard during the week, they partied on the weekends, carousing at juke joints and drinking until all times of night. After supper at home with Mac and Floyd, they'd drop off the boys at friends' houses, returning in the wee hours to pick them up. That went on for several years until one day in 1956, Miss Ethel just decided to *stop*—no more running around drinking and carrying on. Mac had no idea what prompted it, but Walter kept going without her.

Now that Miss Ethel had gotten the McCollough household in order, Mac and Floyd could go to school. In July 1952, they showed up at Mt. Zion School, a two-room schoolhouse on the grounds of Featherstone AME Church in Senatobia. Unlike the school year for white children, Black children's school year began in July because it was structured around the planting and harvesting seasons. While white children were on summer break, Black children were attending classes, returning to the fields when harvest began in September. They worked through much of the fall and went back to the classroom after Thanksgiving, where they remained while the fields lay dormant. In May, they went out to the fields again for the planting season and stayed there until the new school year began in July.

Nine-year-old Mac and seven-year-old Floyd were beginning their schooling late. But Mr. Mane wouldn't be starting at all. At thirteen, he had a job and wasn't about to begin going to school now. The time for that had passed.

Mac was ecstatic to arrive at the little schoolhouse, no more than sixty by ninety feet. The only part of the school that was painted, inside or out, was the blackboard. Inside, an accordion-like partition divided the lower grades in the front from the upper grades in the back, and the bathroom was an outhouse on the edge of the church cemetery. Many years later, Mac would learn that some of his mother's relatives had founded the church. Some of the headstones he'd sat on and clambered over had belonged to them.

On the first day of school, the teacher wasn't sure where to place Floyd and Mac, but Mac announced, "I'm in second grade, and my little brother's in first."

How he arrived at that conclusion was a mystery, but the teacher followed his directive.

He loved school. His teachers cultivated his intellectual curiosity, finding opportunities to give him special responsibilities. Mr. Wallace, his third-grade teacher and the school principal, assigned him fifth-grade work and sometimes had him recite it in front of the fifth-grade class. Mac would remember some of the assignments for the rest of his life, like the story of Samson he had to memorize. It built up his self-esteem and showed him his efforts meant something.

Mr. Wallace noticed that Mac and Floyd needed an extra hand, so he paid them a small salary to build a fire in the schoolhouse's coal-burning heater first thing in the morning and clean the soot out of the stove and chimney at the end of each week. It gave them extra money that they sorely needed, but it also taught them what it meant to have people depending on you to do something important.

Mr. Wallace wound up getting in trouble with the law—something to do with a cotton theft ring. While he was in jail, he made Mac a baseball card scrapbook and had one of his visitors deliver it. Mac never forgot his kindness and belief in him

Mac and Floyd began attending Sunday school at St. Peter Church, and at twelve, Mac was invited to help teach by Mr. Sam Lucky, a deacon and Walter's good friend. Honored, Mac readily agreed.

He admired Mr. Lucky, an upstanding yet kind and easygoing man. Mr. Lucky didn't partake in too much drinking, just an occasional sip from a liquor bottle. He had a coon dog he took hunting at night, sometimes returning with raccoons and possums for Miss Ethel to cook. And he always made sure Mac and Floyd had a way to church, often driving them there himself. Though a sharecropper, he seemed better off than most people in the community. He was someone people respected.

The St. Peter Church deacon board twice appointed Mac as one of the church's Sunday school junior superintendents. The post required him to represent the church at an annual statewide Sunday school convention and report on it to the church when he returned. It made him feel important, like they expected great things from him.

6.

World View

In 1955, Mac didn't know much about civil rights beyond the fact that he didn't have the same ones as white folks. But he and the other children sensed a change coming, a hope that manifested like a shift in the wind or the angle of sunlight. They picked it up in grown folks' conversations, from the things people said, and things they didn't say.

"What you gone do when you get your equal rights?" was the question on their lips.

It expressed a hope for something that was surely coming, as if they heard a faint train whistle on the wind though they didn't yet see the train.

A white man once asked Mac that question, what he'd do when he got equal rights. Though he said little in response, he did have plans.

I'm gonna have me a good job, he thought. *I'm gonna build me a nice house and live wherever I want to live.*

He dreamed of a large home with lots of glass, entire walls of glass he could gaze through at the world.

In the fall of 1955, Walter moved the family from the Cahill place to a farm near Strayhorn, where he started sharecropping for Old Man Davis, a white man who lived in nearby Senatobia. The farm had about forty acres of land, ten for cotton cultivation and the balance for pasture. The McColloughs were the only family living there. Together with Davis they worked the entire ten acres of cotton, Walter and his two mules alongside Davis and his tractor. The children chopped and picked cotton. At harvest, the McColloughs and Davis split the crop.

That summer, a gang of white men murdered fourteen-year-old Emmett Till in the not-too-distant town of Money. Mac was eleven. Some of the grown folks, including Mr. Lucky, used the story as a lesson for the boys.

"You got to be careful how you act around white folks," he'd say. "Remember Emmett Till and that white woman. They killed him for that."

It sounded to Mac like blaming the victim, as if Till somehow brought the murder on himself. But he also understood they were doing their best to protect him, to keep him alive. It was their way of making him understand there were mean, evil people out there, and minding one's behavior was a life and death matter. Sheriff Joe Taylor's murder of their family friend Alonzo that year underscored the point.

Once in a while, Miss Ethel talked about the bloodthirsty lynch mobs of her youth who rampaged through Black areas. There was also a story from his mother's side of the family about a cousin who killed a white man, and in response, a white mob came looking for him and his relatives. They fled to Arkansas and remained there for years before finally returning to Mississippi.

Mac never experienced lynch mobs or Klan activity, though he did know about the White Citizens' Council, a white supremacist group that respectable white folks joined. Walter warned him they were the same as the Klan.

But Mac and Floyd did have an encounter with terror one morning that year as they walked the six or so miles down Highway 4 to their friend's house. A pickup truck full of white boys appeared and swerved toward them, forcing them to dive into the roadside brush. As they hid, crouching and trembling, the truck screeched a U-turn and sped down the road the other way.

In Tate County, everything was segregated—schools, restaurants, movie theaters, even mortuaries, where the white section was in front and the colored section was in back. In Senatobia, there was a colored side of town and a white side, though most of the shopping was downtown along Main Street.

To Mac, it all had an air of normalcy about it because it was all he knew. There were colored and white water fountains and restrooms, but not so close together that he saw them juxtaposed. Though there was a drugstore with a lunch counter, Black folks knew not to go near it, so it wasn't something he thought about. But it did stand out in his mind that when his family did their Saturday shopping on Main Street, the white patrons tried on clothes in the dressing rooms and the Black patrons didn't. And the white patrons went to the front of the checkout line.

The only truly jarring experience he could recall was at the doctor's office when he was thirteen and had a terrible bout of pneumonia. He'd fallen ill on Easter Sunday, and by Wednesday he was so sick that Walter hauled him to Senatobia to see Dr. Ethel. She gave him a shot and some medicine, and he pulled through. He was convinced she saved his life. But he never forgot sitting on the colored side of the room and Dr. Ethel zigzagging over from the white side.

As far as Mac could tell, nobody challenged segregation or even talked about it much. The boycotts and marches happening in various places seemed a world away. It was like living on an island. At school, the teachers taught from the textbooks and never got into what was going on around them societally. They never mentioned voting rights or whether segregation was just. Folks just accepted the way things were—or at least acquiesced.

It wasn't merely that people didn't engage with civil rights, but that the press censored coverage of it, too. Walter kept up with the news as best he could, subscribing to Memphis's *Commercial Appeal*, but the newspaper presented the anti-civil rights point of view. You couldn't get a true picture of things by reading it.

Still, a sense of defiance was emerging all the same among some of the young adults, particularly some of the young Black men who'd moved to Memphis and come back. They carried with them a mood that seemed to challenge things.

It felt like déjà vu when Miss Ethel had a stroke in 1956 and had to spend time in the hospital. When she came home, she was bedridden for weeks, barely able to use her right side. But she immediately set about rehabilitating herself, beginning with her right hand, which she'd exercise by rolling a rubber ball. After a few months she'd recovered so well that when she looked out the window one day and saw a fox chasing the chickens, she was able to throw the ball close enough to frighten it away. After that, she was back to walking and talking and doing housework, though she still suffered some lingering effects.

Her doctor advised her to get plenty of poultry in her diet, so she'd sit at the kitchen table, her plate piled high with fried chicken, telling Mac and Floyd between bites, "I don't want this, but the doctor told me to eat it so I'm forcing myself."

Mac and Floyd laughed.

"Miss Ethel," Mac said, "If you can force yourself to eat six pieces of chicken, you can at least save us one!"

———

After the first harvest at Old Man Davis's place in 1956, Walter moved the family back to Cahill Farm. Mac didn't know why, whether it was money or something else. What he did know was that he wanted two items with all his twelve-year-old heart: a shotgun and pair of leather engineer boots with the buckle across the front. He got the shotgun but could hardly hide his disappointment when he saw the boots Walter bought him. They were cheap knockoffs, with no straps across the front and cheaply glued soles. Mac set about destroying them immediately, holding his feet close to the fire in an effort to melt the glue holding them together. But his scheme backfired. When the soles loosened, Walter wouldn't buy him a new pair, instead making Mac insert pieces of cardboard to reinforce them.

———

In the summer of 1958, Mr. Mane died at nineteen. He got sick on a Wednesday, and by the weekend, he was gone. The doctors said it was jaundice from liver failure, but nobody knew what caused it. Perhaps he'd picked up something from working with the cattle, from the unsanitary conditions there.

His death hit Mac and Floyd especially hard. Nobody and nothing could replace their big brother. Another piece of their lives was gone.

The next year, Mac began working day labor at Cahill Farm, filling up a sprayer tank with malathion pesticide and water and using a highboy tractor to spray the cotton fields. Floyd started doing day labor, too, skipping class to drive the highboy. It made him feel like he was grown.

The foreman was Raymond, a White Citizens' Council member who drove around with a rifle in his pickup truck's rear window. Raymond and Floyd got along fine, but he made Mac's life miserable.

For one thing, he didn't like that Mac went to school. He wanted Mac out in the fields regardless of whether classes were in session. Mac told him no, he wanted to go to school. Floyd, on the other hand, preferred working to attending school. Raymond liked that.

"You got to do one of two things," Walter had told Mac and Floyd. "You got to go to school, or if you not going to school, you can go to work. But as long you go to school, I can protect you, because you have the right to go."

He said that because landowners often pressured families into putting their children to work in the fields.

The highlight of Mac's week was playing baseball on Saturday, so he tried to arrange his work week to begin on Monday and finish on Friday. But Raymond saw things differently—and not for any valid reasons, as far as Mac could tell. Raymond wanted him to start work on Wednesday and continue through Saturday. Mac thought it had to be out of spite, that Raymond knew he loved baseball and was determined to keep him from playing.

And Raymond always seemed to find fault with him in other ways. Mac wasn't quick to show deference and say "Yes, sir" and such, and he could tell Raymond didn't like that. Looking back, Mac wondered if he bore much of the blame for their strained relationship, if he'd been somehow at fault by waging his own passive-aggressive war against Raymond. But if so, it was out of self-preservation as much as anything. The man was trying to whip him until he broke—not his body but his mind.

One time, he and Raymond got into it about something, and Raymond sent him home. "You're *fired*."

But Mac came back the next day, and they went on as before.

There were brief moments when it seemed like they might be able to get along. So when they were out in Raymond's truck one day and he decided to stop at a burger place, Mac went along with it and followed him in. But as soon as they crossed the threshold, the white man behind the counter went ballistic.

"What are you doing bringing that nigger in here?" the man screamed. "Get him outta here!"

Terrified, Mac ran out the door and back to the truck.

Decades later, Mac and Floyd would discuss what motivated Walter to send Mac to live with his older brother Sammy in Missouri in the fall of 1962. Floyd's theory was that Walter felt the winds of change blowing. After all, the Freedom Riders had journeyed across the South the previous year, greeted by beatings, arrests, and a firebombing. The previous year, the Greensboro Four had ushered in a wave of sit-ins that began to catch on in other towns. Floyd believed their father wanted to get Mac out of Mississippi to protect him from the strife that was sure to come his way—especially given how he'd been butting heads with Raymond. With the independence Mac was showing, Walter probably thought it best to send him away to a different environment where he'd have more freedom to become who he was becoming.

But the official story was that Sammy was sick, suffering from painful stomach ulcers, and he needed help in his work as a janitor for five apartment complexes. That was partially true, as he did sometimes suffer from pain spells from his ulcers. But it never seemed to slow him down much.

Though his house was in East St. Louis, a predominantly Black town across the Mississippi River from St. Louis, Sammy usually stayed in his one-bedroom basement apartment in one of the buildings he serviced in the nearby suburb of Clayton. Mac went to live with him there. It was the first time he'd ever set foot outside Mississippi.

Sammy was a tall, solidly built man with the appearance and demeanor of a deacon, which he was at the church he pressured Mac to attend with him and his wife, Martha, every Sunday. Aunt Martha lived in their East St. Louis house, and Sammy would spend weekends there with her.

The move to Clayton was a culture shock in just about every way, though Mac adjusted quickly. The food was different. Instead of biscuits, fatback, and molasses for breakfast, he ate corn flakes and milk, a modern change. At the grocery store, he discovered macaroni and cheese and an array of canned dishes—bachelor food for him and Sammy. He came to hate one of Sammy's mainstays, canned Salisbury steak, after seeing the gorillas at the St. Louis Zoo and realizing they smelled a lot like that canned steak.

In September 1962, Mac began his sophomore year of high school while living in a racially integrated environment for the first time. At his old school, all teachers, staff, and students were Black, but Clayton High was almost entirely white, and he became one of four Black students in a student body of around 750. Its angular and sprawling three-story building featured an enormous sculpture of a globe near the front entrance, making it feel like a launchpad to new worlds.

On the first day of school, one of his teachers asked for a show of hands of the students who'd be absent for Rosh Hashanah, and more than half the class raised their hands. Sitting up near the front, Mac surveyed them with amazement. He was now in the middle of a predominantly Jewish community anchored by a Reform synagogue.

School had come easily to him before, and he'd been an A student with little effort. But as one of the nation's top high schools, Clayton High was more rigorous, and he was chilled to receive his first C there. He gradually adjusted, eventually earning Bs and then As, along with a C here or there.

Before school, he got up at 4:30 in the morning to do janitorial work at three of the five buildings for which Sammy was responsible—blocky brick buildings with about fifty dwellings inside. Before heading to school, he made the rounds, emptying the garbage cans from each apartment, taking them down to the dumpsters, and bringing them back. He'd return after school if there were additional jobs, like minor painting or fixing leaky faucets.

Otherwise, his friends would drop him off at his uncle's apartment after school. The building had a side door leading directly to the basement where he lived, but he'd have them let him out at the building's palatial front entrance instead, waving goodbye from there. He was embarrassed to live in the custodian's basement apartment, though his classmates undoubtedly picked up on the many clues as to his living situation.

Mac's schedule was grueling, but he made sure he reserved some time for fun. He got involved in team sports like track and basketball, and while he was no great athlete, he enjoyed himself. He made friends right away, most of them white. It wasn't that he was uninterested in the other Black students, but aside from the fact that there were only four of them in the entire student body, they didn't seem to have much in common.

Jim Steinberg was the first of his classmates to introduce himself. He welcomed Mac into his close-knit social circle, and after school and on weekends, they went places that ran the gamut from restaurants to wrestling matches. Once, they all went to a spaghetti restaurant, where they shared a big platter of spaghetti and meatballs. Mac had never been to a restaurant like that before. Feeling self-conscious that he didn't know the rules of etiquette, he watched his friends for clues about how to do things. When they put their napkins on their laps, he put his on his lap. As they ate, they dabbed their faces with their napkins from time to time. When he reached for his napkin to do the same, he discovered it had fallen to the floor. He was too embarrassed to ask for another one, imagining what the others might think: *That fool dropped his napkin!*

So he left it on the floor, and for the remainder of the meal, he made himself miserable worrying that he had spaghetti sauce on his lips while everyone else dabbed away, carefree as they pleased. Afterward, he swore to himself that he'd never let embarrassment take hold of him again, that he'd confront every issue head-on, no matter the consequences. He wouldn't just sit there and suffer.

He became close friends with a girl, Susan. They saw each other only in school, and though he wanted to date her, that seemed out of the question, even in relatively progressive Clayton. They often walked to classes together, and he carried her books as they ambled down the hallway. They exchanged tikis, small charms that were fashionable to wear on necklaces, but left their feelings about each other mostly unsaid.

Though Mac felt freer than he ever had in his life, little things happened every now and then that reminded him of how some white people—even there—looked at him. There was the time he and his friends were hanging out on the school's back steps when a white girl he knew dropped an armload of books. He went over to help her pick them up, and a boy he didn't know claimed Mac had lifted the girl's skirt.

"I was just helping her pick up her books!" Mac said. He was furious, and he also knew he needed to shut down the claim fast.

"No, I saw you!" the boy said.

The girl stood there stunned, saying nothing.

In 1962, around Christmastime, Sammy enticed Walter to join Mac and him in Clayton with the promise of a good living doing the kind of janitorial work he was doing for apartment buildings. He promised to find Walter buildings of his own to work. Compared to the never-ending grind of day labor, Walter deemed it a good bet.

But he seemed to chafe as soon as he got there. He never said what was bothering him, but it was soon apparent that Sammy wasn't finding him any jobs as he claimed he would. By March or so of 1963, Walter went back to Mississippi.

Things seemed to carry on normally after that for a couple of months, until Sammy confronted Mac out of the blue, furious, one Sunday.

"Why have you been lying on me to my wife, telling her I'm going around with women at the church?"

"What? I never said that!" Mac's head was reeling.

He had no idea what Sammy was talking about, though occasionally when he answered the phone, the person at the other end would hang up. After that happened a few times, the person on the other end finally spoke. It was a woman—and not Aunt Martha—who asked to speak to Sammy. But none of that had anything to do with Mac, and he never discussed it with Martha or anyone else.

"I just don't understand why you'd tell her something like that!" Sammy said.

"I didn't!"

"That's what she told me you said!"

Around they went, with Sammy refusing to accept anything he said. Then he lodged more complaints against Mac, that he didn't go to church and ran around too much with white folks.

Mac couldn't grasp what was happening—where the story about the women from church came from and how the other grievances got caught up in it. He tried to do everything his uncle asked of him, other than going to church every single Sunday.

Was Sammy just tired of having him as a guest? If so, Mac wished he'd have just said that. But to throw a false story in his face, that cut to the core.

"Pack your bags and get out," Sammy said.

Not knowing what to do, Mac called Sammy's daughter Roberta, who lived in downtown St. Louis.

"Come on over," she said. "You can stay with me."

He lived with her until he finished the school year.

After finishing his sophomore year of high school in spring 1963, Mac returned to Mississippi to live with Walter, Miss Ethel, and Floyd, who'd since moved from Cahill Farm to the J. D. Thomas place in Lake Cormorant, near Walls. The operation dwarfed the Cahill place, with so much happening that it had two foremen managing the work rather than one. Much of the work was mechanized, and it went on seven days a week—even Sundays—unlike Cahill Farm, where people typically worked five days a week and rested on weekends.

As before, Walter was doing day labor, joined by Floyd, who by now had dropped out of school and was working full time. The new accommodations were like those at the Cahill place: a three-room shotgun house without indoor plumbing.

Mac began his junior year at Delta Center High in Walls as a young man who'd seen something of the world. He felt culture shock again, this time in reverse.

"Hey, St. Louis!" someone called out to him in the hallway one day. "You're regressing, huh?"

Mac didn't *feel* like he was regressing. As much as he'd enjoyed the St. Louis area's exciting integrated world, he was glad to be back in Mississippi, reuniting with family and old friends. He remembered his Clayton High friends fondly, but he didn't pine for them.

Some people couldn't help but point out how Mac had changed, and one obvious difference was his manner of speaking. At Clayton High, he'd picked up some of the speech patterns of the white kids, and his soft Northern Mississippi accent began to fall away. After church one Sunday, one of his cousins ran outside after talking with him, and he overheard her say, "Mama, Marrell is back, and he's sitting there talking just like a little white boy!"

While Mac didn't long for integrated spaces like those he'd frequented before, he was beginning to feel a strong sense of unfairness in the way things were in Walls. The civil rights movement was in full swing, and students were finally discussing it in classrooms—segregation versus integration, violence versus nonviolence. Some of the students deemed the fight for integration a waste of time. Most of the teachers still weren't saying much, but one of them, Mr. Epps, told them to focus on their *own* history, culture, and dignity.

Mr. Epps was a short, solid, mustachioed man with eyes that bulged with expression. He'd talk to the students outside the classroom, at recess, or after class.

Nonviolence was a fool's game, he told them. "Dr. King can have that, but as for you and me? If a white man lays a *hand* on you, I want him to draw back a nub."

Mac had never heard anyone speak that way before. The other adults never discussed Black folks' second-class status, much less how to respond. But Mr. Epps did, and he also gave them materials to read outside of school, like a book about African dynasties with kings and queens. He called integrationists "pork chop niggas," because they only cared about having enough money to buy pork chops from the grocery store, he said. As long as they were comfortable, they thought all was well. He spoke favorably of Malcolm X and a group called Fruit of Islam, but said Dr. King and the integrationists were "knocking on the door of a burning house."

Mac admired Mr. Epps and agreed with what he was saying, as did the other students. But they didn't have many occasions to test his ideas in Walls. Protests of any kind were unheard of, and though there were white residents, the town was so segregated that as far as Mac and his peers were concerned, it was 100 percent Black. The white folks had their schools, and the Black folks had theirs. There were no lunch counters, restaurants, stores, or even a traffic light—just a bank and two service stations. People went to Senatobia or Memphis for most everything else.

Mac fell back into the rhythms of the place with ease, going to school during the week and working on the Thomas place during breaks and on weekends. He drove Miss Ethel to St. Peter Church in Walter's black Chevrolet every fourth Sunday, or for special programs like Mother's Day or a Dixie Nightingales gospel concert. Walter hardly ever set foot on church grounds, and if he did, he stayed in the parking lot, socializing with the men. But mostly, he stayed home and had Mac drive Miss Ethel.

It was at church that Mac became reacquainted with a friend he'd known since childhood, a girl named Nellie. But things were different now. Now, they were fascinated with each other. One Sunday, they went off alone during the services, to Walter's Chevrolet.

7.

Induction

As required by law, Mac registered for the selective service at age eighteen, in 1962. But it wasn't until the next year that he got his call-up notice in the mail to appear at the Senatobia draft board in July 1963. Though he was beginning his junior year of high school due to his late start, he was legally an adult.

When he arrived at the draft board, he saw a large group of boys he knew, including a couple of cousins. From there, they took a charter bus up to Memphis for the examination. Throughout the ride, there was chatter about things they could do to avoid qualifying for service. One such scheme involved drinking shoe polish, which supposedly threw off your blood pressure. The bus dropped them off at the YMCA, where the draft board would be putting them up for the night. After an early dinner of sandwiches, some of the boys went out on the town and got drunk, but Mac stayed behind and played basketball in the gym. He didn't drink, plus he wanted to serve so he could use the GI Bill to go to college. There was a purpose in it for him.

The next day, the bus picked up the boys and took them to a large medical center, where they stripped down and the staff gave them complete physicals. The boys also took a written examination that tested their basic academic skills. That took up most of the day, and in the late afternoon, the bus brought them back to Senatobia. A few weeks later, he got his classification in the mail: 1-A. Available for service.

In late fall, a uniformed army recruiter knocked on his front door. He sat down with Mac and Walter and gave them a sales pitch on all the army had to offer. Mac's main concern was finishing high school and going on to college.

"Oh yes, the U.S. Army is an *excellent* choice if you want to continue your education. The first thing we'll do is make sure you get through school, because that'll make you a better soldier." He gushed about how Mac would be able to keep going to class as he did now, graduate on time, and receive his diploma while serving.

Mac had a choice: volunteer to serve or wait to be drafted. Volunteering seemed like the obvious way to go. Given that he'd probably soon be drafted anyway, why not choose the army rather than have it chosen for him? Three of his older brothers had served, and it was practically a family tradition. Plus, there was no other way to pay for school, and he didn't have the means to get a loan.

There was nothing to think over. He signed the enlistment papers then and there.

The sky was overcast on the morning of March 24, 1964, when Walter drove Mac to the Walls bus stop, a forlorn spot on the highway next to a gas station. There, he'd board the bus that came up from Tunica and take it to Memphis. The day had arrived for processing through the army induction center.

Walter didn't say much, and Mac followed suit. It had been that way since breakfast. Anyway, there wasn't much to say. Mac was going off to the army as his older brothers had.

Mac couldn't remember ever feeling that kind of gnawing sadness in his life. He'd left home before, of course, but he always knew he'd be coming back, and now he didn't know that. There were no guarantees when you were going off to be a soldier.

Still, he knew he'd made the right decision for his future. He wanted to go to college, and the GI Bill was the only way. His brothers had good things to say about serving, and besides, he didn't want to stay in Mississippi forever, did he? If he was going to leave, this was the way to do it. New frontiers beckoned. And yet, a homesick feeling devoured his gut as they rumbled down the highway. The air hung heavy and humid under the sheet of clouds above them. A storm was rolling in from the west.

They pulled over by the side of the road near the bus stop. If they'd tuned in to a pop station, they probably would've heard a Beatles song like "I Want to Hold Your Hand" or "She Loves You" or "Please Please Me," as the group held the top three spots on the U.S. pop charts for the second week in a row. If they'd been listening to a blues station, as they would've been more likely to do, they might have heard tracks from one of the three LPs B. B. King had released the previous year. But no one turned on the radio. They sat in silence.

After what felt like a long while, the bus appeared in the rearview mirror and eased up to the stop. Mac hugged Walter tight and grabbed his bag, clutching the ticket the army had sent him. On the bus, he took a window seat a couple of rows past the center, toward the back. He dared not look back at Walter. He didn't want his father to see him wracked with weeping.

The ride to Memphis took less than an hour, and when Mac arrived at the bus terminal around one in the afternoon, he found a car from the army induction center awaiting him. At the center, he joined a crowd of recruits in the reception area waiting to be sworn in.

A young white man walked over and sat beside him, introducing himself as Wayne. He explained that he'd hitchhiked all the way from somewhere up in East Tennessee.

"I took the bus from Mississippi," Mac said.

"I'm so happy I finally made it," Wayne said. "It took me forever to get down here." He made a few more remarks about his trip that made it sound like it had taken a couple of days.

Mac listened with interest, and soon his sorrow over leaving home began to fade. The two of them bantered back and forth, passing the time as they waited for the next thing to happen.

Eventually, someone came in and told the recruits to stand for the oath.

Together, they swore to defend the Constitution and protect the country from all enemies, foreign and domestic. The words had a weight to them.

Someone brought in sandwiches, and the group had an evening snack. Then it was time to head to the Memphis Metropolitan Airport to board a flight to Fort Jackson in South Carolina, where they'd complete the remainder of the induction process. As they made their way to the airport, the storm that had been brewing since that morning began, and rain poured from the sky.

They boarded a small, twin engine propeller plane. This was Mac's first flight, and it should've been exciting, but the turbulent conditions made the experience worse than he ever imagined. As the plane heaved and shuddered its way to South Carolina through lightning and peals of thunder, he quickly discovered the sickness bags. He never wound up having to use one, but he sure was glad they were there.

After what felt like many hours—though in reality, it was a short flight—the plane landed, and a military bus took them to the base. Around nine in the evening, they gathered in a large auditorium, and soldiers began passing out papers to them. What followed was a battery of tests in math, reading, and an entire section on Morse code, something Mac knew nothing about.

He was freezing. They hadn't yet been issued their uniforms, so everyone was still wearing their civilian clothes. Mac was dressed fine for a March day in Walls, but his short-sleeved shirt and thin trousers, still damp from rain, weren't nearly enough for an evening in that chilly auditorium. He powered through the tests. He just wanted to get them over with, get out of his damp clothes, go to sleep. He finally finished sometime after midnight, then went as directed to the barracks, exhausted and unaware that the hours of testing he'd just endured would determine his placement for the next three years.

———

The recruits were awakened at five the next morning, assembled outside the barracks, and marched to the cafeteria. Mac felt a pang of sadness return when he saw what they were serving for breakfast: burnt toast with chipped beef slopped onto it, alongside runny eggs. At home, he always had a say in how his eggs were cooked, and he almost always chose scrambled. He'd never eaten a runny egg in his life. But here he had no choice, and maybe he'd never have a choice.

What have I gotten myself into? he thought.

After breakfast, they got a little free time in the barracks before they were marched over to the barber to have their hair shorn. Again, no choice, just *bzzz bzzz bzzz* and "Next!"

Mac was overjoyed when they were finally issued their uniforms: boots, socks, underwear, long johns, shirts, pants, field jackets. He took off the clothes and shoes he'd worn from Mississippi and threw them in a trash can.

A few days later, they were transported by bus to Fort Gordon, Georgia, for eight weeks of basic training, where they learned hand-to-hand combat and all about firearms—cleaning, loading and unloading, marksmanship. Though the army was transitioning its standard rifle from the M14 to the M16, the class was given old surplus M1s from World War II. The rifles were notorious for knocking off a thumbnail if you weren't careful loading the clip, an embarrassing injury that was so common it had a nickname: the M1 Thumb. Mac managed to make it through almost the entire eight weeks without having it happen to him, but disaster finally struck. Fortunately, no one saw it because it was right before his class went on leave.

There weren't many Black recruits—they probably made up less than 5 percent of the class—but Mac got to be friendly with a group of white guys from the Boston area. One night, they went off base to check out downtown Augusta, and as they strolled up and down the streets, a bar caught their eye. They were under twenty-one, too young to drink in the state of Georgia, but curiosity got the better of them. They decided to go inside. No sooner had they crossed the threshold than the barkeep came running out from behind the bar.

"You know you're not allowed in here! Get out!"

He charged them, baseball bat in hand.

Mac and the guys sprinted out the door and made it a good ways down the street before they realized someone was missing from their group. Later, they learned what happened: The barkeep had held one young man and called the police, who arrested him. Now he was gone, recycled out of the class.

After completing basic training in spring 1964, Mac received the orders that would set the course for his career in the army and beyond: military police school. Like basic training, it was located at Fort Gordon and would last for eight weeks. But first, he'd get a two-week furlough to visit home.

He boarded a bus in Augusta that would take him to Senatobia, Mississippi, with a stop in Birmingham, Alabama. Arriving in Birmingham, he found that the station was completely segregated, though federal regulations had prohibited segregation three years earlier. But there, it was as if the regulations didn't exist. The white passengers walked right into the station's main terminal, while Mac, in his army uniform, couldn't go that way.

Many wearisome hours later, the bus passed through Memphis and down to Mississippi, finally crossing into Tate County. Once it entered Senatobia city limits, Mac expected it to turn down the road leading to the heart of town and make its usual stop at the drugstore on the corner of Main Street. Instead, it pulled onto the shoulder of Highway 51.

"Senatobia," the driver said.

The doors opened with a hissing sound.

Mac wondered why the bus was stopping there. He rose and walked to the front. "Excuse me, sir, aren't we going to the station in town?"

"This is the only stop in Senatobia now."

A grim realization struck Mac—they must've shut down the station in town rather than integrate.

He descended the steps and walked over to the luggage compartment. The driver met him there and dragged out Mac's seventy-pound pack before hopping back into his seat. The bus pulled back onto the highway with a groan. Mac stood frozen for a moment in the haze of dust and exhaust fumes. He did the only thing he could think to do—he started walking.

He'd just spent eight weeks training to protect the country, plus another week taking the oath and getting tested and having his head shaved and eating slop, and it all culminated in a bus leaving him by the side of the highway in uniform with his pack on his back. It was a tragic absurdity, an obscenity.

By the time he got to the center of town on Main Street, he was drenched with sweat. But he was in the ideal place for somebody he knew—a former neighbor, family friend, or St. Peter Church parishioner—to see him standing there and give him a ride in the direction of Walter and Ethel's place. Sure enough, somebody from the church spotted him and brought him to their home, where Walter picked him up.

When he finally walked through Walter and Miss Ethel's front door, Miss Ethel greeted him with a big chocolate cake. He was home again.

At dinner, Mac regaled them with tales of what he'd experienced over the past two months, from meeting Wayne to the turbulent flight through the thunderstorm to the new skills he'd learned in basic training. Every couple of sentences, Miss Ethel interrupted him.

"Watch your language, boy."

Without realizing it, he'd peppered his stories with profanity. It dawned on him that his speech had changed a lot since he'd been gone.

There wasn't much for Mac to do out there in the country during his stay. Walter let him drive his car, but there was nowhere to go. Most of his friends were still in school during the day. The biggest thing that happened was his high school prom came around while he was there, so he got to attend. He took his high school girlfriend, having kept in touch with her while he was away. He wore his uniform, knowing he looked sharp.

He had a joyful reunion with friends and family at St. Peter Church on Sunday, but he got the shock of his life when he saw his friend Nellie.

She was visibly pregnant. She said the baby was his.

As shocking as the news was, it didn't surprise him. After all, it was a natural result of what they'd done at that very church a few months earlier. While they never had a relationship, or wanted one, there was no question in his mind that he was going to take care of that child.

Military police school was like basic training in terms of the physical exercise, but there was also a classroom component where they learned about military justice and police procedures. For the first few weeks, they spent nearly every day in the classroom before moving to hands-on training. First aid was big. So was marksmanship, but with a .45 sidearm rather than a long gun. They learned techniques for physical restraint, as well as hand-to-hand combat—but differently than they'd been taught before. Previously, they were told to let out a yell if they were being thrown to the ground to clear the lungs of air and help prevent injury. But now that rule was out the window.

"I know they taught you that you got to scream when you fall," the trainer said. "Well, we don't want our military police hollering and screaming."

Instead, he taught, they should let their triceps hit the ground first, then the forearms, and then roll forward—without the scream.

During the program's first week, Mac was returning to the barracks from class when he saw Wayne, the hitchhiking recruit he'd met at the Memphis induction center, standing on the steps. They hadn't seen each other since that day, having been assigned to different basic training units, but he'd somehow found where Mac was living and waited for him to come back from class. They had a long talk about what they'd been doing. Wayne had been placed in lineman school, learning about electrical power systems. That evening was the last time Mac ever saw him.

In late summer 1964, after his eight weeks of military police school were up, his orders sent him to Fort Ritchie, Maryland, to guard a classified communications facility. For that, he needed a security clearance. His FBI background check was already underway by the time he graduated from military police school, and a week or so later, he had his clearance. The job was a monotonous routine of securing entrances, checking passes, and patrolling on foot, or driving around the perimeter by car. Certain points required the MPs to punch a clock to show what time they'd passed by the location while making the rounds. On icy winter days, some of them would take the clocks to the guard house and spend the day there, periodically punching in.

Now that Mac was done with basic training and military police school, he thought he'd be able to complete his senior year of high school like the recruiter said. But this was when he discovered the sales pitch had been a lie.

"The recruiter told me I was going to be able to finish high school," Mac said to a superior officer. "When can I do that?"

"We've got classes here, but they're at night," the officer said.

These were GED classes, not high school. And Mac was free to attend them, but he had to work his shift first. When he worked the day shift, he attended night classes, and vice versa when he worked the night shift. He never let doubt take over, or the anger crouching in the corner of his mind that whispered the recruiter should've told him the truth, that he'd been eligible for a deferment until he finished high school.

In May 1965, he turned twenty-one. He went out on the town in nearby Frederick, Maryland, to celebrate, stumbling back to the base just before sunrise. After a quick shower, he reported for duty.

His sergeant scowled when he saw him. "I'm really surprised at you. I never thought you'd show up here in this condition."

Mac kept his mouth shut. The sergeant could probably smell the alcohol wafting out of his pores. But the man took pity on him and assigned him to just sit and watch the gate.

Sometimes Mac patrolled the streets around the base in a Dodge Carryall, a job nearly as dull as all the others. But one day, he spotted a car speeding on a street parallel to his. He turned down a side street, switched on his lights, and pulled over the car. An exasperated looking white woman sat behind the wheel.

"License and registration?"

"What are you doing?" she asked.

"You were speeding."

"Well if I was, I was only going a couple of miles over the speed limit. Don't you have something better to do with your time?"

He wasn't sure what to say. Maybe she was right, maybe there *were* better uses of his time. He let her go with a warning, feeling about two feet tall.

His next posting took him to West Germany by slow troop ship in the fall of 1965, where he joined the 558th Military Police Company guarding the army's special weapons depot in Kriegsfeld. Behind a double-fenced perimeter and underneath eleven twenty-foot guard towers, a dozen earth-covered bunkers housed a cache of tactical nuclear warheads for deployment throughout the North Atlantic Treaty Organization. It was a site so secret that the soldiers weren't allowed to disclose where they were or what they were doing.

Mind-numbing duties filled his days. The place was isolated and cold, and there seemed to be snow on the ground from Thanksgiving through Easter. Time and again, he patrolled the secured weapons facility or sat in a freezing guard shack watching next to nothing happen. Most evenings, the soldiers partied in the barracks—if a group of men sitting around in their underwear drinking, playing cards, and occasionally lighting flatulence on fire could be considered a party. But with the drudgery came a new vantage point on the world. He now had the chance to visit places he'd only read about in books. On a three-day pass, he could see Amsterdam, or Frankfurt, or the nearby town of Kaiserslautern.

The base included a PX, a movie theater, and a small library, but the most popular spot was the Enlisted Men Club, or EM for short. Beer was twenty-five cents a can, and there was no limit on purchases. The military brought in musical acts—usually German or British bands covering British rock n' roll hits—to play on the club's expansive stage, and the bands often brought in go-go dancers. On a typical night, there was a band playing, dancers dancing, and a club packed with young soldiers, full of beer and ogling the dancers.

After a day's work, Mac would head over to the EM with his new buddies, white guys like the great majority of the MPs in his unit, though the company they supported did include a good number of Black soldiers. One night, his choice of friends got him into trouble.

He'd been sitting at a table talking and laughing when he got up to go to the bar. A Black soldier stepped in front of him, blocking his way.

"Why are you sitting over there with them?" the man asked.

"They're my friends."

"You too good to come over here with us?"

He pushed the man aside. "Let me pass."

The man punched him, and Mac punched back, knocking him down. The man's friends rushed over to pick him up and bring him back to their table. Meanwhile, Mac got his drink from the bar and went back to his table, giving the fight no further thought.

A couple of hours later, Mac left the EM alone. He was walking to his barracks when he heard footsteps behind him. He got the feeling he needed to turn around. The moment he did, he saw stars.

Someone had punched him in the face, and now he was on the ground, on his back. A group of guys—he couldn't tell how many—encircled him, kicking and beating him. He curled into a ball, trying to shield himself. Then he heard yelling and the shuffling of footsteps. His attackers fled just as several guys from his unit ran over. They helped him to his feet and accompanied him the rest of the way to the barracks.

Inside the building, he broke away from the group and went to the arms room, looking around until he found his M14. His face smeared with blood, he went back outside and hunted for his attackers. His adrenaline subsided after a while, and he returned to the barracks.

It was then that he realized how badly he was hurt. His nose was broken, and his face throbbed with pain. An attendant in the dispensary packed his nose with cotton, gave him two aspirin, and sent him to bed.

The next morning, two officers from the army's criminal investigation division came to his room and questioned him about what happened. He told them about the confrontation in the EM and how the group ganged up on him afterward and beat him up, conveniently omitting the part where he'd tried to hunt them down—nobody knew about that anyway. The matter seemed to end there, though he later heard a rumor that his attackers had been identified and transferred elsewhere.

He never understood why those guys cared so much about who he associated with. What was it to them? He might've understood it if he'd shunned other Black folks, but he hadn't. But that was just it—those guys didn't know him. The whole thing started because they saw him with his friends and didn't like the looks of it.

Before Mac knew it, it was 1967, and his three years of service were ending—just as the war in Vietnam was intensifying. He wasn't itching to see combat, but he knew guys who were, folks who were putting in 1049s and *asking* to be sent there. You had to have at least thirteen months left on your military commitment to do that, so some of them extended their tours, wanting to go where the fighting was. The topic was coming up with increasing frequency.

"You got your 1049 in?" someone would ask.

"Oh yeah," some said.

"No, and don't intend to," said others.

Mac was in the latter camp. He'd done his duty, and now he was moving on. There were more than enough guys getting drafted to fill the ranks. The military was bringing in every man they could get their hands on.

In February, Mac got orders to report back to CONUS, the continental United States, for separation from the army. He turned in his equipment and surplus clothes, holding onto his boots, field jacket, and the uniform on his back. Then he boarded a charter flight from Frankfurt to Newark via Goose Bay, Canada, for processing through Fort Monmouth. The separation took a week, which seemed to drag on endlessly because he had no access to the facilities, just the barracks and the mess hall. His only duty was police calls—MP-speak for picking up trash.

Finally, he got his flight voucher for Memphis, where he'd be living with his older sister Pirl and her husband, Sonny. He'd already arranged things with her and given the army her address so they could mail his DD Form 214, his report of separation, there. He had other family in Memphis, too, including his younger siblings Joyce and Floyd and his cousin Eugene. Walter and Miss Ethel had moved and were living in Sarah, Mississippi, about an hour's drive south.

When Mac arrived in Memphis, finding a job was near the top of his list of priorities, but first he had to take care of another more urgent matter. He borrowed Eugene's car and drove it down to Delta Center High School in Walls.

"I've got my GED now," he told the principal, Mr. Johnson. "I'd like to walk with the class at graduation, if I may."

Mr. Johnson gave him an enthusiastic yes. It wasn't Mac's class—that would've been 1965—but it made no difference.

When he finally got to walk across the gymnasium floor wearing his cap and gown, diploma in hand, his feet barely touched the ground. Though Eugene was the only relative in the audience cheering him on—Walter and Miss Ethel couldn't attend—it was enough. Mac felt like he'd completed something big but was also embarking on something bigger. He knew he'd more than earned the diploma he clutched, and he tingled with pride and possibility. The road to that day was longer than he thought it would be, and the cost higher, but there was no telling what life held in store now.

8.

Everybody's Guilty, Everybody's Innocent

I held my breath as I dialed on the phone's slippery screen, my pulse hammering in my ears. After two rings, a woman answered.

"Young residence."

I gave my name and said I was Marrell McCollough's daughter. "I understand that Ambassador Young wanted to get in touch with my father."

The woman paused. "McCollough?"

After taking a deep breath, I explained that Andrew Young, a member of Martin Luther King Jr.'s inner circle who was at the scene of his assassination in Memphis, had reached out to my father several years ago through one of my mother's colleagues at *The Commercial Appeal*.

Though Young had asked the reporter to give Dad his phone number—along with the message to call, day or night, if he ever wanted to talk—it was I who'd ended up calling. When I'd told Dad about the message, he quickly dismissed the proposal.

As I spoke, I tried not to sound winded. On this bright and blustery afternoon in May 2015, I'd been doing high intensity interval training with an exercise video on the third-story deck of my vacation home-turned-primary residence. The video provided for thirty-second breaks between intervals, but I tended to be more generous with myself, taking one whenever I felt too exhausted to continue, or just wanted to take a swig of coffee and surf the internet on my tablet. I'd been on one of these breaks, leaning against a deck chair and chugging coffee, when through the glare of my tablet's smudgy screen, I read a jarring headline in a British tabloid: FORMER ATLANTA MAYOR ANDREW YOUNG ESCAPES DEATH BUT IS HOSPITALIZED AFTER TRAFFIC ACCIDENT WITH CEMENT TRUCK.

After scanning the article and searching more reputable sources, I learned that Young, then eighty-three, was doing fine and resting at home. A single thought seized me: *I have to contact him.*

My mind snapped to the email I'd received from Ma more than four years earlier passing along Young's message to Dad via her colleague. A quick search of my inbox uncovered it, and I instantly felt better about my practice of rarely deleting emails.

"Alright. Please hold."

A tinny, singsong tune began to play, and I used that time to reflect on what I was doing. Calling Young was impulsive, and I'd done so without giving much thought as to why. I suppose I wanted to contact him while I still had a chance. News of the accident reminded me that it wasn't a chance I'd always have, that not calling might be riskier than calling. I wanted to know why he'd reached out to Dad, even if Dad didn't care to find out.

The woman returned to the phone. "Mr. Young will speak with you."

Oh, no, I thought. I was expecting to leave a message.

The tinny music started again, and my mind scrambled to conjure up something sensible to say. I ran across the room to my desk and grabbed a notebook and pen.

"Hello?" said a voice that reminded me of Granddaddy's.

I introduced myself and told him who my father was. "I just read that you were in an accident yesterday. Are you feeling all right?"

"I'm fine."

"Well, I'm calling because I learned that you reached out to my father through a Memphis reporter."

"That was a long time ago, but I wanted to tie up some loose ends."

I wondered what that meant, but I didn't want to be pushy. I was already on shaky ground by calling him out of the blue.

"I think my dad wants some closure about this as well," I said. I told him I was planning to write a book about Dad, including what happened at the assassination. I mentioned a bestselling book I'd read about it to kick off my research.

"Oh, you believe that?"

He described the atmosphere on April 4, 1968, when King gathered with him and his other aides in Memphis.

"Everybody was confused. I didn't know your father, but I heard his name around. I just knew him as the brother with the car." He went on to say he felt that "something was supposed to happen," and it probably happened at the right time.

"Well, I want to know what happened." I felt my mouth getting ahead of me, but I couldn't stop myself.

"No you don't."

He became discursive, noting that FBI director James Comey kept a Lucite-embedded order issued in 1963 by Attorney General Robert Kennedy, authorizing the wiretapping of King and the Southern Christian Leadership Conference, on his desk. Comey deemed the FBI's interactions with King a low point in its history, Young said, so the director required all new agents to read the order and visit King's memorial in Washington. "Hoover's distortions poisoned everything."

I'd read about J. Edgar Hoover's personal, pathological hatred of King. It made me wonder how far he and the FBI went to bring King down. After all, it was Hoover's FBI that sent King a letter in 1964, packaged with purported tapes of his sexual dalliances, that by all appearances urged him to kill himself.

"But the SCLC had nothing to hide," he continued. He described how, as recently as 2004, he'd found leftover wires from a government wiretap at his home when he had fencing installed around his property.

I asked if he'd been surprised by the somewhat recent revelation that famed civil rights photographer Ernest Withers—a fixture at civil rights gatherings who enjoyed intimate access to the movement's leaders—had been a paid FBI informant. On the evening of the assassination, Withers had been in King's room at the Lorraine.

"I wasn't surprised," Young said. In any event, he said, two known FBI informants had worked in the SCLC's Atlanta offices. He believed one of them, the former financial secretary, had previously worked for the CIA in Europe. Young said he'd warned King about him, but King was unconcerned. Even after the man was caught using the office credit card to pay for his girlfriend's trips to Las Vegas, King refused to fire him. The FBI was paying the man $500 a month for his services. "That was as much as my entire SCLC salary," he said with an ironic laugh.

Still, he said he forgave the man, noting that he spotted him around Atlanta from time to time. "We have to forgive others so we can receive forgiveness from God."

I agreed. "But I want to know the truth," I said. As the words left my mouth, their naiveté embarrassed me.

"No, you don't." His tone became heavy, his words hitting me like lightning. "I don't want to be in a position to think that high officials in our government arranged to kill my friend." After a beat of silence, he added, "I liked that *Selma* movie. Everybody comes out looking good."

My chest tightened. I couldn't speak.

He continued, "We can't know the truth. It isn't black and white; it's gray. Everybody's guilty, and everybody's innocent."

Before we hung up, he asked me to invite Dad to call him. I said I would.

———

A couple of hours later, I called Ma at work. I was worried that she might not agree with what I'd done, that I might have made a mistake I couldn't yet see. As we spoke, I paced from one end of the kitchen to the other.

"Leta, I had a premonition this would happen." Just a day or two before, she said, she'd been struck by the recurring thought that I needed to talk to Young. "But you know, I'm a little bit psychic like your Grandma was."

"If you get a feeling like that again, tell me so I'll know what I'm going to do next!"

———

A few hours after I spoke with Ma, I called my brother Micah.

"Whoa, that's amazing," he said. "So are you going to tell Dad?"

"I guess I have to." I wondered if Dad would be angry I'd spoken to Young without consulting him first. But just because Dad hadn't wanted to talk to him a few years ago didn't mean I couldn't—right? "I'm not sure how to do it, though. I'm trying to think of a way to ease into it."

"In my experience with that dude, the best way is just to tell him straight. Don't try to soft-pedal it."

"I know, I know, but I have to be comfortable, too." My face prickled with emotion. "It's like getting into a hot bath. You don't just stick your booty straight in the water—you have to start with the toes!"

We broke into laughter.

"You think he's awake now?" I asked. Like Micah, Dad lived three time zones away from me.

"Yeah, he just posted on Facebook that he's watching the playoffs."

"Then won't I be disturbing him if I call?"

"Nah, just call him. And let me know what he says."

I was nervous to tell Dad about my phone call with Andrew Young, but I knew that the longer I let it go unmentioned, the more awkward the discussion would become—though a certain level of awkwardness was inevitable. As soon as I hung up with Micah, I called Dad.

"Hey Dad, how's it going?"

"Miss Leta! I'm doing fine, just watching the game."

After a weak attempt to make chitchat about basketball, I launched into an inelegant segue. "Well, you'll never believe what happened today." I told him about my conversation with Young, beginning with the high intensity interval training and the tabloid headline. "He says you should call him if you want. Would you be interested in that?"

I felt like I had when I tried downhill skiing for the first time that winter—adrenaline-loaded and plunging into unknown terrain.

Dad chuckled softly. "Not at this time."

9.

Strike

The Vietnam War was raging as Mac began classes at the Memphis Police Training Academy in September 1967, as were denouncements of it, perhaps most notably Dr. Martin Luther King Jr.'s. In a speech titled "Beyond Vietnam: A Time to Break Silence," delivered at New York's Riverside Church on April 4—a year to the day before his assassination—he called for an end to the war, condemning the U.S. government as "the greatest purveyor of violence in the world today." The speech drew swift and bitter criticism in newspapers across the nation, including Memphis's *Commercial Appeal*, where an editorial announced that "[p]rofound shifts in the centers of power within the civil rights movement are occurring in the wake of Martin Luther King's decision to go all the way in his bid for the favor of Negro extremism."

The nation was wrestling with more than just the war—there was plenty of domestic unrest, too. In what the media dubbed "The Long, Hot Summer," more than 150 urban uprisings had recently rocked the nation, many precipitated by police violence. Memphis had escaped any notable strife, though it felt like an uneasy peace to anyone paying attention.

None of this managed to permeate the walls of the police academy, where for sixteen weeks instructors trained recruits with no mention of the racial, social, or political climate, much less the dynamics of social problems or how to handle civil disturbances. Even so, Mac was well aware of what was happening. There was no escaping it: The old ways of doing things were ending and the changes were accelerating. He could see it in the way people dressed and groomed themselves, with their free and easy clothes and hair. He could hear it in the frank way they spoke, and the things they *didn't* say—like how "colored" and "Negro" gave way to "Black." He picked it up in song lyrics, like Bob Dylan's "Blowin' in the Wind."

He agreed with the changes—not just the stylistic ones but the deeper shifts they reflected. He supported the movements for civil rights and peace; he just didn't have much chance to show it, having gone from three years in the army to searching for employment to long hours in low-wage jobs to his current reality in the police academy. As far as he could tell, Memphis didn't have much of a protest scene, but if it had, he wouldn't have been able to take part. His path sidelined him. Once he enlisted in the army, he was out of play as far as activism went. And now he was on his way to becoming part of the very establishment some folks were protesting.

———

Police academy classes began the day after Labor Day at the Claude A. Armour Fire and Police Training Center, a no-frills building in a semi-industrial neighborhood near the Mid-South Fairgrounds. On the first day, cadets assembled for the welcome ceremony, where they were cautioned that some would succeed while others wouldn't. They were advised that they were expected to do classwork, plus physical conditioning. For Mac and a good number of the others with military backgrounds, this was nothing new. And unlike basic training in the army, police academy training came with a substantial paycheck, around $500 a month. Mac used the money to finance a brand new car, a blue Volkswagen Fastback, through the city employees' credit union.

Class began at 8:00 a.m., with an hour-long lunch break at noon. Physical training ran from 3:00 to 5:00 p.m., Monday through Friday, and exams were on Fridays. Those who passed the exams returned the following Monday, while those who failed were dismissed. To Mac, it was like the army in one major respect: if he fell in line and met expectations, he did fine.

Friendships formed almost immediately. The physical training in particular lent itself to that, with many of the exercises requiring the cadets to pair off. Mac befriended Jim Shotwell, a gregarious, square-jawed ex-Marine and one of three fellow Black recruits. Though he wasn't quite as tall as Mac, he was muscular enough to bounce him around like a rag doll in the early days of training. But Mac got stronger as they worked together, and soon he was bouncing Jim around, too.

The academic work was slightly more challenging than the physical training, but Mac found that he performed well by just showing up, paying attention, and applying himself. Many of the classes consisted of guest speakers, mostly police officers, giving lectures on everything from the Tennessee Code Annotated to how officers should conduct themselves. The U.S. Supreme Court had just handed down the *Miranda v. Arizona* decision in June 1966, and theirs was only the second class to receive instruction on reading suspects their Miranda rights. It was a big deal. They also spent a lot of time on probable cause—what it was and what it took to get there.

The instructors taught cadets to respect the rights of all citizens, take their complaints seriously, and uphold the law. But when a conflict arose, they needed to take charge of the situation. That meant barking authoritative commands in a harsh tone, using profanity. Officers didn't ask, "Please stand against the wall"; they shouted, "Up against the wall, motherfucker!"

When it came to making arrests, instructors focused on subduing combative suspects with holds and takedowns. Run-of-the-mill encounters with suspects who complied? Not covered. Officers were to use the level of force necessary to subdue the subject. If the person escalated, then the officer should escalate. The order of escalation went from the hand to Mace—which the department would provide to officers beginning December 1—to the nightstick or flashlight. That was the extent of the non-lethal options.

As a new weapon in the department's arsenal, Mace drew much interest and attention, not only within the department but in the press. In an editorial titled "MACE, A Humane Weapon," *The Commercial Appeal* praised it for its ability to "immobilize a man, or crowd of rioters, but without physical harm or lasting effects." Though the liquid tear gas caused "extreme irritation to skin, nostrils and body extremities," the article reassured readers that it "cannot be labeled as 'brutal,'" because "[n]o one arrested through the use of liquid gas will appear in court with bruises, bandages or after-effects."

After non-lethal weapons came deadly force, appropriate only to protect the life of the officer or someone else, or to stop a fleeing felon. An officer shouldn't pull his gun from his holster unless he intended to use it, instructors taught. And if an officer shot someone because he thought the person had a weapon, he should say the person had a "shiny object," the instructors cautioned. He should not say "I saw a weapon," let alone try to identify a specific weapon.

The instructors gave them pointers on testifying in court, like answering only the question asked and not volunteering information. Officers should always keep a pen and a notebook, they taught, and the notebook should contain police matters only—not unrelated information like their girlfriend's name and number. If the contents came up at trial, the defense had a right to see it, and extraneous notes could open the door to all kinds of new questions.

Another major component of the program was firearms training. The department had only two types: the Smith & Wesson Model 10 revolver and the Model 10 shotgun. They practiced firing at seven feet, then fifteen, then twenty-five, then thirty, though the instructors cautioned them that most armed encounters took place within seven feet or so.

Mac enjoyed the academy, especially compared to the army or manual labor. Some people considered policing a calling, but he disagreed. To him it was a *profession*, an occupation that required certain skills, training, and discipline. It wasn't about domination, but restraint—not only of wrongdoers, but of himself, too.

He particularly enjoyed getting out of the classroom to learn the practical side of things, like the ride-alongs with commissioned officers during the program's penultimate week. That Sunday, he rode with officers who set up a radar in one of the Black neighborhoods to catch speeders running late to church. At the end of their shift, they drove past a group of kids holding up a large cardboard sign. It read, RADAR AHEAD.

One theme Mac carried away from the academy settled strangely in his mind. It was best stated by one of the instructors during a lecture about the relationship between officers and the department: "You might agree or disagree with the way certain things are done. If you disagree, you can speak up, and you can leave. But if you don't speak up, and you don't leave, be loyal."

Related to that idea was a phrase—a question, really—instructors in the academy often repeated: "Who can you ride with?" Every officer needed someone to ride with, someone to be their trusted partner. The work could be dangerous, and they needed to be able to trust their colleagues 100 percent, all the time. That was the code of loyalty, and an officer who didn't abide by it would become someone the others wouldn't ride with. If you found yourself in that situation, you wouldn't last long in the department.

The message stuck with Mac. He took it to mean that an officer who didn't agree with the department's practices should leave rather than obstruct its activities. And if the officer hadn't spoken up about whatever the issue was, they shouldn't criticize in the first place. They should be forthright, not two-faced.

He didn't hear it as a warning against trying to fix problems, but as an appeal to group loyalty, which was something he understood viscerally, going back to his earliest years and through his army days. The cadets would be pledging to make the department the best it could be. They'd all be risking their lives to protect the city, and mutual trust was paramount. While trying to make reforms was a good thing, turning on the group was not. Mac could've pondered the proposition more deeply, mentally running through all kinds of hypothetical scenarios to test its limits, but he didn't. He just accepted it, making it sound logical in his mind.

On December 6, 1967, the academy held its graduation ceremony in the training center gym, furnished with folding chairs for the occasion. Robert G. Jensen, special agent in charge of the FBI's Memphis office, gave the keynote speech. In attendance were Mayor-elect Henry Loeb and the newly appointed fire and police director, Frank Holloman, as a *Commercial Appeal* article listing the names of all thirty-nine graduates would announce the following day.

Mac looked out into the stands and spotted Walter, Miss Ethel, Eugene, and his brother-in-law Sonny, who was there without Pirl because she was at the hospital in labor. Mac's family was beaming, and so was he.

He hadn't been far off the mark when he told Eugene the department wouldn't hire a Negro, as it had hired few since it began with a single town constable in 1827. His graduating class was only the fourth racially integrated one in the academy's history. As it stood, only about fifty of the department's nine hundred or so officers were Black—5.5 percent of the force, though Memphis' population was about one-third Black. And Mac now claimed a place among their ranks.

———

A few days after graduation, Mac was on the phone with Miss Ethel when she mentioned the money order for his uniform and revolver.

"I had to get every bit of money I had out of my savings for that. Your father gave me some money, too."

"Well, it should've been easy to get the money because I sent it to him in bonds. He should've just cashed them out."

"He never said nothing about no bonds. We had to struggle to get it."

Mac fell silent for a moment, confused. Then he understood, and the realization crushed him. Walter had spent the money from the bonds. Many of them hadn't even reached maturity.

Mac didn't begrudge him the money, which he must have sorely needed to do something so desperate. Mac hoped he'd at least shared some of it with Miss Ethel, though. Now all he could do was protect her feelings.

"Oh," was all he could say.

———

Two days after graduation, the newly minted cadets were gathered for a training exercise when a lieutenant appeared out of nowhere and sprayed Mac and several others with a blast of Mace. As they staggered around, coughing and choking, another man snapped away on his camera.

The next day, *The Commercial Appeal* ran a brief story about the episode near the popular *Hambone's Meditations* cartoon, named for its stereotypical Black central figure. (That day's meditation: "Some folks don' mo'n git dey finguh in de pie twell dey tries t' git de pie in dey *pocket*!!")

The article described the attack with a combination of fascination and awe:

> The effects of a bit of Mace in the face were vividly demonstrated at the Shelby County Penal Farm yesterday when Lt. John Coletta pounced with a canister of the new mobilization gas in a surprise attack on some members of the new police recruit class. One, Morrell [sic] McCollough, staggered away, rested while the tears rolled down his face and then told the approaching officer that he'd had enough. Each policeman will carry a canister of the gas, which is being used in several cities.

Accompanying the article were four large photographs of Mac in various stages of distress: doubled over, stumbling, crying, and kneeling.

On December 7, 1967, the day after graduation, Mac's shift commander gave him his first assignment: foot patrol in the Lamar–Airways Shopping Center in the historically Black Orange Mound neighborhood. A strip mall of twenty or so shops, it was a popular spot to shop for clothes, toys, and sundries. Mac would be working the swing shift, from three in the afternoon until eleven at night.

The commander paired him with Patrolman Tom Clark as his senior training officer—not that there was a formal training program. The department expected rookie officers to pick up tips from their more experienced partners, who weren't necessarily selected for their training ability. By watching the senior officer, the rookie was to learn the practical side of law enforcement—an officer's expected behavior and how things were supposed to work. Though some of this was captured in the written rules, much more remained unwritten, passed down by custom and practice from class to class.

Tall and wiry, Clark was in his early forties and had been a patrolman for over fifteen years. He had two brothers on the force—an older one named Earl who was a lieutenant in charge of the shooting range and a younger one named David who, like Tom, was a patrolman. As required by the rules on personal appearance, Tom was clean-shaven with short and well-groomed black hair under his police hat, which had to be worn at all times while on duty.

Day after day, Mac and Clark walked from one end of the shopping center to the other and back again, surveying the jovial crowds, taking in the festive sights and sounds, greeting the shopkeepers here and there. Gleaming Christmas decorations festooned the shops as the sidewalks bustled with cheerful shoppers and piped-in music wafted through the chilly air. All the hallmarks of the holiday season were there in plentitude—including shoplifters and pickpockets.

For the most part, foot patrol was easy work. The main responsibility of the job was to be visible, which in itself would help deter criminal activity and make people feel safe. Mac enjoyed it, especially the attention he got from women. But besides flirting, there wasn't much in the way of excitement.

That changed one evening just days before Christmas. Mac was standing in the Rexall drugstore—Clark had gone off somewhere—when an elderly man walked up to him, looking distraught. His voice and demeanor telegraphed urgency.

"Some boys stole my car in South Memphis, and now they have it right here in the parking lot!"

He led Mac out of the drugstore and pointed toward a long sedan filled with teenagers creeping across the pavement.

After telling the man to get Clark, who had just entered the drugstore, Mac approached the car and motioned for it to stop.

The driver, who looked to be about seventeen, pulled over to the curb. Mac ordered the occupants out of the car.

As he walked around the back of the car to its front driver's side, the front and rear passenger-side doors flew open. Kids jumped out and tore off in different directions—except the driver, who remained behind the wheel.

Just then, Mac saw Clark walking down the middle of the parking lot toward the stopped car.

The driver punched the accelerator, and the car screeched away from the curb, straight at Clark. Mac and Clark drew their guns and fired. The car skidded into a lamppost.

The driver sprang out and sprinted out of the parking lot. Mac took off behind him.

They tore across Park Avenue, reaching a stretch of railroad tracks illuminated by dim ambient light that grew increasingly faint as he chased the boy down the tracks. Soon they were running in complete darkness. Mac following the sound of the boy's panting, his drumming footfalls on the tracks. The boy was talking between breaths, but Mac couldn't make out what he was saying, only that he was crying.

The breathing, talking, and crying grew louder. What was going on? Mac knew he couldn't be catching up to him that quickly. Then the boy appeared in front of him, weeping and bleeding from the shoulder. He'd been shot and had reversed course.

Mac put his arm around him and led him back to the shopping center, where squad cars now filled the parking lot. Sweating and winded, Mac handed the boy over to two white officers. One of them struck the boy across the face before shoving him into the back of a patrol car.

When Mac saw it, he felt a flash of anger. But in the heat of his outrage, he also felt the sting of powerlessness, knowing that as a Black rookie fresh out of the academy, there was nothing he could do about it. Who would he complain to, and what would it accomplish?

Mac and Clark went downtown to police headquarters to write incident report letters, expanded police reports addressed to the chief explaining an extraordinary event in the course of duty. It was a dreaded task Mac had heard about in the academy, though he hadn't been trained how to write one. He knew the chief would scrutinize his words, that it needed to be as close to perfect as possible. Under the station's harsh lights, he stared at the blank sheet of white paper on the desk for a moment, then began writing.

The next day, an article about the incident appeared in *The Commercial Appeal.* Mentioning Mac and Clark by name, it noted that "[a] youth charged with auto theft was held to the state yesterday while his 17-year-old brother was in good condition at John Gaston Hospital with a policeman's bullet wound in his left shoulder."

During his off hours, Mac spent as much time as he could with his family. He'd drive by Pirl and Sonny's house when his shift ended, and if the lights were on, he'd stop in, have a snack, and chat for a bit before heading back to the room he rented in a house not far from there. Then he'd watch a little television before going to sleep.

He had two days a week off from work, which he also spent visiting Pirl and Sonny, plus his younger brother Floyd. Sometimes he and Floyd would go out to nightclubs and take in the scene. He saw Eugene only occasionally now due to their different schedules. Once a month or so, he'd visit Walter and Miss Ethel down in Mississippi, and also his son Terry, who lived with Nellie near St. Peter Church.

Mac saw her in one of the strip mall shops buying gifts one evening. She was tall and modestly dressed with glowing brown skin and black hair that swept over her shoulders. When she headed to the checkout stand, he worked up the nerve to approach her.

"Let me help you to your car," he said as the cashier placed her purchases in several large bags.

"That's okay. I can manage." She glanced at him with a slight smile.

He summoned every drop of charm he could muster. "Miss, helping shoppers is part of my job."

Her name was Linda, he learned as they walked to her compact car, and she worked as a special education teacher in the Memphis City Schools. She was a prize.

He got more time with her a few days later when she returned to do more shopping. When he spotted her, his heart started pounding. He sidled up beside her, quick and smooth, and together they strolled past the cheerful shop windows. He did his best to dazzle her with his words.

She told him she lived with her mother on Clementine Street, not far from the shopping center. "Would you like to come over for dinner?"

He smiled broadly.

The following week, shortly before Christmas, they had that dinner. Her mother, Miss Elizabeth, wore her long hair parted down the middle and braided in two long plaits wound around her head. She had American Indian heritage, Linda said. Linda's father was long dead, killed in a logging accident.

The house, the sturdy furniture—Miss Elizabeth's, from Natchez—and most of all Linda's teaching career placed them squarely in Memphis's upwardly mobile Black middle class. She also had a brother who was a postal worker—another high-potential career among Black folks.

Mac, Linda, and Miss Elizabeth shared a beautiful chicken dinner that Linda prepared. While Mac and Linda talked, Miss Elizabeth said little. Mac raved about the chicken, which was so delicious, so well-seasoned, maybe the best chicken he'd had since he was a boy.

———

A few days before Christmas 1967, Mac's supervisors reassigned him from foot patrol to car patrols—Car 15 in the Orange Mound, Castalia, and Glenview neighborhoods of southeast Memphis and Car 42 in North Memphis's Hollywood neighborhood. His base would be the Armour substation where he'd gone through the police academy.

In Car 15, he was paired once again with Clark. His partner in Car 42 was Bull Wheeler, who like Clark had been a patrolman for over fifteen years. A tall, broad-bellied man, he would've resembled Santa Claus if the uniforms, with their thigh-length jackets, had been red instead of blue.

Three officers were assigned to each car, and they patrolled in pairs on a rotating basis, depending on who had the day off. They took turns driving from one day to the next. Both Clark and Bull had regular partners they rode with, and Mac was the third wheel.

When both of Mac's cars were fully staffed, he drove the paddy wagon, a police van outfitted for transporting multiple prisoners or officers. He continued to work the swing shift—from mid-afternoon through the late evening—and he also picked up an overnight shift.

The patrol cars were raggedy old Ford Fairlanes that were hard to drive and even harder to stop. Just getting them to travel in a straight line down the road was a challenge, as they tended to weave from side to side, and the brakes heated up fast. If an officer in a high-speed chase needed to slow down, he had to be sure to pump the brakes—but if he pumped them too many times, they'd get hot and fail. Then he wouldn't be able to stop.

The car patrols introduced Mac to the tapestry of neighborhoods that made up Black Memphis, with their modest homes, schools and churches, commercial districts, and nightlife. The oldest of these was Orange Mound, one of the nation's first communities built by and for Black people.

In addition to its quiet residential areas, it featured a lively business district with barbershops, pool halls, and nightclubs. This was the section that generated most of Car 15's calls, usually for complaints of disturbing the peace and disorderly conduct, along with the occasional stolen vehicle report, shooting, or residential burglary. The nearby neighborhoods of Castalia and Glenview, being mostly residential, were quieter.

Night by night, Mac and Clark cruised the light-studded avenues and dusky side streets, making themselves visible, scoping things out, shaking the locks on businesses here and there to make sure the doors were secured. Sometimes they'd walk into a corner store or restaurant or beauty shop, saying hello and showing their faces.

Every now and then, the dispatcher would call on the radio. "Car 15, see a complainant at Orange Mound Grill, drunk loitering."

The officer who wasn't driving would acknowledge the call. "Okay, Car 15."

They'd head to the scene, take a look, and perhaps find someone sitting with their head resting on a table. Public drunkenness almost always ended in arrest.

They'd handcuff the person, put them in the back of the car, and take them to Armour Station for booking and holding. For a misdemeanor like that, they'd write up the arrest report in the car, though they wrote up longer felony reports back at the station.

Hollywood also had its peaceful residential areas and lively business district, and the calls were generally the same. For both patrols, weekday nights tended to be quiet, with calls picking up on Friday evenings. Then calls would come in back-to-back, and the officers would go from one place to the next, mostly responding to reports of fighting and drunken behavior.

The many hours spent riding created a deep familiarity between officers, and with Clark, Mac saw things he hadn't noticed when they walked foot patrol—things he didn't like. What Mac had previously taken for breeziness became merely coldness. Clark's sharp and imperious side emerged.

He took to calling Mac "Meece," a silly diminutive form of "Mouse," to highlight Mac's lowly rookie status. He probably took the name from the *Huckleberry Hound* cartoon, which featured a cat with a famous tagline about two mice he routinely chased: "I hate meeces to pieces!"

They normally kept their conversation superficial and cordial, but one evening, the topic of Black police officers came up. Clark radiated disdain.

"You know, Meece, you think your uniform is as blue as mine, but it's not."

Mac swallowed his rising anger. The panel of top brass at the civil service exam had made a point of asking what he'd do if somebody on the street called him a nigger, but they never asked about one of his fellow officers calling him one.

"That's what you say," Mac said, "but I *did* graduate from the same academy." He kept his voice measured.

Perhaps what stung the most about Clark's remark was that it was true. Mac didn't have the same authority as a white officer in the same uniform. How could he? Despite the legal changes, the pretense of rising equality, Memphis was still segregated. He need look no further than the police department, which refused to assign Black officers to white neighborhoods like out in East Memphis. To be Black and in uniform was to wear a giant asterisk. Your legitimacy was always in question.

Then there was the way Clark treated civilians. Mac's probationary period ran for a year from graduation, so he was still a trainee, and Clark's written evaluation would help determine whether he kept his job. Mac had to be careful. But some of the things Clark did disgusted him. Like the time they arrested a guy in Orange Mound for disorderly conduct—a catch-all charge when police wanted to lock somebody up, Mac learned. The man was handcuffed in the backseat of the cruiser, talking nonstop.

"Shut up," Clark barked. He was riding in the passenger seat while Mac drove.

The man kept talking.

"I said shut up."

The man continued on.

Clark turned around and Maced him in the face.

It sickened Mac—both the act and his own inability to intervene. But what good would it do now to chastise Clark? The man didn't respect him, as he'd plainly said. Nothing Mac said or did would change the way Clark operated, and the only thing he'd succeed in doing was jeopardizing his own career. It came down to the question raised by the police academy instructors: "Who can you ride with?"

There were no such tense moments in Car 42 with Bull. He loved food, and riding with him was a culinary tour of Hollywood. Between calls, they'd drive down Chelsea Avenue past pool halls and hole-in-the-wall nightclubs to a guy standing on the street selling hot tamales wrapped in newspapers. Bull would buy three at a time and spread out the newspaper to catch the dripping red sauce. A few hours later, they might stop by a grocery store for cold cuts, then swing by the Wonder Bread factory downtown for a freshly baked loaf. At dinnertime, it was back to Chelsea for a plate of barbecue from Lil Bob's—considered by many to be Hollywood's best.

One day, Linda called Mac and told him to drive by her house, which was in the Car 15 patrol area, and check the mailbox. There, he found a fragrant roast chicken neatly wrapped in foil on a plate. As its delectable aroma filled the car, he felt like the luckiest patrolman there ever was.

He and Linda saw each other every free night he had, dining at her house with Miss Elizabeth. Sometimes they went from there to the movies, but more often than not, they went back to his place. Linda had been raised to be what folks called "sanctified" and wasn't one to frequent bars and nightclubs. There were only so many places he could take her. Fortunately for them, Miss Elizabeth went to bed early and was asleep when Linda got home in the wee hours.

Within a few weeks' time, he brought Linda down to Mississippi to visit Walter and Miss Ethel. She dazzled them, and his chest swelled with pride. They knew he must be doing something right to get a woman like her.

———

From time to time, Clark would pull over on Park Avenue to pick up an older Black man waiting at the curb. "Hop in, Sug."

Everige "Sug" Jones was one of Memphis's first Black officers, having been hired in the late 1940s after the city's all-white force came under fire for police brutality. Back then, Black officers were segregated from the rest of the force and prohibited from arresting white people, and Sug's patrol was limited to Beale Street and its environs. He earned a fearsome reputation for abusing people as he made his rounds.

Riding in the back seat as Mac and Clark continued their patrol, Sug stared out the window, scanning the streets, muttering his contempt for Black folks who entered his line of sight.

"Look at those *niggers*."

Mac sat there without saying a word, a stony expression fixed on his face.

Clark laughed. "How'd you keep 'em in line, Sug?"

"Man, when I was out there, I'd go upside a nigger's head so fast!" He erupted in laughter. Then he launched into tales from his Beale Street days, doling out beatings and making arrests.

Mac rode in silence, fuming.

As a longtime Orange Mound resident, Sug knew every inch of the neighborhood—where the illegal liquor was sold and who ran the craps games. Occasionally, he'd drop nuggets of information about that, but he mostly talked about his glory days terrorizing Beale Street.

Mac knew Sug's ride-alongs were Clark's way of putting Mac in his place, showing him what his role was. But how could Mac challenge it? He had to weigh the cost. Was he prepared to leave the department over it?

Right before New Year's Eve 1967, the shift commander assigned Clark and Mac to conduct a sting operation targeting an illegal liquor racket in Castalia. The department sent out undercover officers every so often to try to make buys and arrest the culprits.

Mac was excited about his first undercover operation. He was to dress like a rural field worker who'd traveled to the neighborhood to buy liquor on a Sunday—also a crime. He'd be driving his own car, the Volkswagen. Dressed in a work shirt and overalls, he parked on a quiet side street and ambled down the sidewalk in search of alcohol.

He saw several young men standing on the corner. They began walking toward him, their faces contorted in anger. "Hey man, get the fuck outta here!"

He backed up a few feet, wondering why they were acting so hostile.

They kept walking toward him, swearing and making threatening gestures. He had no choice but to run.

When he got back to his car, he saw what the problem was, and it made him sick with disappointment. On the rear bumper was a sticker he'd put there when he bought the car and forgotten about: SUPPORT YOUR LOCAL POLICE.

The sanitation strike seemed to come out of nowhere, though in many ways it was overdue. On February 12, 1968, the garbage didn't get picked up. Then another day, and another.

From newspapers and word of mouth, he learned what happened.

White supervisors had been running the sanitation department like a plantation, calling the mostly Black workforce "boys," keeping them in menial positions, favoring the white workers over them. Black workers were subject to termination for talking back or even being one minute late for work. They weren't allowed to take breaks, and the only shelter they had from the pouring rain or the scorching sun was the garbage truck.

Their wages depended on the number of routes worked rather than hours, and they weren't paid overtime. Though Federal minimum wage was one dollar an hour, they were making as little as ninety-four cents. Yet they had to supply their own work clothing and gloves, and some of them had to rummage through the trash they carried for clothes and boots. Many worked extra jobs or went on public assistance.

And all that for what? The privilege of hauling the city's garbage. Six days a week, the 1,100 sanitation workers toted 2,500 tons of garbage a day, walking up to each individual house, hoisting the stinking aluminum cans, and carrying them to the trucks to dump their foul contents, sometimes getting splashed in the process. People didn't want to walk downwind of them, let alone stand next to them on the bus.

A grisly accident sparked the strike. Nearly two weeks earlier, sanitation workers Echol Cole and Robert Walker climbed into their garbage truck's compactor to escape a downpour because there was no room for them to take shelter inside the truck's cab. The compactor malfunctioned, crushing them to death.

After their deaths, the overwhelming majority of the workers asked the public works commissioner for union recognition, safer working conditions, and better pay. The commissioner dismissed their concerns.

The workers didn't need to hold a formal vote to decide what to do next. On February 11, they agreed among themselves to stop showing up for work. Three days into the strike, only four sanitation trucks were operating, and rotting garbage began piling up.

Mac knew what it was like to work grueling hours and have nothing to show for it, or even less than nothing. Sanitation work sounded like the urban version of sharecropping.

By the end of the strike's first week, the city was hiring scab workers to collect the trash, and stories about strikers harassing the scabs immediately began to circulate, including reports of gunfire around the trucks. The police department assigned officers extra shifts escorting the trucks, and Mac picked up a twelve-hour shift doing this in addition to his regular car patrols.

Riding with an officer he didn't know, he trailed the trucks through the streets. Occasionally, he'd hear a report over the radio of interference with the trucks, but he never saw anything. He and his new partner didn't talk about the strike or much else. Especially after his run-in with Clark, he knew better than to discuss social issues on the job. He made a discipline of not thinking about all that while on duty, of keeping his opinions separate from his work.

Which isn't to say he didn't have opinions. Like most Black people in Memphis, he sympathized with the sanitation workers. He knew the city was treating them unfairly. He'd heard about how Mayor Henry Loeb scolded them like rebellious children, refusing to engage in meaningful negotiations with them. He understood all too well what that kind of treatment felt like. But he had a duty to protect the scabs, and that's what he did.

He knew society was changing anyway. No matter how hard the city fought, it couldn't be stopped. He had a good job, one he felt lucky to have, and though he didn't yet own a nice house and certainly couldn't live in any neighborhood he chose, he still sensed a slow but inexorable forward push toward equal rights. The unprecedented strike among the sanitation workers—a group most people would write off as powerless—was proof of that. The strikers had their role to play, and he had his, which was to uphold the law. There didn't need to be a conflict.

Try as they might, officials couldn't attract enough scabs for the size of the job. Most Black folks weren't about to break the strike, and most white folks believed sanitation work to be beneath them. The desperate souls who did step in had to learn fast, and that had consequences—as when a garbage truck rolled backward into Mac's squad car after the inexperienced driver failed to engage the parking brake.

After about a week of escorting the trucks, Mac's shift commander reassigned him to guard the entrance to one of the city's two landfills, the one near the airport. For twelve-hour shifts, he and another officer stood inside a temporary shelter provided by the city, watching the trucks come and go and breathing the fetid air. He never saw any strikers, only trucks.

Early one morning in late February 1968, Mac was guarding the landfill when a call came in for him in the site's small office. Assistant Police Chief Henry Lux wanted to see him in his office right away. Mac didn't know what to think—was he in trouble? He'd been a little late that morning. Exhausted from the extra twelve-hour shifts, he'd overslept.

When he walked into Lux's spacious office, five other officers were already there: Inspector Graydon Tines, Lieutenant Eli Arkin, Detective Jerry Davis, and two Black officers, Detective Ed Redditt and Patrolman Willie Richmond. Tines, Arkin, and Davis were from the department's Domestic Intelligence Bureau.

Lux offered Mac a seat. "We were discussing all the trouble around this sanitation strike and how we can try to get out in front of it." He explained that the strikers were holding regular meetings, including one scheduled for noon at a downtown church, Clayborn Temple. "I need you and Richmond to go down there and find out what they're planning."

Mac agreed. It would be the most intriguing assignment he'd gotten thus far—much more compelling than standing in a hut at a landfill, or escorting garbage trucks, or patrolling the same neighborhoods night after night.

Maybe he could do some good here, not just for the department but for the city, too. The more information the police had about plans to interfere with the trucks, the easier it would be to focus on any troublemakers. With better information, the police could deal with the lawbreakers and leave everybody else alone.

Of course, the only reason he was on the assistant chief's radar was because he was Black and therefore one of the few officers who *could* blend in with the strikers and their supporters. For once, his race put him in good stead in the department. He wasn't going to squander his chance to show that he could perform as well as any other officer—or better.

From Lux's office, Mac went back to his apartment. He changed out of his uniform and into jeans and a sweater. Then he went to Clayborn Temple, its limestone walls looming over the downtown corner of Pontotoc and Hernando. It had originally housed a white congregation, the Second Presbyterian Church, but they moved out to East Memphis in the 1940s and sold the building to the African Methodist Episcopal Church. Now home to a Black congregation under the leadership of Rev. Malcolm Blackburn, a white man, it had become a key gathering place for the striking sanitation workers and their supporters.

Mac walked in and found an empty spot in one of the sanctuary's crowded pews. He spotted Richmond on the other side of the room. As the mass meeting got going, the place hummed with the crowd's righteous anger. Most of the people there seemed to be strikers, and they cheered enthusiastically as someone thundered from the pulpit. Folks took turns speaking, discussing fundraising efforts to support the strikers, who were now deprived of what little earnings they would have received had they been working. They also talked about plans for marches and protests.

The meeting continued for about half an hour, and when it ended, Mac and Richmond separately made their way back to police headquarters. They reported all they'd observed back to Arkin, who commended them on a job well done. He asked them to attend the next meeting the following day.

Over the next several days, Mac and Richmond returned to Clayborn Temple as instructed. The mass meetings were two parts planning session and one part revival, filling the sanctuary with energetic activists. Mac and Richmond noted no significant developments until one afternoon about a week after their first visit, when Mac felt a change in the tension-charged air.

A young man seated in the middle of the crowd sprang to his feet. "We got police in here! And all they're doing is listening in and reporting back to Loeb!"

His voice echoed through the sanctuary, and a commotion rippled across the crowd.

Another young man near the first one stood. "We know you here! Why don't you just get up and announce yourselves?"

A wave of murmurs mixed with laughter overtook the room.

Oh, shit, Mac thought. *Should I stand? They already know we're here.*

"Here he is right here!" The first man pointed to Richmond.

Mac's eyes darted to his fellow plainclothes officer, who looked terrified. Slowly, Richmond rose from his seat as the two young men began to move in his direction. Then Richmond took off running, slamming through a rear door as the two men chased him.

Mac jumped up and ran behind them, afraid that if they caught Richmond, they might beat him half to death. He sprinted as fast as he could down the aisle, through a rear door, and out onto Hernando Street, catching up with the two men on a corner about a block away. Richmond had escaped.

Beads of sweat rolling down his forehead, Mac walked back to the church and slunk into a pew, wondering if he'd be called out next. He did his best to keep cool.

Tines and Arkin were impressed that Mac had maintained his cover after Richmond's disastrous outing. The two of them decided Mac should continue to attend the meetings. And he could accomplish something further, too: gathering information about a local Black power group called the Invaders.

Mac hadn't heard of the group, though a reporter for the afternoon newspaper, *The Memphis Press-Scimitar*, was making a splash with her sensationalized coverage of them, making them out to be dangerous militants.

Tines and Arkin told him Invaders had been coming down to the temple and inserting themselves into the strike controversy, which could lead to all kinds of problems. They wondered if he might be able to get inside the organization.

He said he'd do his best.

As February turned to March, the sanitation strike gathered steam, with Mayor Loeb taking the position that the strike was illegal because state law disallowed strikes against the public. The city council couldn't have helped if it wanted to, because under the recently introduced mayor-council system, Loeb's powers were nearly absolute, giving him control of city operations and veto power over legislation. Though the city council could still pass ordinances, approve budgets, and override his veto, it couldn't hire its own staff or seek legal counsel. If it came down to a fight with him, they were outgunned.

Black people did have some representation on the council, three out of the thirteen seats. A Black man, Fred Davis, chaired its public works committee, which governed the sanitation department. On February 22—ten days after the strike began—he held a hearing on the workers' concerns. His committee adopted a resolution recommending union recognition and an option allowing automatic deduction of union dues from workers' paychecks. But the next day, the full city council rejected the resolution, finding that only the mayor—not the city council—could negotiate contracts on the city's behalf.

Around seven hundred sanitation workers were sitting in the chambers when the city council rejected the recommendation. In response, they stormed out. Mac wasn't there, but he and the whole city heard about it later. The strikers wanted to hold a march right then and there, but a tight line of police officers outside city hall blocked their way. The officers let them through only after getting word from Mayor Loeb and fire and police director Holloman that it was allowed.

But the police weren't done with them yet. They used their squad cars to corral the strikers into a narrow passageway along the street, inching closer and closer to the protesters, and then too close, running over a woman's foot. Some of the marchers encircled the offending squad car and began rocking it, perhaps to free the woman's foot from underneath the tire. Police countered by spraying the entire crowd with Mace and clubbing them with nightsticks.

On an evening in early March, Assistant Chief Lux, Inspector Tines, Lieutenant Arkin, Detective Davis, and Mac gathered around Lux's kitchen table to craft Mac's cover story. It would become the Domestic Intelligence Bureau's first real undercover operation. Lacking experience, a handbook, or any apparent guidance on how to pull it off, they put their heads together and figured things out.

They decided to pull some elements from Mac's real background and fabricate others to round out the story. He'd go by his real first name, Marrell, and as in real life, he'd be from Mississippi. Having just been discharged from the army, he'd come to Memphis to find a job and attend school. Arkin and Davis had arranged for cover employment with a business that was friendly with the police department, an electrical repair shop. That would provide him with paystubs and other pocket litter.

He'd need to make a clean break with his previous life. That meant finding a new place to live—practically everyone on his street knew he was a police officer—and a new phone number. He'd have to separate himself from the department's visible operations. No more setting foot in a police station—not as an officer, anyway. His only contact with the department would be over the phone, calling in his reports to Davis and Arkin. The city finance office would remove him from the police department payroll, transferring him to a generic ledger with a confidential code for his activities. Rather than receive his paychecks by mail, the city would deposit the funds directly into his account. His car would be scrubbed of all dealer markings, decals, and bumper stickers.

The operation would have two objectives: to gather intelligence that would help the police better understand the Invaders' goals and methods, and to collect evidence of any crimes they committed for later prosecution. It required a wait-and-see attitude. They had to let events unfurl as naturally as possible without interference. Mac had to remain an observer only, never injecting himself into the Invaders' decision-making process. Under no circumstances could he be a catalyst for their actions, an agent provocateur. He could neither suggest they commit crimes nor create opportunities for them to do so. His role was to watch and report, not make things happen. That meant he had to assume a passive stance, the demeanor of a follower. He'd be the quiet, bland guy who wanted to be in the Invaders' orbit.

When Mac mentioned to his landlady that he needed to move, she told him she had a vacancy in a rooming house she owned in South Memphis on Third Street. She never asked him why he needed to move, nor did she ask why he'd stopped wearing his uniform, shaving, and getting haircuts. He took to wearing jeans and a loose-fitting top that was reminiscent of a dashiki, perfect for concealing the .25 caliber pistol he kept tucked in his waistband.

His new place in the rooming house, one of five bedrooms off a long hallway on the second floor, was as spartan as his newly streamlined existence. He got a new, unlisted phone number—the line he'd use to call in his daily reports to Arkin or Davis at their desks first thing in the morning, or at home during nonwork hours if there were some urgency.

Mac and Linda talked on most days, so she'd known about his evolving duties, from escorting the sanitation trucks to his new undercover role. She seemed to look at it as just another part of the job. While he never explicitly told her to keep it a secret, she knew better than to go around telling people. But she must've mentioned it to her family, because she later told him one of her brothers warned her Mac was playing with fire and putting them all in danger.

"He said you were gonna get found out, and they'd kill you," she said.

10.

Be Concerned About Your Brother

Days after Mac moved into his new apartment in early March 1968, the phone rang in the wee hours. Half asleep, his voice was gruff when he answered. "Yeah?"

"Patrolman McCollough?"

"Yeah."

"We know what you're doing." It was a male voice Mac didn't recognize, but he thought it sounded like a Black man. He still had the phone to his ear when the caller hung up, leaving him with the *bap-bap-bap* of the disconnect tone.

Who would call him and say something like that? And what did it mean? He couldn't think of anyone outside the Intelligence Bureau who even had his new number, which was unlisted.

The next morning, he called Arkin to report what happened.

"Seems like a threat, all right," Arkin said. "Nothing direct or specific, though."

Mac agreed. He was unsettled, but not scared.

"Let's continue with the plan," Arkin said. "Just keep watch for anything strange."

By mid-March, Mac was a regular attendee at Clayborn Temple's daily mass meetings. Within a couple of weeks of his initial visit, he'd met the strike's key community organizers, a group of prominent ministers who'd formed an organization called Community on the Move for Equality—or COME, as most people called it—to conduct strategy meetings, raise money for the strikers, and mobilize community support.

Mac threw himself into the group's activities, showing up before scheduled meetings or demonstrations to lend a hand. Some of COME's activities took place in the Minimum Salary Building next door to the church, where the African Methodist Episcopal Church's administrative offices were located. He became a fixture there, helping someone run off flyers in the mimeograph machine one minute, and operating the machine himself the next. Or he was stacking flyers, or just standing around chatting with people, getting to know them.

He met all the major strike organizers, some of Memphis's most respected reverends like James Lawson, H. Ralph Jackson, J. O. Patterson, Harold Middlebrook, and Clayborn Temple's own Malcolm Blackburn. He met a radio preacher who'd come up from Texas to help. The man kept his show going by excusing himself from time to time for around twenty minutes to tape a sermon in an office closet. Through the door, Mac could hear him as he began his message soberly, then worked up to a rhapsodic crescendo, only to stop, play back the tape, decide he didn't like something about it, and retape the crescendo again until it sounded like he wanted.

COME led marches after some mass meetings, with seventy-five or so strikers pouring out of the church and onto Hernando to walk an established route two blocks north to Beale, then three blocks west to Main, then ten or so blocks north on Main to city hall, and then back to the church. Mac marched right alongside them.

Every so often, he'd see a face that looked familiar. He'd try hard to avoid that person, hanging back or changing direction or facing away as the circumstances permitted. There was one person in particular he saw more than once, a woman he remembered from his Car 15 patrol. Her name was Tarlease, and she worked in one of the beauty shops on Park.

Many of the demonstrators carried signs with various slogans, but there was one that appeared again and again: I AM A MAN. Rev. Blackburn had them printed by the hundreds. The phrase was a real attention-getter, a reminder of what was at stake. It went to the heart of what the protest was about, what the Black struggle in America had always been about: self-determination, equity, human rights. White city leaders, who'd already robbed the sanitation workers of their rights, were now trying to rob them of their human dignity. And as Rev. Lawson had noted, "At the heart of racism is the idea that a man is not a man, that a person is not a person."

An ardent segregationist, Mayor Loeb had run a law-and-order campaign in the most recent election, promising to allow voters to "be proud again"—as if that pride must come from a time before now, with all the recent strides toward equality. Everyone knew what that meant. Not to mention that for three generations, his family had built its laundry business on exploited Black labor—though there were whispers that his brother William, who operated the laundries as well as a chain of restaurants, had contributed money to the SCLC and even the Invaders. But the mayor, even if he tried, couldn't mask his disdain for Black people and unions, much less Black people who wanted to unionize. Everything about his handling of the strike said to the sanitation workers, "Stop misbehaving and go back to work, boy." The workers responded with signs raised in admonition, each placard a declaration of agency and self respect.

Mac believed in the message and the cause the signs represented, but he didn't carry one, choosing instead to disappear into the crowd and size up the demonstrators. He was looking for Invaders, who stood out with their big afros, denim or leather jackets, and rebellious swaggers. But with hundreds of young people around town who'd adopted the same style, it was hard to spot a true militant.

He had his eye on a few guys with the requisite look who showed up at the temple, but he needed a strategy to integrate into their group. He had one major asset—his car.

He kept his approach subtle, sitting near them during the meetings and making conversation as he walked out with them at the end. "I'm going to South Memphis if anybody needs a ride."

His blue Volkswagen, parked near the church, gleamed in the sun. Ten minutes later, he was pulling up to a plain-looking apartment building with a carload of Invaders. They exited with a chorus of "Thanks, brother."

This apartment was their main hangout, a place they called "the crib." If he were to learn anything useful about them, he needed an invitation inside.

After a week or so of giving them rides, he didn't need to offer anymore. Anyone who wanted a ride just followed him down the church steps to his car. Soon he got the invitation he'd been waiting for.

"You wanna come up to the crib?"

Once inside, he settled into a chair as the small group of guys talked about nothing in particular, skirting around the day's events and mentioning vague revolutionary goals like "liberation" and "the unification of our people." Some of them sipped from little bottles of Robitussin AC cough syrup with codeine, a drug they called "syrup" that turned them lethargic and heavy-lidded. After a while, Mac decided he'd seen enough for one evening. He told them he had to get going because he had to be at work early the next morning.

Did he feel guilty about pretending to befriend them? Not at all. He was just gathering information. He didn't wish them any harm or even think of himself as adverse to them. It wasn't about them as individuals. They had their agenda, and he had his. After all, they wanted something out of him, too: rides in his car. But that was okay—they could ride in his car all they wanted, but he'd be right there in their midst, seeing and hearing what they did.

Bit by bit, Mac learned the Invaders' history. It was one of a number of groups affiliated with—some might say organized under the umbrella of—the Black Organizing Project (BOP), which Charles Cabbage, John Burl Smith, and Coby Smith had formed in the summer of 1967. Their goals: to organize Memphis's Black youth, build Black institutions, and fight for liberation from America's racist power structure.

As the BOP gained members, its leaders' vision took shape. They dreamed of revitalizing the community, providing economic opportunities, hosting cultural events, training people to organize, and much more. They devised what sounded to them like the right organizational structure for an entity that could achieve this, but their grand ideas had a big price tag—an estimated $2 million a year, even with minimal overhead expenditures.

Their recent attempts to generate funding had proven unsuccessful, but they were working on it.

What they lacked in finances, they made up for in an alphabet soup of affiliates: the Afro-American Brotherhood (AAB), students at historically Black Owen College; the Black Student Association (BSA) at Memphis State; the Intercollegiate Chapter of the NAACP at historically Black LeMoyne College; the City Organizers, underemployed young adults; and the Invaders, largely high school students and dropouts. To this, they added another acronym—BUF, for Black United Front—that the leaders sometimes used to refer to this collection of groups. Because if Black people needed anything, they believed, it was a united front. The BUF was the entity that would centralize their resources, coordinate their plans.

They believed the hearts and minds of the city's young people were with them. Law enforcement worried they might be right.

Though the Invaders were only one of BOP's affiliate organizations, in the media and on the streets, "Invaders" became shorthand for the entire organization. The name was synonymous with Black Power in Memphis, and that's what drew the police department's attention. Part of the reason people focused on them was likely the attention-getting name itself, which evoked ominous images of mysterious and hostile intruders. It captured people's imaginations far more than the bureaucratic-sounding BOP. And the group wanted to be provocative, right down to the name, which they took from a popular television show about space alien infiltrators who passed for regular human beings. If you saw them out on the street, they might be just regular guys, or they might be on a revolutionary mission.

All told, BOP and its affiliates had around a hundred members, making it Memphis's foremost Black militant organization. But as far as Mac could tell, there weren't more than ten or so serious adherents—even if plenty of young people around town adopted their style. In the public spotlight, the small group cast long shadows.

In mimeographed newsletters, they proclaimed their objectives and raison d'être:

> It is the purpose of BOP to organize the people of the black community

> into an effective political structure in an effort to gain complete liberation and freedom for African-American blacks. Due to the deeply embedded Christian influence and capitalistic orientation of freedom fighters of earlier generations, and the confinement of their struggle to civil rights, it is necessary for young blacks to create, maintain and operate their own political organizations. America cannot give these rights to our people unless the entire system of government is completely destroyed and rebuilt along socialistic lines with a redistribution and re-management of power. To meet the demands of the civil rights protestors and organizations would require the whites to surrender the very basis of power which allows them to control and rape the world. To allow blacks to be free would mean the demise of capitalistic America. The black communities of this country are no longer seeking aid and free gifts of civil rights from the cracker. Ours is a struggle for liberation, a human rights struggle entwined and interlocked with the struggles for national liberation being waged by 2/3 of the world's population against the oppressor of all mankind—the racist, inhuman, cowardly white man.

They believed they were the right group to advance their soaring ideals because they, unlike the Black bourgeoisie and the civil rights preachers, were of the people. They knew from experience that nobody listened to young people, the poor, the unemployed, dropouts, convicts, or hustlers, which was why they believed existing community programs never seemed to accomplish much. Their programs weren't revolutionary, the Invaders said, but only pacified the people, co-opting them into accepting things the way they were. The Invaders wanted change, and they understood what was needed because they lived it. The downtrodden was *them*.

Mac's assessment of the group could be summed up by the daily routine he soon fell into. He'd leave Clayborn Temple in the late afternoon with one or more Invaders in tow and head to the crib, where they smoked marijuana, took swigs of syrup, and rapped in the style of H. Rap Brown and other revolutionaries they esteemed.

"What you gone do when the revolution come?"

On the revolution, they never talked specifics—gaining adherents, acquiring munitions, strategic objectives. Instead, they tended toward wry observations and punchlines, like when they were riding down the street past a sign for STP motor oil additive, and someone remarked, “Look, it’s STP: Snitching To Police.”

In fact, they didn’t seem particularly interested in overthrowing the U.S. government at all. At the heart of what they advocated was something more amorphous and idealized—Black power—which perhaps was another way of getting at the same idea as “I am a man.”

It didn’t take long for Mac to earn an official post in the group: “Minister of Transportation.” He knew it was a farce, that they were just flattering him for free rides, but that was just how he wanted it. He’d be the quiet hanger-on, the patsy with a car, the guy they made feel important.

The guys would sometimes pool the little money they had and get him to run them down to Beale Street to buy marijuana, Dilaudid—an opiate four times as potent as morphine—and syrup from dealers prowling the sidewalks, then go back to the crib and get high. Most of them went for the marijuana and syrup, but only a few used Dilaudid, because you had to melt down the pills and shoot them up—hardcore stuff. It was easy for Mac to hang back when folks started doing that. To fit in, he pretended to smoke marijuana.

To his surprise and horror, the group’s heaviest Dilaudid user turned out to be a cousin of his sister Joyce’s husband, Percy. Mac pieced it together from his remarks. The guy didn’t seem to realize the connection, thank goodness.

When Mac arrived at Clayborn Temple on a mid-March afternoon, everyone was abuzz with the news: Dr. Martin Luther King Jr. was coming to Memphis to help the sanitation workers. People recognized it as a crucial new stage of the strike. In a situation where nothing seemed able to break the sanitation workers’ impasse with Mayor Loeb, King’s involvement gave the strike supporters a measure of hope.

Weeks had passed since the trouble with the police at city hall, and the union was getting nowhere in their attempts to negotiate with Loeb. COME continued to hold regular mass meetings and marches, and they also started a boycott of downtown businesses and the local daily newspapers (which, to no one's surprise, were biased in Loeb's favor). Still, the mayor didn't budge. The Black community was applying its full weight to the workers' side, but to little effect.

Neither Cole and Walker's horrific deaths in their garbage truck, nor the strike supporters' sizable demonstrations, nor the police department's beatings and Mace had been enough to shine a national media spotlight on the sanitation workers' battle with the city. The ministers behind COME knew they had to bring even more pressure to bear. That was where King came into play.

COME's leader, Rev. James Lawson, had a long-standing friendship with King, still the nation's preeminent civil rights leader, though his popularity was fading in some Black communities. But in Memphis, he was as celebrated as ever, and with his moral authority and international standing, he could bring unprecedented attention to the strike. Lawson asked him to come to Memphis to lend a hand to the workers, and he said yes.

The news may have excited the folks at Clayborn Temple, but not the Invaders. They had no confidence in any of the mainstream civil rights leaders, including King. *Especially* someone like King—coming in from the outside, lacking an intimate understanding of the situation on the ground. To them, much of the civil rights movement amounted to little more than a bid for acceptance among people who would never accept them. Why do all that marching and singing spirituals and taking beatings for the privilege of sitting next to people who hated you?

What the Invaders wanted was a revolution, even if they didn't have concrete ideas about how to get there. They wanted power, *Black* power, like Stokely Carmichael and Huey Newton were talking about. That was what would make a difference, the Invaders believed—not intermingling with whites. Power was the only thing white folks or anybody else respected. It was currency, legal tender for all debts public and private.

As the days wore on, Mac realized his cover legend wasn't serving him well. It limited his freedom during the day, forcing him to fritter away hours until his fictitious shift ended, time he could have put into investigating the Invaders. He needed a story that gave him more flexibility.

Of course, this was a consequence of how his undercover assignment had developed. His legend wasn't much more than a thin backstory to accommodate the evolving nature of his assignment. The Intelligence Bureau hadn't put any forethought into it; they'd merely extracted him from his real life and given him a story to get by. And to a certain extent, it worked. He fit the role of a stranger coming to town, having recently arrived in Memphis after his army discharge. The Intelligence Bureau used that to their advantage in crafting the cover, but they hadn't accounted for the fact that numerous people had seen him in uniform during his foot and car patrols. Not to mention that he'd been identified in *The Commercial Appeal* as a police officer in three articles: the police academy graduation, the Mace ambush—accompanied by a large photo spread—and the shopping center shooting.

Had his cover been planned, he wouldn't have gone through the police academy with all the other recruits and walked in the graduation, nor would he have worked foot patrol in a shopping center at the height of the Christmas shopping season and car patrol in two different cars, nor would he have escorted garbage trucks during the sanitation strike. Each element had introduced a measure of exposure, and it all added up to a lot of risk.

Plus he had his own goals that transcended the department, dreams of pursuing higher education. That was one of the main reasons he'd volunteered to enlist in the army—to pay for college with the GI Bill. The army had barely given him time to get his GED, and he wondered when this job was going to allow him to take college courses. An adjustment to his cover legend could be an opportunity to work toward a degree while giving his story some much-needed heft. In fact, he'd be leaning further into the legend, retrofitting his identity with parts from the one the police department created.

He brought it up to Lieutenant Arkin during a call, and they decided Mac should enroll at Memphis State University. It worked especially well because the Intelligence Bureau had its eye on a group of students they believed were associated with the Students for a Democratic Society, (or SDS, as it was commonly known)—a rogue's gallery of hippies, communists, and misfit rabble-rousers in the police department's eyes. SDS chapters had sprung up at schools nationwide, spearheading protests against the Vietnam War. They marched, held teach-ins, coordinated student strikes, even took over college administrative buildings, as they did at Columbia University, forcing it to scrap its partnership with a Defense Department-affiliated think tank. And there were murmurs that something more sinister was brewing in the group. A group of Memphis State students seemed to be connected to the organization and its ideologies, if not formally, then in spirit.

So Mac was finally going to be a college student, something he'd been working toward since his days in the two-room schoolhouse. And he wouldn't be going to just any college but to a university where he could study practically anything he wanted. Growing up, the agricultural sciences intrigued him, but at this point, police administration seemed like an obvious choice.

It was nearly 8:30 p.m. on March 18, and King's speech about the sanitation workers' plight was about to start. The location was Mason Temple—the South's largest Black-owned-and-operated venue and central headquarters of the world's largest Black Pentecostal denomination, the Church of God in Christ. Though it was a Monday night, the auditorium was packed with more than ten thousand eager attendees. Mac had never seen so many Black folks gathered in one place in his entire life. He arrived early to be sure he got a good seat, finding one a few rows from the front and not too far off to the side. As always, he was on the lookout for militants. He spotted a good number of young people dressed in the popular urban guerrilla style, but that didn't necessarily mean they were militant, of course.

Shortly after nine, Dr. King took the pulpit. He began by complimenting the strikers and their supporters on their solidarity. "You are demonstrating that we are all tied in a single garment of destiny." His voice rose to fill the auditorium. "We can all get more organized together than we can apart. This is the way to gain power. Power is the ability to achieve purpose. Power is the ability to effect change. *We need power.*"

Shouts of "Amen!" rose from the audience.

His voice booming, he called for a citywide work stoppage if the government refused to grant the strikers' demands for decent wages, union recognition, and a dues check-off. "The city of Memphis will not be able to function that day. All I'm saying is, you've got to put the pressure on. That is why we have decided to go to Washington."

The crowd erupted in cheering and applause, punctuated by shouts of agreement.

He described his plan to take great masses of poor people to Washington, D.C., where they'd demand that the nation make good on its promise of life, liberty, and the pursuit of happiness:

> America hasn't lived up to this. She gave the Black man a bad check that's been bouncing all around. We are going to demand our check, to say to this nation, "We know that that check shouldn't have bounced because you have the resources in the federal treasury." We are going to also say, "You are even unjustly spending five hundred thousand dollars to kill a single Vietcong soldier, while you spend only fifty-three dollars a year per person for every person categorized as poverty stricken."

He said he'd lead a brigade to build a shantytown in Washington and name it "City of Hope." The people would march around Capitol Hill's walls every Sunday until "the walls of injustice come tumbling down."

The auditorium quaked with the clapping and cheering of thousands, and Mac joined in. He knew something about that bouncing check. Sometimes his halcyon early childhood memories gave way to a patchwork of bleak scenes, like how Walter would say, "We almost made it" after coming back from seeing the landlord's books. But they never did make it. They never got out of debt.

He knew what it was like to pledge his loyalty to the writer of that bad check, only to have his service and humanity count for nothing. He knew what it was like to struggle to make a living. Somehow, he'd managed to claw his way onto the police force, the odds of which were probably about the same as being struck by lightning. And while he could list the succession of events that brought him there that evening, larger forces had set them in motion: the socioeconomic factors that led him to the military and law enforcement, the political currents that placed him in his undercover role, perhaps even the shadowy hand of fate.

Overlying all of this was his sheer force of will, his drive to live out the potential of his abilities. Finding nearly every other opportunity foreclosed, he chose the army, then the police force as his path. These choices required him to submit to certain constraints, like sitting in an audience listening to King speak, but as an undercover police officer—Mac the patrolman playing the role of Marrell the Invader. He had to split himself in two.

After finishing his speech, King sat, spoke briefly with aides, and took the pulpit again to announce that he was coming back to Memphis to lead a demonstration that Friday, March 22. Mac marked that day in his mind. If troublemakers were going to intervene in the strike, that would be the time for them to do it.

The first snowflakes fluttered down from the clouds over Memphis on the afternoon of Thursday, March 21, the day before King's planned demonstration. It had begun as a hard rain, though the weather service predicted one to two inches of snow—a rarity in Memphis at any time, especially in March. The rainfall became a rain and snow mix, which became billowing flakes tumbling down like something out of a Christmas movie. The expected inch fell, then two, but it just kept falling, continuing through the night and into the next day. The following morning, it greeted the city like a once charming guest overstaying their welcome. It finally stopped more than twenty hours after it began, leaving more than a foot of snow on the ground.

Memphians were aghast. The city almost never got that much snow and wasn't equipped to handle it. What had begun as a novelty had become an emergency, and the city had no choice but to shut down. Employers told workers to stay home, and to the delight of children all over town, schools closed. It went without saying that King's demonstration would have to be postponed—and with all the momentum that had been building, the freak snowstorm was about the only thing that could've stopped it. Folks would have to wait a little longer. It was as if nature had decided to keep Memphis on ice.

11.

Occupier

Just before nine in the morning on Thursday, March 28, 1968, Clayborn Temple was abuzz with strike supporters. Postponed from a week earlier due to the freak snowstorm, the day had finally come for the march that King was to lead through the downtown streets from the church to city hall. Memphis was brimming with pent-up anticipation, and the police department expected anywhere from ten to twenty thousand protesters. Leaflets announcing the new date for the march had passed from hand to eager hand in high schools all over town, and the major Black-owned businesses—including the insurance companies Universal Life, North Carolina Mutual, and Union Protective Life, as the insurance industry was one of the few avenues for building wealth in the community—told their employees to skip work and participate in the march instead. Word traveled down streets and around corners, urging folks to leave behind their quotidian lives and join King in the march. It would be the most important duty of the year, maybe of a lifetime, and the people were ready.

Mac ambled around the church's perimeter, sizing up the crowd as thousands poured onto the streets from all directions. Though the hour was early, the temperature had already reached sixty degrees. It was guaranteed to be a hot day. People of all ages showed up, from high schoolers to the elderly, and a smattering of white folks. But where were the Invaders?

An hour passed. King was supposed to have arrived at ten, but there was still no sign of him. There were easily ten thousand people gathered on the sidewalks and streets, the temperature creeping up by the minute. A rumor was spreading among the crowd that police had beaten a girl at one of the high schools as students were leaving to attend the march.

Mac finally spotted a couple of Invaders, Charles Cabbage and John Burl Smith, helping pass out I AM A MAN placards mounted on two-foot-long wooden sticks. Mac could hear them grumbling about the march, saying it wasn't going to work and nonviolence didn't make any sense. Just before eleven, John entered the church.

Moments later, John's voice blared from the church's public address system. "These preachers don't know what they're doing! Nonviolence is doomed to fail! If y'all want to fight, y'all better be prepared to fight!"

His announcement didn't draw much of a reaction from the crowd.

A short time later, a rumble among the crowd became a roar. King had arrived, and people rushed over to catch a glimpse. Already restless, the throngs of demonstrators became frenetic, with people crushing against each other on the sidewalk. Rev. Lawson, an expert organizer, was supposed to be in charge, but the situation seemed to be getting out of control.

Where were the marshals charged with keeping order? And where were the police? Every so often a police helicopter whirred overhead, but Mac didn't see any officers on the ground.

The marchers rambled down Hernando toward Beale Street. Mac couldn't see what was happening at the front, his view obscured by a sea of people. They turned left onto Beale, picking up speed as they crossed Main Street. That was when he heard the first sickening sounds of crashing glass.

He turned and saw men wielding wooden sticks that had been protest sign handles, their placards torn off and discarded. The men stepped through large shop windows as alarm bells clanged, grabbing armloads of whatever they could find—shoes, clothes, bolts of fabric. Soon, Beale Street reverberated with more shattered windows and alarms.

Mac finally spotted the marshals, who were running up and down the street trying to collect discarded protest signs before they could be used as weapons. But it was too late. The jewelry stores and fancy boutiques were sitting ducks behind plates of glass.

Chaos descended. Rocks and bottles sailed through the air as several people ran down the street, laden with plunder. A few others reveled in the mindless destruction.

"Burn it down!" someone shouted.

Mac tried to make out who the troublemakers were, but they weren't people he recognized. They looked to be vagrants, the down-and-out denizens of Beale Street he might ordinarily walk past without giving a second look.

Police officers appeared, wearing gas masks. Tear gas filled the air; people ran in every direction. Mac began to cough and choke.

This was much more than he had bargained for when he went undercover, he thought, and maybe it was time to hang it up. Police headquarters was only a short distance away, if he could get down Second Street. He could run back to headquarters, tell them what he saw, end the operation. He'd more than done his duty.

But a tight line of police officers was blocking the street. There was no way he'd make it through. There was no path out.

Police began charging the protesters, billy clubs raised. Some of the marchers tried to fight back with their placard handles. Mac turned around and found himself face to face with one of the officers, who blasted his face with Mace. Mac doubled back and sprinted in the direction of Clayborn Temple, leaving behind the panicked demonstrators and the dull *thunk, thunk* of billy clubs against their bodies.

As soon as Mac got home, he called in his report to Detective Davis, describing everything from the tense and disorganized beginning to the disastrous end. He knew the police would think the Invaders had something to do with it, so he made sure to note that he didn't see any Invaders participating in the disorder. The Intelligence Bureau had been waiting for them to start something like this, and for their part, the Invaders had been advocating for chaos in the streets.

Now the city was under martial law, a 7:00 p.m. curfew enforced by four thousand helmeted National Guard troops called in by Mayor Loeb and the governor. Armed with bayonet-tipped rifles and .50 caliber machine guns, they rode down the streets of Black neighborhoods in tanks. It was the machinery of war.

When Mac saw the troops, a visceral rage seized him. Never did he think he'd see with his own eyes his country using its military power against its own people—against *him*—treating *them* like the enemy.

For much of the past three years, Mac had worn some kind of uniform, first army and then Memphis Police Department. He knew a few yards of fabric could never negate his race, as his run-in with Clark had made clear. But out of uniform? He was just another Black man. They'd kill him as sure as they'd kill any other Black person they decided was stepping out of line, or perhaps for no reason at all. And they'd do it with impunity.

In fact, police had already killed someone that day over nothing, a Black teenager named Larry Payne. Officers followed him from a Sears and Roebuck to the public housing complex where his mother lived, claiming he'd stolen a television. They chased him, but he escaped behind a basement door. After they pounded on the door, he came out, but police said he didn't put his hands in the air as they'd ordered but instead pulled out a large knife. One of the officers explained that he'd feared for his life when he pressed his 12-gauge shotgun into Payne's belly.

Eyewitnesses said Payne did raise his hands and didn't have a knife. They said he'd pleaded for his life. According to his mother, who arrived at the scene distraught, one of the officers brandished his gun at her and called her a nigger.

When the Invaders arrived in Room 306 of the Lorraine Motel on April 3, a contingent of boldface names from the SCLC greeted them: King and his brother, A. D., Ralph Abernathy, Jesse Jackson, Andrew Young, and Hosea Williams. Accompanying them was a youth coordinator whose name Mac didn't catch. Representing the Invaders were Charles Cabbage, John Burl Smith, Oree McKenzie, Verdell Brooks, Coby Smith, Edwinna Harrell, and Mac.

The previous week's catastrophic march had unleashed a torrent of bad press about King, including a *Commercial Appeal* headline dubbing him "Chicken a la King." A narrative emerged that King had gotten in over his head toying with violent forces he couldn't control, then run like a coward—to the plush, white-owned-and-operated Rivermont Hotel, no less. The truth was that associates had to convince him to take a ride to safety offered by a Good Samaritan to escape the chaos unfolding around him. He had no reasonable alternative to the Rivermont, given the few routes available through downtown's blocked-off streets. But the facts mattered little once the stories started flying, and the picture they painted endangered his Poor People's Campaign in Washington. As the argument went, if he couldn't successfully lead a peaceful demonstration in relatively sleepy Memphis, how could he possibly shepherd tens of thousands of protesters in the nation's capital?

In response, King announced that he'd return to Memphis to lead another march, and this one would be peaceful. One thing was clear: he couldn't afford another disaster.

King welcomed the Invaders, saying he understood they'd offered to help him have a peaceful march. He radiated peace, his eyes gentle and his gaze placid.

Yes, they said.

King described his philosophy of nonviolence. He said he was bringing his Poor People's Campaign to Washington, D.C. in the next few weeks, and it had to be done peacefully. But first, they had to show they could have a peaceful march in Memphis. The youth coordinator spoke next, noting the importance of youth involvement in the civil rights movement.

Now it was the Invaders' turn to speak. Mac hung back while the leadership told King they could help ensure a peaceful march, but they needed money—Mac thought he heard $500—and cars to reach the city's youth, to convince them to keep the peace. Cab did a lot of the talking.

It sounded like extortion to Mac, and also a scam, because in reality, they couldn't do anything to control whether the march was peaceful. While the Invaders wanted King to believe they or people they could influence had caused the disorder at the previous march, that wasn't true. It had been opportunistic criminals who hung around Beale Street. But it seemed to Mac that the Invaders thought they had King over a barrel. The failed march had humiliated him, and the press was on the attack, endangering his next big objective.

King listened to the request and didn't respond right away. When he did, his voice was soft. He thanked them for meeting with him. He said he'd take it under advisement. Mac took that as a no.

The Invaders filed back to the rooms the SCLC had rented for them. To Mac's surprise, they weren't disappointed at all but hopeful.

The evening of April 3, Mac squeezed in with the crush of people at Mason Temple to hear King address a rally in support of the sanitation strike. The weather was awful. Rain poured down in sheets, and the National Weather Service had issued a tornado warning. But none of that stopped the thousands of attendees from crowding into the seats. Mac looked around and saw a few other Invaders, Oree and John among them. Facing the podium, Mac sat to the right, near the front.

The air hung heavy with a sense of foreboding as King's voice reverberated through the sanctuary:

> Like anybody, I would like to live a long life. Longevity has its place. But I'm not concerned about that now. I just want to do God's will. And He's allowed me to go up to the mountain. And I've seen the promised land. I may not get there with you. But I want you to know tonight, that we, as a people, will get to the promised land!

Deafening applause filled the church. Mac clapped too, his spirit soaring with the audience's cascading cheers and shouts. He believed it—Black folks *would* get to the promised land. And what was this promised land, this place he'd striven for all his life, before the police academy and the army? Wasn't it the place he'd daydreamed about as a young boy, where he could have a good job and live in the house with the big windows, looking out on the world? It was a place where it didn't take so much struggle to get what you earned, where the Raymonds and Clarks and Loebs of the world didn't have so much power over people.

Some might've found his presence there ironic, sitting among people fighting for changes that would benefit him, but as an agent of the forces opposing those changes. But he didn't get tangled up in the seeming contradictions. To make the job work, he had to think in terms of clear demarcations, not ambiguities. His mission was to investigate the Invaders, nothing more and nothing less.

12.

MEM, ATL

In April 2017, I took part in a reunion I never dreamed would happen. Ambassador Andrew Young and my father sat just a few feet apart in Young's living room, forty-nine years after their last encounter on a Lorraine Motel balcony. It felt like a miracle, and certainly not the outcome I had expected from my chance phone call with Young two years earlier. At the end of that call, Young invited Dad to contact him, but when I mentioned it to Dad, he declined. And there things stood—until another happenstance call shook things loose.

A March 2017 phone conversation with Hampton Sides, author of the gripping and meticulously researched book about the assassination, *Hellhound on His Trail*, moved me to arrange the meeting. He inspired me to consider the import—not only historical but personal—of an exchange between them. Dad and Young were part of an ever-dwindling group of people captured in the famous photograph from that day. What would they have to say to each other, and where might it lead?

After talking with Sides, I called Dad and asked if he'd be willing to meet with Young. I expected him to say no again, but to my surprise and delight, he said yes. I'm not sure what changed his mind this time, and I didn't ask; I just moved forward.

After talking to Young and getting a yes from him, plus an invitation to meet at his home, the plan was in place. Maybe this trip Dad and I were about to take was what Young had meant when he'd mentioned "tying up loose ends" during our first phone call. In any event, it felt right.

Two weeks later, I was driving down a two-lane mountain highway in the pitch dark through swirls of snow to get to Reno, where I'd be catching a 5:30 a.m. flight to Atlanta the next morning. A spring snowstorm was raging, so I'd booked an overnight stay at a casino near the Reno airport in case the roads in Tahoe closed. As I approached the Sierra pass, the wind and flying snow merged into opaque white sheets that whipped my windshield, concealing from view everything in my path except the pulsating brake lights of the snowplow ahead of me. For the first time in nearly three years of driving that route, I didn't think I could make it safely down the mountain. I did my best to make sure no headlights approached in the opposite lane, then hung a U-turn and doubled back the way I came. I'd have to take a different, longer route to town.

As I made my way toward I-80's brightly lit lanes, I thought about another drive I'd made down that two-lane mountain highway a couple of years earlier. It was another spring when snow was falling, and the temptation to abandon Dad's story—again—crept up on me as I negotiated the icy hairpin turns. The prospect of plumbing the depths of what happened, of interrogating the facts and following where they led, felt a lot like navigating the slick bends on the mountain's edge. But I kept going then, just as I'd keep going now. Not only that, but I was getting as close to something like closure as I could ever reasonably expect. I was getting closer to the whole story, gathering pieces that had never been told. It was these missing pieces, however small, that helped to remove ambiguities and distortions in the whole.

Arriving at Atlanta's Hartsfield-Jackson airport the next morning, I thought about an insight I'd gained while living overseas: you can tell a lot about a city by its airport. The name of this one alone provided important clues, as it honored both the city's longest-serving mayor, William B. Hartsfield, and the first Black person to hold that office, Maynard Jackson. The enormous terminal gleamed as throngs of people bustled through. It was the very picture of the slogan Atlanta's business leaders had crafted decades earlier: "The city too busy to hate."

I thought back to my dreary arrivals at the quiet and diminishing Memphis International Airport. Memphis, it seemed, had some time on its hands.

My brother Micah and his family lived in a suburb about half an hour south of town, and that's where I'd be picking up Dad. When I arrived, I saw that Dad and I were dressed in similar outfits—collared shirts and navy blazers—though my shirt was white and I paired it with jeans, while he wore a blue shirt and gray slacks.

"We look like cops," I joked.

The drive to Young's house was quiet. We tried chatting a little bit, but our banter was punctuated by silences. I was focused on navigating the tangle of highways, while Dad mostly looked straight ahead.

Young was smiling when we met him on the doorstep of his ranch-style home nestled in a quiet, leafy suburb. He led us through his kitchen, where we said a quick hello to his mother-in-law, and down a carpeted staircase, taking each step deliberately. In the plush den below, he sat in a tall-backed, deep-cushioned armchair with outward curving arms while Dad and I sat in elegant armchairs facing him. Exquisite African art filled the room, and I could've spent the better part of the afternoon perusing it.

As he and Dad made small talk, I set up my smartphone on a tripod to record a video of the meeting. This was history, and I didn't want to miss a frame of it. When I settled in, Young was discussing the Reagan administration's evisceration of government. The topic quickly turned to something called Operation Hope, which helped rebuild communities in the wake of Los Angeles's Rodney King uprisings.

"They organized a bankers' bus tour. Well, the bankers wouldn't come out there by themselves, but you get a group of them, and they did pretty good."

Young seemed to be suffering from a cold and sniffled every now and then. He drew a contrast between himself and the bankers, noting that he never made much money. The SCLC paid him only $6,000 a year, and living on that low salary left his credit in tatters. "I'd been the mayor and a congressman and an ambassador, and still, not only was I broke, I was in debt." One of his fellow church parishioners helped him get his finances in shape.

His cell phone rang.

"Let me see what they're talking about—excuse me," he said to us. Moments later, he spoke into the phone. "How you doin', Madam Prime Minister?"

I caught an impressed-looking grin on Dad's face as my gaze traveled from statue to statue. A short while later, Young was off the phone. "So how long have you been retired?"

"Since 1999," Dad said. "Well, then I went back contract until 2010, so seven full years and eighteen semi."

They talked about Dad's Mississippi roots, where he served in the military, and how he wound up living in Memphis.

"You know, I did everything I could—in fact, all of us did—to keep Dr. King from coming to Memphis," Young said. "But he insisted on it."

"Destiny," Dad said. "Sometimes you just can't—"

"And I mean, I think he kind of knew his days were numbered, and he wanted to give his life for poor people." Young described how King brushed off Young's arguments against leading the march in Memphis that turned disastrous. "And it didn't make any difference who killed him. We knew *what* killed him."

Young wasn't convinced that James Earl Ray pulled the trigger, either. "There was too much going on around," he said, waving his hands. "There were too many people being killed in strange accidents, you know, but it all related to the movement."

He noted other suspicious deaths around the time of King's assassination, like those of labor leader Walter Reuther, clergyman and activist Robert Spike, philanthropists and civil rights supporters Stephen and Audrey Bruce Currier, "and then the person that was one of the influences on King on the war in Vietnam, Thomas Merton, a Catholic priest."

The long list of suspicious deaths staggered me. It was hard to hear that and think it was all coincidence.

"So how long had you been in Memphis when we got there?" Young asked Dad.

"I got to Memphis in February of '67, so I'd been there about a year, a little over a year," Dad said. "You know, I guess it's an appropriate time to personally thank you for the work that you and Dr. King and everybody else did for civil rights." He leaned forward, his eyes intent on Young's. "I remember as a kid growing up in Senatobia, we knew what was going on in Montgomery and other places around us. Not in the sense of being involved in it, but we knew there was a change coming, and it gave us a lot of hope and a lot of energy, and this is the first time I've met you, and so I think it's appropriate to say thank you."

"Thank you," I echoed, nodding.

"But anyway, let me go back," Dad said, "because obviously, you know as well as I do that there's a lot of information that's been put out there about my work with the Memphis police that's totally erroneous and totally, absolutely wrong."

Here we go, I thought.

"One is about the allegation that Memphis police, including myself, were somehow involved in the assassination of Dr. King. Nothing could be further from the truth."

He talked about how he had to testify before the House Select Committee on Assassinations in 1978 and cooperated with a Department of Justice investigation in the '90s. "Which I totally disagreed with, number one, because of the time that had passed, and any trail in the investigation is long gone. Secondly, it was based on the allegation from this guy who said, oh, there was an FBI agent and Memphis police—including myself—in this café, and he overhead a conversation where we were talking about the assassination. And if you know Memphis and know that café, you know African Americans were not *in* there."

Young listened quietly.

Dad continued. "The source, this guy, Jowers, he—his reputation. I felt that I had served in the military, I had served on the Memphis police, I had served, at that time, twenty-plus years in the CIA, and then I have to go and take polygraph tests to refute something that some criminal said? That was just a slap in the face, if you ask me."

I thought I saw a glimmer of understanding on Young's face.

"The guy Pepper," Dad said, spitting out the name, "he sells a book talking about me being in the military, getting out, and then being in some unit that had a license to go out assassinating people. Well, that's absolutely wrong, too. I served in the military, I sure did. I did three years, and then I was completely out—wasn't even involved in the reserve. So that unit he cites, I don't even know if it exists—"

"Well, the only way I found out about it was an Associated Press writer brought me the pages where somebody, he said, told him I was supposed to be shot," Young said. "I tried not to worry about it. And it—the only evidence I have is that when we came back from the hospital, they were cutting those bushes down, and the big guy, James Orange—"

"Baby Jesus," Dad interjected.

"—had always said *that* was where he saw smoke come from, those bushes. And so we went back there, and the Parks Department had cut the bushes down and had swept that whole area clean."

Dad opened his mouth as if to interrupt but didn't.

Young continued. "And so we said the Memphis police destroyed a crime scene, at the very least."

I silently agreed. Dad tilted his head to the side.

"But I don't even like to get into it," Young said. "I wanted to get as far beyond that as I could."

"Right, right," Dad said. That was something they could agree on.

"In fact, when I go to Memphis, I don't even go to the Lorraine Motel," Young said.

Dad talked about his experience of that day—arriving at the Lorraine from the shopping trip, hearing the shot, seeing King's wound, and determining the direction from which the shot came. Young listened intently.

They talked about the gunshot itself. Young said he didn't think King even heard it. Dad pointed out its explosion-like sound.

"Well, I even say to my kids—well, Ralph's sermon for his eulogy was from Genesis where Joseph's brothers sell him into slavery, and they say, 'Let us slay the dreamer, and we'll see then what will become of his dreams,'" Young said. "I focus on what becomes of his dreams."

Dad asked about the origins of the Poor People's Campaign, and I wondered why, until it dawned on me that it began in response to the kind of deep poverty he experienced during childhood.

"Oh, Marian Wright Edelman came over to see us from Mississippi," Young said. "She had just organized the Children's Defense Fund." This occurred in the wake of newly passed farm subsidy legislation that allowed farmers to receive payments for their land if they didn't grow anything.

"I know about that," Dad said.

"The thing was that the people who had been sharecroppers needed to grow at least a couple of acres of corn to feed the chickens and cows and things. And landlords were putting them off the land. And Marian asked us if we could come over and help. And we decided to start in Marks, Mississippi, which was in the poorest county in America back then. The idea was we'd go by mule train and pick people up along the way."

But it didn't pan out. "What made Birmingham successful was not so much the marches but that three-hundred thousand Black people didn't buy anything but food or medicine for ninety days," Young said.

The Poor People's Campaign was different. This time, larger forces had coalesced against King and the SCLC. "I think Hoover realized that, I think there are eight bridges going across the Potomac, and there are two other roads coming in from Baltimore and Virginia. And so with ten bridges, three thousand people, that we could've shut down the city. And I think that's the reason. And, I mean, I have to believe the FBI did it, see, and it—they had been after us too long."

By "it," he seemed to mean the assassination.

"When Dr. King won the Nobel Prize, they had made a recording of him and, well, several of us at the Willard Hotel. And then we were all in there, talking and clowning, and I mean, everybody was happy after the March on Washington." He and King's cohorts "all had rooms on the floor where our wives were. But we had this one apartment, it was an office where he wrote his speech. Somebody went in there with somebody and had sexual intercourse. And it was recorded."

I held my breath, mentally melting into my armchair.

"They sent it to Coretta, see, and with a letter trying to get him—saying that this is going to be released, and the only way he could stop it is to commit suicide. And she listened to it before any of the rest of us did, and she said, 'I don't know where they got this from, but this is not my husband,' she said."

Young had additional reasons to distrust the FBI.

"I was always getting reports from the newspaper people, *The New York Times* and *The Washington Post*, where FBI agents would tell them the—three things they said was that he was a communist, and I didn't know any communists; that he had millions of dollars in Swiss banks, see—well we, I mean, we didn't have any money; and the other thing, they said—they tried to say that Martin and Ralph were gay. They just put out all kinds of rumors."

"Disinformation," Dad said.

Young gestured toward the window. "And, I mean, when I put up that fence out here—that was about, well, it was not long after my mother-in-law came in here, so that's about ten years ago at most. We had to put it on a phone line. And so the guy said, 'How many lines do you have in this house?' And I said, 'We have four.' He said, 'No, you have five.'"

Young traced the fifth phone line to a house down the street where, "when we moved here, there were white folks who lived there." One of his wife's sorority sisters lived there now, and when they talked on the phone, "they always have trouble on the line."

But FBI surveillance didn't scare Young or the SCLC. "Our position was that we weren't doing anything wrong or that we were ashamed of, and we wanted them to know it."

That sounded like the flip side of Dad's sentiments about spying on the Invaders—that he was merely reporting the truth of what happened.

Soon, Young and Dad were discussing mortality and fate. Young said King seemed to sense death was near, which was why he wanted to go to Memphis.

"You remember the first march that ended in violence?" Dad asked.

"I didn't—see, I wasn't there for the first march."

"You weren't there for it, but you know about it," Dad said. "Will you tell Leta about the meeting that the Invaders had with Dr. King and you guys in the Lorraine Motel?" Then he turned to me. "I want you to listen and see if it tracks with what I told you."

"I just remember one boy by the name of Charles Cabbage," Young said.

"Mmm-hmm, he was there."

"Who'd gone to Morehouse. And what they told us was that somebody had paid them to disrupt the march."

That was the first I'd heard of this claim. Paid by whom? Among other things, wouldn't that raise a host of questions about their involvement in COINTELPRO dirty tricks against King? COINTELPRO—short for Counter Intelligence Program—was the the FBI's program of harassment and dirty tricks targeting activists and political organizations.

"The preachers, they didn't like the preachers," Young said.

Dad nodded. "Right, they didn't like the preachers."

"When we came in, they asked—well, we asked them to join us and help with the march, and they said in order to get them to join, they needed two station wagons."

Dad smiled and held up two fingers. "Two conditions that they were asking you guys for: They wanted cars."

"They wanted cars, and they wanted M-O-N-*money*," Young said.

"Money. That's right. I was in that meeting."

"And we tried to say that we didn't, you know, we didn't have that kind of money," Young said, shrugging.

"I was proud because you guys flatly turned them down. And then they left. My characterization of that, it was like they were strong-arming you guys because what they were telling you was not true."

They'd tried to give the impression they could control what happened, Dad said, "but they didn't cause that violence, in my opinion." He pinned the blame on petty criminals who routinely loitered on and around Beale Street. The Invaders, on the other hand, "were trying to sell the fact to you guys that they could control it, all they needed to do is be given the cars for transportation and money for pocket money to go out and take care of their business. So that was the upshot of what was going on at that point."

When the discussion began to flag, I seized the opportunity to ask about something that had been gnawing at me.

"Mr. Young," I said, silently castigating myself for forgetting to address him as Ambassador Young, "did you say they told you they had been offered money or paid money to disrupt?"

"Well, that's what they told me."

Dad wasn't letting that claim stand. "Yeah, but Leta, you hear from me, they didn't *cause* that. I know—I was there."

"Right," I said. Of course, I knew Dad's account, but I was still interested in the claim. I did understand Dad's frustration, though. We weren't merely discussing old claims, but one of his traumatic experiences.

"I don't know," Young said. "I try not to dredge up that period."

"Yeah," Dad said.

"Because it's, it's too many *angles*, see," Young said. "I mean, I've heard so much that I don't wanna believe any of it."

He mentioned James Earl Ray's last-ditch efforts to change his guilty plea and get a retrial. The case wound up before Judge Joe Brown, now of television court show fame but then a Memphis criminal court judge. "And Judge Joe Brown had been, he'd been in the military, and he could—he knew a little something about the way markings on barrels and things work. And when they came up with a rifle and barrel—I mean with, and bullets—they offered him their job on television."

As I recalled it, Judge Brown was forced off the case, though I didn't know the particulars.

Dad leaned forward. "So you're saying, wait a minute now, let's be absolutely clear on this—"

"And they put—it might've had nothing, it might be strictly coincidence," Young said. "But when he got that gun and sent it out for ballistics analysis or something, he suddenly got an offer from Hollywood."

"And dropped it," Dad said.

"And he dropped the case."

I wondered if I should interject that I thought he was pushed off the case but decided it wouldn't have changed Young's underlying point, and actually might have reinforced it.

"And I mean, everything that happened in Atlanta was the spirit of Martin Luther King. See, I mean, no other city has grown like this one," Young said, giving credit to former mayor Maynard Jackson. Young and Dad noted their own ages—Young was eighty-five and Dad was seventy-two.

"I've reaped the harvest of the fruits of the labor that you guys put into the movement," Dad said.

They talked about their military service—how Dad's army service didn't take him to Vietnam, and how Young would've volunteered for Korea, but his sergeant told him to seek a medical discharge because a childhood injury kept him from holding his rifle properly.

Silence descended. Dad pursed his lips. "You know, going back to what you were saying, that you don't focus on what happened in '68, I have one comment, I guess, and two opinions. One is, as you know, I spent all my career—all my life, in some form or another—in the government. And it's hard for me to believe I served a government that was capable of assassinating its citizens, including Dr. King. But still, I know the history. I know the history of the FBI's hatred, I know the history of the counterintelligence program."

"Also a lot of assassinations going on around him," Young said.

"Yeah, all over. Just to finish up, what I'm saying is that I find it really difficult to believe that there was a program of assassination to that degree. But still, that's not the definitive answer, because a lot of stuff happened, like with the Agency, I retired from the Central Intelligence Agency, and I know their policy, their assassination policy—"

"But by that time, though, the Mondale Commission came on and they wiped all that out. They made it illegal for—"

"Yeah, the Church Commission is what I'm talking about, the Church Commission," Dad said. "They just said no, you can't do that. But all I know is what I had personal knowledge of, and my role, and what I—my duty with the Memphis Police Department."

He contrasted the police department's handling of militants with that of other police departments that used heavier-handed tactics, including violence. "We never—I was never asked to engage in dirty tricks. Now, is that a definitive statement saying they didn't do it? All I can say, no, from my standpoint, it didn't happen, but I'm only one. I was only one officer."

Young found common ground, mentioning an undercover program the Atlanta police department started when he was mayor to combat sexual harassment on downtown streets. Women officers dressed in plain clothes, "and if anybody said anything to them, they just talked into the microphone: 'Get the guy in the yellow vest up there.' And we took 'em down and fingerprinted 'em and booked 'em but let 'em go. But we made eighty-five arrests in a week." After that, he said, the problem largely abated.

The room fell quiet again. I recognized the lull as my chance to ask a question, though I was nervous to speak. "So I know you had tried to get in contact with Dad over the years a while ago—"

"I really hadn't," Young said.

That didn't square with my understanding. After all, his reaching out to Dad through a reporter was how I wound up with his phone number in the first place. I was going to ask him *why* he wanted to speak with Dad, but now the premise was gone.

"The only way I knew you," he continued, looking at Dad, "was through Lou Donaldson, the reporter."

I decided he meant Sam Donaldson, the *Primetime Live* host.

"And I said, all I knew about you was that you had a car and we needed to get around. But I didn't know you, and I didn't remember you in any meetings or anything."

He said he'd spent much of the day of the assassination in court seeking permission for King to hold his second march. He recounted how King greeted him when he returned to the Lorraine that afternoon. "I'd been in the courtroom all day, and King, he was just feeling crazy, and what he said was, 'Where you been, little nigga?' He picked up a pillow off the bed and started, you know, beating at me." Young pantomimed how King swatted at him with the pillow.

Dad and I erupted in laughter. The story's seeming incongruity with King's popular image made it even funnier. This wasn't the stern and sanitized portrait of King that appeared in children's textbooks or on murals, but an intimate sketch of a man who lampooned his friends and had pillow fights. It was funny, but also heartrending. King was brutally murdered within hours of that pillow fight.

On the drive back to Micah's house, Dad seemed lighter, as if he'd just removed a heavy pack from his back. Even the air around us felt lighter, the sun's rays more gossamer. We talked a little about the meeting but mostly basked in the easy quiet. I didn't need to ask him how he felt about the meeting because the answer was all around us.

It seemed like Young believed what Dad said about not being involved in the assassination or knowing about any government involvement. At least I couldn't imagine him sitting there talking politely with us otherwise.

But that wasn't the point. Dad didn't need Young to believe him. At the same time, I could see it meant a lot to Dad to look Young in the eye and tell his side of things, regardless of how Young received it. To our grateful delight, he listened with grace.

I came away from our meeting with a new question: If Young was right that Atlanta's development reflected King's spirit, then what spirit did Memphis's reflect?

Memphis historian Wayne Dowdy wrote that after King's murder, "[t]he national media vilified the city, describing it as a 'decaying Mississippi River Town,' 'a city that never wants to change,' and 'the Sun Belt's dark spot.'" The city's tarnished image harmed its economy, he wrote, but it also added to its "collective inferiority complex."

The Memphis where I grew up was certainly a city with low self-esteem. Its residential and commercial development, which hollowed out the middle of town to push ever outward toward the suburbs, seemed to point to a deeper truth: It was fleeing from its own heart. And at its heart sat the Lorraine Motel.

The conventional wisdom seemed to be that Memphis never recovered in the decades following King's assassination, lagging economically, socially, and culturally while Atlanta boomed. It felt true, but was it?

How did Memphis and Atlanta compare in terms of population growth? It made sense to start with 1968, the year of King's assassination, as the baseline. That year, the Memphis metropolitan area had a population of around 641,000, a 1.9 percent increase over the previous year, while

Metro Atlanta's population stood at 1,089,000, a 4.3 percent increase over the same period. So even back then, Atlanta was both more populous and had a faster growing population. That trend only magnified over time, with Memphis's 2020 metro population reaching 1,150,000—a 0.5 percent increase over the previous year and a 79 percent increase since 1968. Meanwhile, Metro Atlanta's 2020 population was 5,803,000—an increase of 2 percent and 433 percent, respectively, over the same periods.

When it came to population growth, Atlanta sizzled and Memphis . . . did okay. (By way of comparison, both the New York metropolitan area and Los Angeles saw less population growth than Memphis from 1968 to 2020, with New York's at less than 19 percent and Los Angeles's at 56 percent.)

But population growth was only a small part of the story. What about median income? According to the U.S. Census Bureau's latest statistics, Memphis's median household income was $41,228, while Atlanta's was significantly higher at $59,948.

A few other facts from the Census Bureau stood out. I was surprised to see that Atlanta proper had a smaller population than Memphis proper (507,000, versus 651,000 in Memphis), and a significantly smaller percentage of its population was Black—51 percent, versus 64 percent in Memphis. Atlanta's median home value was well over double that of Memphis, and larger percentages of its population held high school diplomas and college degrees. In Memphis, a larger percentage of people lived in poverty—25 percent, versus 21 percent of Atlantans.

Overall, Memphis was Blacker and poorer, with less educational attainment. But other statistics looked similar—the percentages of foreign-born residents (6 percent in Memphis versus 8 percent in Atlanta), people in the civilian labor force (63 percent versus 66 percent, respectively), and rates of owner-occupied housing (46.6 percent and 43.5 percent, respectively).

What about the cost of living? Unsurprisingly, Atlanta's was 28 percent higher, exceeding the national average by 0.3 percent, while Memphis's fell below the national average by 16 percent. Did Atlanta's vaunted career opportunities make up for that?

Maybe. A Memphian earning the city's median income of $41,228 would need to earn $52,573—less than Atlanta's $59,948 median salary—to maintain the same living standard in Atlanta. But of course, you'd have to get one of those good jobs to live well. In early 2021, Atlanta's job market offered 72,500 fewer positions than it had the previous January as the economy recovered from pandemic-related shutdowns, though it was adding positions in construction, education, retail, and remote tech work. So perhaps the city did offer a chance at greater economic prosperity.

But these numbers didn't tell the whole story of the differences between the two cities, just as people can't be fully assessed based on résumés or test scores. Like people, cities have personalities. They have souls.

I was turning all this over in my mind when I stumbled upon a discussion thread on a website called Citydata.com titled "Is Atlanta just a bigger Memphis?" The comments ran the gamut, from disparaging the question itself ("Atlanta is much more progressive, rapidly-growing, seeing tons of investment in the city proper as well as the 'burbs, has a significantly larger business base, has tons more to see and do, etc. It's such a silly thing to say so if that's your present mindset, you honestly may be better off just staying in Memphis.") to harsh critiques of Memphis ("The Memphis that my friends left behind didn't seem like much, which is why they are no longer there.") to high praise of Atlanta ("Atlanta feels much more fresh, energetic, and it feels like what it's been for the last 3 decades, a booming southern metropolis that sees high job growth and development.")

It bothered me to read the unfavorable comparisons between Atlanta and Memphis, though I'd lodged some of the same criticisms myself. But the difference was that I *knew* Memphis. I grew up with it, and because of that, I loved it. In fact, it was this level of intimacy that granted it the ability and opportunity to hurt me.

As much as I complained about Memphis, put it down, even fled from it, I missed it as if it were a person. Arriving in the Memphis International Airport was like walking into a relative's living room, where I remembered the walls and furniture. Apart from a few jarring gentrification efforts, the neighborhoods looked mostly like they did when I was a child. The old landmarks still stood—the Peabody Hotel, the Orpheum Theatre, the now-repurposed Sears Crosstown building.

So what spirit did Memphis's development represent? I'd posed the question in anger, I realized. My thoughts took me down brick-paved Beale Street, past its flashing neon signs to Robert R. Church Park—a small green space named in honor of the trailblazing entrepreneur and landowner believed to be the South's first Black millionaire. I could remember walking past the park as a small child and wondering who this Church man was. Occasionally, I attended a church across the street—Pentecostal Temple Church of God in Christ—with Grandma and Granddaddy, and I wondered if that Church had something to do with *their* church.

A historical marker nearby honored pioneering Black journalist Ida B. Wells, who risked her life to launch powerful attacks on white supremacist violence. As a child, I had the idea that she might be associated with Grandma and Granddaddy's church, too. Surely, a woman with a historical marker that close to Pentecostal Temple belonged among the sharp-dressed church mothers with their soaring hats.

Those legacies and many more—including Grandma's, Granddaddy's, Ma's, Dad's, and King's, too—were alive in Memphis. They all had a hand in making me who I was, as did the city itself, which after all was also a living, breathing entity, inhaling and exhaling land and people and culture. If I couldn't love Memphis, then I couldn't love myself.

And there was this, as a commenter noted in the Citydata.com discussion thread:

> I seen BURGER KING have a MEMPHIS BBQ burger . . . I got to Krogers grocery and see Memphis BBQ sauce. I've seen Domino's have a MEMPHIS BBQ pizza, heck I even seen Memphis on the Travel channel doing a special on Memphis cuisine . . . I'm sorry I've never seen McDonald's have a ATL salad, burger or Anything.

13.

Triggerman

In the days following King's assassination in April 1968, Memphis looked something like a war zone, with National Guard soldiers rolling through the streets as they had after King's first and final march. Again, the governor declared martial law, and convoys of police cars patrolled in tactical units.

There hadn't been nearly as much trouble as Mac expected. Buildings burned here and there, and a handful of businesses were vandalized, but it was nothing compared to what was going on in other cities, like D.C., Baltimore, Chicago, Detroit, and New York City.

By comparison, the reaction in Memphis had been subdued, especially given that it was the site of King's murder, the place he was trying to help when he was killed. The prevailing mood wasn't anger but numbing grief bordering on despair. His widow, Coretta Scott King, came to town on April 8 and led a peaceful mass march. With immense pressure bearing down on Mayor Loeb from the federal government, civic groups, and business interests, he had no choice but to settle the strike and make a few concessions to the sanitation workers. Something resembling peace settled over the city.

On April 27, 1968, Mac and Linda decided to elope. When she gave him the news she was pregnant, his heart soared. They were going to be a family—the young police officer, his beautiful schoolteacher wife, and now a child. It was like something out of a magazine, a dream. It was time to do the respectable thing. They'd be Officer and Mrs. McCollough, a thought that made him smile.

Because of his undercover assignment, a big ceremony was never an option. There could be no church filled with family and friends celebrating their union, no printed wedding announcements, no photos of them in regal white gown and dashing tuxedo. They told no one of their news, or their plans, except Mac's little brother Floyd, who'd serve as their witness.

They decided to seal the deal on a Saturday, when neither of them had to work. Floyd met them at their house, all three of them wearing casual clothes. Then they set off to find a justice of the peace. With no Saturday options in Memphis, their first stop was the naval base community of Millington, about half an hour's drive north on Highway 51, but that office was closed, too. They drove still farther north for another forty-five minutes or so to the small town of Ripley, where the justice of the peace was on duty.

They said their "I dos" around noon. Afterward, they had lunch, then took the scenic route back to Memphis, cutting across the lush countryside on back roads until they reached Interstate 40. That would have to do for their honeymoon.

On a warm afternoon in late April, Mac and a few of the guys decided to stop by the Kentucky Fried Chicken on South Third. As they stood in line, he noticed the cashier, a young, thin Black woman, staring at him. She looked bemused, her expression searching.

When Mac reached the counter, she smirked. "Marrell, your daddy is telling everybody you a police officer, but just look at you! Here you are an Invader!"

He could feel everyone's eyes on him—the people behind the counter, the guys he was with, the other people in line. Who was she, and how did she know his father? She must have been from around the St. Peter Church community. Word traveled fast there, and it wasn't all that far from Memphis.

Mac let out a stiff laugh. "That old man? Only thing I can think of, maybe he's talking about when I was a military policeman in the army."

After a few beats, she laughed. "I knew nobody could believe that old man."

None of the guys with Mac said a word. After the guys picked up their orders and got back in Mac's car, they went back to their usual loud banter. Nobody mentioned what happened.

Mac's anxiety about someone blowing his cover, usually a low background hum, hit an inflection point. If the woman in the chicken joint recognized him, how many other people around town would?

He'd thought about this before, coming up with techniques to deal with the risk. Unfortunately, they wouldn't have worked in the restaurant, as they were more fitting in situations where he saw someone he knew from afar. If that happened, he told himself, he'd try to take a few steps ahead of whoever he was with and greet the person, see what they were going to say.

He'd ask, "Hey, how you doin?"

If they were going to greet him as Mac the police officer, he needed it to happen before his companions heard it. Regardless, he'd keep the encounter brief and brisk.

"Oh, I'm doing good. Okay, good to see you!"

It was either that or avoid the person altogether. The point was to control the situation as best he could. He hadn't yet had occasion to use these tactics, but he kept them in his back pocket, just in case.

Mac called Arkin that evening and told him about his encounter with the chicken joint cashier. The next day, police department detectives and FBI agents showed up at the restaurant and asked to speak with her. They showed her several photos of Mac, telling her he was the prime suspect in a series of bank robberies in Memphis and Northern Mississippi. They questioned her closely. After that, Mac didn't hear anything else about it.

The home of Memphis State University president Cecil Humphreys looked like Mac would've envisioned it—large and elegant, its shelves brimming with books. Until recently, he wouldn't have imagined himself sitting in it on a late spring evening, working out the details of his enrollment beginning in the summer session. After all, he'd dropped out of high school—not because he didn't want to continue his education but because he so desperately *wanted* to continue it that an army recruiter was able to hoodwink him.

A tall, avuncular man with a kindly demeanor, Humphreys listened as Davis and Arkin explained their plan to have Mac enroll at MSU to keep an eye on the SDS-friendly students and their fellow travelers.

"But I want to be a real student earning credits towards a real degree," Mac said.

"That will be fine," Humphreys replied. "You will need to sit for the ACT, though."

Humphreys mentioned another group he wanted to keep an eye on, a new organization called the Black Student Association, or BSA. Arkin and Davis told him that wouldn't be a problem.

Humphreys turned to Mac. "How do you intend to carry out this operation?"

Mac said he planned to take on a full course load, blending in with the students and showing his face around the student union. He'd befriend SDS supporters and BSA members and report back on their intentions. In fact, Davis and Arkin had already given Mac a list of students they wanted to target.

Though Memphis State's 1968 recruitment handbook, *A Viewbook: Memphis State University*, wasn't published until September of that year, the picture of college life it presented was much like what Mac found on his first day of classes in June: spare and angular brick and concrete architecture, and a mostly white and conservative student body. Greek organizations dominated the social scene, between rush week, post-game parties, sing-alongs, and similar activities. The handbook listed twelve national fraternities and thirteen national sororities, two of which—Delta Sigma Theta and Zeta Phi Beta—were historically Black. Below the list was a large color photo of sorority and fraternity members, exclusively white, striking various poses. Several groups displayed bright banners, including one that held a Confederate flag.

Mac attended classes in the mornings beginning around nine, grabbing a Slurpee from 7-Eleven on the way to campus. When he got out at noon, he'd walk over to the student union and scope out the crowd, looking for people dressed like hippies—long hair, scraggly facial hair, or sloppy clothes for men and long or messy hair and long peasant dresses and skirts for women—and Black students. Hippies stood out like beacons, to say nothing of Black folks. He took the same approach as he had when he infiltrated the Invaders, sidling up to them and striking up conversations.

———

Despite what the Invaders took to be promising talks with the SCLC for funding that spring, no money ever came. The militant group had big dreams, but they were broke.

Their best hope was President Johnson's War on Poverty, part of his Great Society initiatives to tackle chronic poverty and racial inequities plaguing the country. Landmark legislation passed in 1964 kicked it off with a $1 billion appropriation for community-guided-and-shaped programs focusing on issues including hunger, legal services, and youth employment. In the next several years, billions more followed.

These federal dollars flowed to community organizations through local War on Poverty committees, and in Memphis, that committee was headed by a Black man, Washington Butler Jr. Though he might've seemed a natural ally of young upstarts like the Invaders, the reality was more complicated.

Funny enough, it was Rev. Lawson—the head of COME whom the Invaders now couldn't stand—who'd hired Charles Cabbage and Coby Smith the previous year to do fieldwork for a South Memphis–based group receiving federal funds through Butler's War on Poverty committee. The Memphis Area Project South, known as MAP-South, sought to improve residents' health, living conditions, and employment prospects, and Lawson became its president in 1966. Familiar with Coby and Cab from the community, he admired their organizing background and zeal. He thought he might be able to mentor them, provide some guidance.

Their job would be to educate renters about tenants' rights, going door-to-door and explaining what to do if they ran into problems with their landlord. But Cab and Coby didn't think the official rights and remedies went far enough. They decided to add their own component, telling tenants to organize rent strikes if their housing wasn't fit to live in. When word got out that workers for a federally funded organization were encouraging rent strikes in federally subsidized housing, the pair quickly found themselves in hot water.

Cab and Coby were swept into congressional hearings about summer 1967's wave of urban unrest, facing questions about whether they were members of a subversive organization. Now in the spotlight, MAP-South and the Memphis War on Poverty Commission (WOPC) felt pressured to act, lest they endanger their federal funding. Whatever Rev. Lawson's personal feelings were about their actions, he sprang to their defense, and at his urging, MAP-South elected to keep them on staff. But the WOPC reversed that decision—Coby and Cab were out. And in some ways, it seemed like they'd been out ever since.

They didn't give up easily, though. In June 1968, they were back in the WOPC's orbit through a new federally funded initiative. Originally conceived as the Community Unification Program and reenvisioned as the Ghetto Organizing Project, the Neighborhood Organizing Project (NOP) got a $20,000 budget to do what the Invaders had dreamed of doing since their founding—to unify and uplift the community, giving young people opportunities and a feeling of pride. It was a chance to have a voice in what was happening, to be taken seriously, to do something that mattered. Nine other local organizations, some of which the Black Organizing Project (BOP) claimed as affiliates, joined the Invaders in steering the NOP's activities—student groups from LeMoyne College, Owen College, Southwestern at Memphis, and Christian Brothers College; Memphis State's Black Student Association and Inter-Religious Council; the City Organizers; the Mayor's Council on Youth Opportunity; and the NAACP's youth group.

Serving as project director was Charles Ballard, one of the original Invaders and an Owen College graduate. Studious and dedicated to the cause of Black power, he wasn't much for rabble-rousing and stayed out of the drug scene, though like everyone, he indulged in marijuana from time to time. He was a thinker, a planner.

The NOP provided cultural events, discussion forums, and Black history education. Its youth board, which handled most governance issues, was dominated by BOP members, and BOP members held seventeen of twenty paid positions. The plan may have looked fine on paper, but problems arose in the translation from the page to reality. Though *The Commercial Appeal*—not inclined to report on the program favorably and playing up concerns that the program would teach insurrection techniques to Black youth—indicated that thirty or forty children were at the NOP center on Florida Street "playing at tables" in July, Mac didn't see much of anything happening when he visited its Thomas Street center in North Memphis.

Then there were budgetary issues. Of the $20,000 budget, $17,000 went to salaries, and $175 per month went toward the rental of a beige Ford Mustang for Ballard to drive to the various sites. The car rental may not have been as decadent as it seemed, though, as Invader and NOP coordinator James Philips told *The Commercial Appeal* on July 11 that transportation was a big challenge for the project.

"We have one car to use all over the city," he said.

Still, these numbers drew scrutiny, as did the Invaders' use of an NOP office street address on Invaders' membership applications.

As the weeks passed and spring turned to summer, not much changed about Mac's daily interactions with the Invaders: Go to the crib, take the guys to buy drugs, return to the crib, use the drugs, and rap. On one such night in June, the cousin of Mac's brother-in-law overdosed on Dilaudid and nearly died. Someone noticed he was lying on the couch unresponsive with only the whites of his eyes visible. They did everything they could to rouse him, but nothing worked. Afraid to call the police, they tried to perform first aid themselves. Mac and a couple other guys picked him up, carried him out to the apartment complex's front lawn, and rolled him around in the grass until he finally came to.

But that didn't change their behavior. On June 23, 1968, Mac and some of the guys drove all over Shelby County and three adjoining counties buying up syrup. By the end of the day, they'd collected nearly a gallon, which they planned to cut with Lipton tea and sell at a profit.

Mac tried to reflect this picture of the Invaders in his phoned-in reports to Arkin and Davis. To Mac, this was a small group of mostly men who engaged in radical talk and drug use but didn't present any kind of militant threat.

Their other interactions with law enforcement bore that out. The most serious criminal incidents among them had been three episodes of unrest at Carver High School, one in March 1968 and two others in May. A good number of Invaders were past and current Carver students, and many lived nearby. They were part of the school community, whether the administration liked it or not, and some—including the principal—did not.

In the first disruption, on March 11, prosecutors charged John Henry Ferguson and another man under a 110-year-old Tennessee statute for "unlawfully disturbing and disquieting a school assemblage," a law that had led to only a single indictment in its entire history. Reportedly, the men had tried to entice students to support the striking sanitation workers by boycotting classes.

In the second one, on May 17, police said three Invaders caused a riot involving at least 200 of the school's 2,400 students. The Invaders said the protests came from the students themselves and from the community. Mac wasn't there and didn't know any more about what happened than what the newspapers were reporting: that students were angry over a prohibition against a student chapter of the Invaders, as well as high cafeteria food prices and the curriculum's omission of Black culture. A disturbance broke out in the cafeteria, and when the principal saw Invaders standing nearby, he called the police.

"I have forbade them admission to the campus, but they come anyway," he told *The Commercial Appeal.*

Students threw rocks and bottles at police when they arrived, slightly injuring an officer's wrist and damaging several police cars, a board of education truck, and two television stations' camera cars. Arrested were John Burl Smith, charged with inciting a riot; Oree McKenzie, charged with disorderly conduct; and Larry Davis, charged with assault.

In a third uprising the following Monday, May 20, an estimated 250 students and others reportedly roamed around the campus throwing stones and shattering upward of 150 windows. Police arrested John Burl and John Henry, along with Womax Lee "Speedy" Stevenson, age seventeen, for causing that disturbance, too. A judge set bond for John Burl and John Henry at $50,000, but a second judge reduced it to $10,000—though prosecutors had sought only $1,500 for John Burl and $2,500 for John Henry.

To Mac this was much ado about relatively little. But by July, a real danger was emerging that he thought police needed to monitor. Ben Berry and Oree McKenzie were saying it was time for the group to start killing police—"offing roaches," as they put it. They were angry about many of the same things that frustrated a lot of Black men in Memphis: brutality, disrespect, stops and searches for no reason, and arbitrary arrests and charges, to name a few.

Berry had been bragging about owning a gun, a .303 British carbine rifle. One June night, he brought it by the crib to show it off. Unlike the guys' normal bluster, the discussion sounded serious this time. They were really entertaining the idea, and they had a weapon in their hands. Reports were already coming in of police being fired on with BB guns—a small matter in itself but one that might signal a trend toward violence. At that very hour, Huey Newton of Oakland's Black Panthers sat in jail for murdering an officer; he was already a folk hero in some quarters.

Back in his apartment at the end of the night, Mac phoned Lieutenant Arkin and described the Invaders' discussion about killing police.

"Did they give any details of what they're planning?" Arkin asked.

"No, it was just a general discussion of doing it."

"We need to be ready with our own plan."

Arkin and Mac decided that if and when the details of an ambush were worked out, Mac would volunteer to be the triggerman, while Arkin would drive the targeted police car. Mac would fire into the back seat of Arkin's car, and Arkin would speed away from the scene.

"We need to put a hot mike in your car so we can pick up recordings of any more discussions," Arkin said. "Bring it down to Armour Station."

Over the course of the following week, Mac continued his normal routine of showing up at the crib and taking the guys to buy drugs. They wove their way down to Beale Street in his car, talking their profanity-laced talk. Whenever they spotted a squad car, the discussion turned to police.

"See them roaches? They need to be *offed*," went a typical comment.

"Just wait till the revolution come," another might say.

Several days into the hot mike operation, Mac found himself high on marijuana, by accident. The guys had been smoking it through a water pipe, and Mac took a couple of fake tokes so as not to arouse anyone's suspicions. But to his horror, he discovered that the pipe didn't contain water, but Ripple. After the marijuana was gone, they passed around the bowl for everyone to drink the remaining liquid. Pretending to smoke was one thing, but there was no way out of this. Raising the bowl to his lips, he powered through his revulsion and sipped the sweet, smoky brew.

When he got home, he called in his report. "Hey Arch, I'm in."

"I'm glad you called, because we got a problem with that radio. It's blasting all over the place. The radio channel you fellas are on, it's the same channel the radar units use. Any time your car is near one, those officers can hear what you're saying. I need you to come down to Armour Station so we can fix this."

"I'm on my way." Mac tried to sound normal. Would anyone be able to tell he was high? He had to act normal.

But he was frustrated, too. How could the technicians have made such a dumb mistake? There were only two frequencies in use—the regular one for the dispatchers to talk to the squad cars, and the one for the radar units that caught speeders. This error could have cost the investigation, and his safety. What if he'd been sitting with a car full of Invaders near one of those radar units, and they all heard their own conversations coming out of the police car? Or what if one of those radar units had been parked at, say, Jack Pirtle's Chicken, with the Invaders' conversation pouring out of the radio for everyone to hear? Surely the Intelligence Bureau could do better than this.

He returned to Armour Station to get the radio problem squared away and carried out the hot mike operation for several more days, but it came to nothing. There was never any more talk about the ambush. He and Arkin decided to scrap it and removed the microphone.

One late July afternoon on a lonely stretch of road beneath an overpass in West Memphis, Arkansas, an unmarked sedan sat parked on the shoulder. Not far behind it was a blue Volkswagen Fastback. Both cars had crossed the Memphis & Arkansas Bridge spanning the Mississippi River, taking the first exit to their rendezvous point. Inside the first car, Mac, Arkin, Detective Davis, and a special agent, either Lawrence or Lowe—depending on which one was available—discussed Mac's recent activities. They had begun meeting this way that summer, when the FBI raised concerns about members of a militant group out of St. Louis, the Black Egyptians, traveling to town to meet with Invaders.

Lawrence and Lowe showed Mac photos of people who moved in the Invaders' orbit, photos that Arkin and Davis didn't have. Mac would put names to the faces and nicknames to government names. He'd also flesh out the reports he'd called in to Arkin and Davis over the past week.

Lasting no more than an hour, the meetings gave Mac a week's worth of psychological sustenance. His undercover existence was lonely, and he'd felt adrift at times, like he was floating at the end of the ever-lengthening tether connecting him to his real identity and purpose. The meetings reeled him back to the ship, reminding him he was still part of the team, fulfilling key duties. For those brief moments, he was himself again—not Marrell the Invader but Mac the police officer.

Sometimes they'd talk about that in their meetings, how Mac's intelligence-gathering was keeping them on top of what was happening with the Invaders.

"You're our eyes and ears," they said. "It's important work."

Mac drew strength from that. It made him say to himself, *I can do this.*

The summer days whirred by like a flipbook of scenes that varied little from day to day—college courses, the crib, clandestine meetings with the Intelligence Bureau and FBI agents under a West Memphis overpass. The Invaders were still holding meetings in the crib—if you could call the casual get-togethers meetings.

Mac's cover was still intact, despite a few close calls. Now that he was a student, his undercover role blended much better with his real life. But it came at a personal cost. He and Linda were almost like strangers now.

Home life had been less idyllic than the romantic mental image he'd painted. Due to their work schedules, he and Linda barely saw each other. And Miss Elizabeth was always there. Though she spent most of her time reading the Bible or praying in her room, her constant presence kept him from feeling fully comfortable and at home. He thought Linda was overly attached to her, too. But how could he complain when he was hardly ever there?

Monday through Saturday, he spent all the free time he had in class, with the SDS-ers, or with the Invaders, not getting home until around midnight most nights. He was living out his backstory as the lone wolf veteran looking for an identity and a purpose. He kept his real life with Linda locked away in a separate compartment in his mind.

The only day he could reserve for his home life was Sunday, using the excuse that his wife's bourgeois family demanded he spend the Lord's day with them rather than his friends. He told the Invaders his wife was so uppity, he could hardly stand her, that he didn't fit in with her family but had to please them to keep the peace. Though he'd concocted this storyline to allow himself that day at home, he repeated it so often that perhaps he began to believe it on some level.

Then there was the pregnancy that prompted him to propose. After they went to the justice of the peace, she never mentioned it again. She'd shown him the swelling in her belly early on, but nothing came of it. She didn't get any bigger, and they didn't discuss it. It just passed, like a dream. Then she started talking about going to the doctor, saying she was having female problems, but she wouldn't let him go with her. Mac didn't know what to say or do, so he just tried to carry on as normal.

He met a white girl on campus, Penny, whose father was a doctor or something. Mac could tell she liked him, though to him, she was just part of the investigation. He met her in one of his classes and discovered she wanted to hang out with the SDS crowd, so he started taking her to meetings. She helped him blend in. Sometimes they held hands, but it didn't feel like a big deal—especially given that one of his buddies in the group, a white guy, had a Black girlfriend.

But one day, Penny came crying to Mac after hearing an earful from her father. She said the FBI told him she'd been making time with a Negro radical, and she was about to get herself in trouble.

"It's okay," Mac told her. "It's your life." But he was puzzled that the FBI raised the matter with her father. They knew he was working.

On the languid night of August 2, the hours at the crib unfurling seemingly without end, a loud bang interrupted the quietude. It was the front door, which now hung wide open as police poured in.

A cacophony of shouting filled the air as the officers rounded up the small group of Invaders and others gathered there. One of the officers set upon Mac, cuffing his wrists behind his back and shoving him in the back of a paddy wagon.

At police headquarters, the prisoners were herded through processing like livestock and pushed into cold cells. Eight had been arrested in the raid: John Burl Smith, charged with possession of marijuana and legend (prescription) drugs; a neighbor, Lizzie, also charged with possession of marijuana and legend drugs; and Oree McKenzie, Charles Ballard, Verdell Brooks, Mac, a woman named Jewel, and an underage girl, all charged with disorderly conduct. Though Mac hadn't expected to get arrested as part of his assignment, he supposed it made sense. If there was one thing he needed to do to blend in with the Invaders, it was get hassled by police.

He wanted to go home, and he knew all it would take was getting the attention of one of the guards and sending word to the Intelligence Bureau. But he knew it would be a mistake. This was something he'd have to endure, at least for a night.

In court the next morning, the judge released him and everyone else except John and Lizzie on $51 bond. Disorderly conduct, as he knew from his car patrol days, was in the eye of the beholder.

———

The news hit Mac like a gut punch: On August 24, snipers ambushed a squad car carrying an officer from his police academy class, Patrolman R. J. Waddell. The bullet went through the front passenger door, piercing Waddell's right leg below the knee. He survived.

Police arrested four Invaders for the crime—Oree McKenzie, Ben Berry, John Gary Williams, and Womax Stevenson. The real shocker of the bunch was John Gary, a Stax recording artist with the hit group the Mad Lads, known for silky ballads like "Don't Have to Shop Around" and "Whatever Hurts You." With his Hollywood looks and honey butter voice, John Gary didn't seem to fit the profile for a police ambush. Mac had never even met him.

The breathless newspaper coverage of the shooting made sure to point out Oree and Ben's employment with the Neighborhood Organizing Project that summer. According to Berry, who later turned state's evidence, the Florida Street NOP office was where they'd planned the ambush. It was revenge for the arrest of fellow Invader John Henry Ferguson, who'd been picked up earlier that evening for brandishing what turned out to be a toy rifle at motorists.

According to Berry, the guys went to his apartment and grabbed three firearms: a Russian 7.62-millimeter Mosin-Nagant rifle, a .303 British carbine, and a .22-250 Remington. But only the .303 carbine was Berry's—the Russian rifle was Charles Cabbage's and the Remington was John Burl Smith's. Next, according to Berry, they returned to the NOP office and got the ammunition, which they kept on a shelf, as well as a 9-millimeter handgun from John Burl Smith. Accompanying them was John Gary's girlfriend, Gloria. She was the one who placed the phone call that set the plan in motion.

Send someone quick, she told the switchboard operator at police headquarters, saying there was trouble in southwest Memphis over by the lumberyard near the railroad tracks. She stressed that they needed to send a squad car.

The minutes passed as Ben, Womax, Oree, and John Gary lay in wait by the railroad tracks, each of them holding a gun. Meanwhile, Gloria sat tight in the getaway car on a nearby street that dead-ended at the tracks. After about fifteen minutes, a squad car showed up.

According to Ben, each of the guys fired one shot into the car. They thought their shots missed, Ben said. And anyway, they weren't specifically trying to kill an officer—they only wanted to hit the car. Now they sat in jail, charged with assault to murder.

On September 10, 1968, a few of the Invaders decided to settle an old score. The target: attorney A. W. Willis, Tennessee's first Black state representative and unsuccessful mayoral candidate against Mayor Loeb the previous November. The Invaders had tried to help Willis back then, doing what they could to promote his candidacy and turn out the voters candidates tended to overlook. After all, he had a chance to become Memphis's first Black mayor. Carl Stokes and Richard Hatcher were serious contenders to make history in Cleveland and Gary, so why couldn't the same happen in Memphis? It was a rare opportunity to bring Black power to bear on the whole city—if Black folks were ready to take that step. The Invaders wanted to do all they could to make it happen.

But disappointment followed. After a bruising loss, plus criticism for his relationship with the Invaders, Willis seemed to distance himself from them. They felt taken for granted, used and thrown away. On top of all that, rumors swirled that his candidacy had been a ruse, that Loeb had paid him $35,000 to enter the race and split the Black vote.

All these months later, several of them were still seething about it, as Mac discovered one afternoon at the crib. Some of the guys—minor players, including a guy they called Lard—were sitting around talking when the topic turned to Willis.

"We oughta teach that Uncle Tom a lesson," somebody said.

Mac just listened.

"What we gone do?" asked another.

"Burn his houses down," said someone else.

They got in Mac's car and told him to take them to a service station on South Parkway, where one of them got the attendant to lend them a five-gallon gas can. After filling it with gasoline, they directed Mac to a street not far from the crib, where there were three homes under construction by a mortgage and realty company headed by Willis. They'd been sold as part of a low-income housing program.

Mac parked, and they entered one of the homes. Then Lard and another guy took turns pouring gasoline on the floors alongside the walls. While everyone else stood back, the guy lit a match and dropped it.

Perhaps he expected the ensuing flame to follow the trail of gasoline, and that's why he just stood there instead of getting ready to run. But it didn't. As soon as the lit match met the fumes, there was a bright flash and a loud *BOOM!*

The man jumped back, barely escaping serious burns. They all sprinted back to the car.

Mac dropped them off at the crib, telling them not to worry about returning the gas can to the service station. "I'll do it."

When he got to the service station, he went to the attendant empty-handed and apologetic. "My friends and I borrowed a gas can earlier, but I don't know what happened to it."

He gave the man a couple of dollars in compensation for the loss. Then he went home and called Arkin.

"Hey Arch, I have some evidence for you."

14.

Blown

By the time late summer 1968 turned to fall, much of the Invaders' old guard was locked up on charges: John Burl Smith, for the drug raid, plus inciting a riot at Carver High School, plus another disturbing the peace charge; John Henry Ferguson, for the Carver disturbances; and Ben Berry, Oree McKenzie, John Gary Williams, and Womax Stevenson, for the police shooting. Charles Cabbage was indicted by a federal grand jury in July for failing to report for army induction the previous May. He was released on $1,500 bond, only to be rearrested the next month on a state charge of burglary and a city charge of carrying a pistol. In fining him $50 on the pistol charge, the judge snapped, "I can't understand why he refuses to carry a rifle for his country but wants to carry a pistol on the streets."

With John Burl's departure, the Invaders lost the crib, so Rev. H. Ralph Jackson, whose duties for the AME Church included managing Clayborn Temple, allowed them to use a vacant office at the church. The NOP, the Invaders-backed children's program, concluded in August and wasn't renewed. The bad press was overwhelming, particularly when the Invaders' arrests hit the newspapers in articles that rarely neglected to mention their connections to the program.

Mac was convinced that failure had been built into the NOP, that the federal government had poured money into it but didn't care where it went or whether the program even did what it was supposed to do. If the government had cared, he thought, they would have provided some oversight.

But instead, he saw none. It looked to him like a lot of the money went to marijuana and syrup—a shameful waste.

With many of the original Invaders out of the picture by summer's end, a leadership vacuum appeared. Almost immediately, a trio of newly active members stepped in to fill it: Lance "Sweet Willie Wine" Watson, Roy Turks, and Ogundele Uwefemi.

Sweet Willie Wine looked every part the telegenic firebrand the press wanted to see, his willowy frame draped in a dashiki and necklaces as he glared from behind dark sunglasses. Cameras flashed as he spat out diatribes like an incensed oracle, his polio-shrunken left arm folded close to his chest. He'd been an Invader for a while, though he'd been in Washington, D.C., for much of the summer. He'd joined the SCLC's Poor People's Campaign, which went on in the wake of King's murder.

Every time Mac turned on the news, there seemed to be reports of rain drenching the campaign's tent city on the National Mall. Some of the Invaders grew suspicious.

"The government's seeding the clouds," went a typical comment.

As thousands of protesters sloshed through the muck and filth in a desperate bid to be seen and heard, out of that morass rose Memphis's own Sweet Willie Wine. He'd been featured in a big publication—*Playboy* or *Look* or something like that, people said. He returned to town a celebrity activist, though before that, he'd been known as a street hustler.

He made his first big splash in local news in mid-August when he led a protest at the SCLC's national convention at Memphis's Mason Temple, the site of King's last speech. The convention ended on an otherwise harmonious note, with Rev. Ralph Abernathy winning a unanimous vote to take over leadership of the organization. Richard Hatcher, who'd won a history-making election the previous year as the first Black mayor of Gary, Indiana, gave a rousing speech calling for the nomination of a Black man for either president or vice president of the United States.

"How do you tell white people that black people are finished being nice, happy, and simple folk?" he asked. "Black people all over this country are saying, 'Ready or not, here we come!'"

But Wine had a different message for the convention's five thousand attendees as he marched into the church with thirty Invaders. A *Commercial Appeal* article about the event written by Calvin Taylor—a young Black reporter who also happened to be an Invader—described Wine as the Invaders' spokesman and detailed his grievances against the SCLC.

The civil rights group hadn't lived up to King's promise to give the Invaders money and "staff support," Wine said. He also claimed the SCLC held the Invaders responsible for a chain of events leading to King's murder—presumably the disorder during King's March 28 demonstration. Charging that Rev. Andrew Young "us[ed] racial epithets in accusing Memphis Negroes of actions that led to the death of Dr. King," Wine demanded that the SCLC "clear their names."

Young struck a conciliatory note, admitting that he'd lost his temper and praising the Invaders for "do[ing] quite a bit to make the Poor People's Campaign a success."

He said the militant group's anger likely stemmed from his and the SCLC's neglect of them. "I think that this is what happens—as soon as we began to neglect them, they began to resent us. The Invaders have been charged not with specific things but rather with being young and more so with being black."

As for King's alleged promises, Rev. Abernathy pledged that the SCLC would live up to every promise King made to the Invaders. "If we go up together, we're certainly going to go down together."

Wine was back in the paper a few days later calling for partners to establish a "Black United Front" of organizations, militant and nonmilitant, to serve as the Black community's spokespeople. The term would have been fresh in the minds of keen observers, as an organization headed by Black organizer and activist Stokely Carmichael called "The Black United Front" had recently issued a statement about the killing of a D.C. police officer, declaring, "[T]he alleged slaying of a honky cop is a justifiable homicide, in the same sense that police are allowed to kill black people and call it justifiable homicide."

In any event, Wine would have known that the prospect of a Black united front—militants and traditional civil rights organizations working in concert—would get everyone's attention.

"And just to let you know that we ain't fooling, SCLC has given us $500 to help us get our program started and has promised us other financial and administrative assistance." *The Commercial Appeal* article described how he brandished the SCLC's $500 check.

The program he was referring to bore the same name and objectives as the Community Unification Program the Invaders had envisioned months before—which evolved into the Neighborhood Organizing Project.

Roy Turks was like a second lieutenant to Wine. Clean-cut and reserved in his jeans and denim jacket, he walked around carrying an attaché case filled with papers like a young and hip businessman, taking notes.

Ogundele Uwefemi was born somewhere down in Mississippi as Melvin Smith. At some point he went to Chicago, then came to Memphis wearing African garb and bearing colorful tales from his Southside Chicago upbringing. He liked to boast that everyone in his family took their names from Yoruba deities.

But Wine was the clear standout, cutting a prophet-like figure as he preached on the street to anyone who'd listen. Mac listened too, but to him it sounded like a lot of catchphrases and platitudes sprinkled with more than a few puzzling statements.

For example, Wine's claim that he didn't mind having Mayor Loeb in office, as he told Memphis State's Black Student Association in an October 1968 speech:

> We want people like Loeb to stay in office as long as he can. We want Wallace as president. In fact, the Black militants are going to vote for him because these kind of people are not going to do anything but cause the Black people to revolt. They are going to bring us together rather than divide us.

But there was more to Wine than drawing crowds and tossing verbal grenades. He showed up for the folks most people in power paid no mind to, making their causes impossible to ignore, at least for a moment. In late August, he was at a city council meeting condemning its delayed decision on a public housing project, saying he "came to speak for the fuse on the powder keg." He'd become a fixture at Clayborn Temple by that time, lending his voice to the cause of aggrieved city hospital workers embroiled in Memphis's biggest labor dispute since the sanitation strike. And in October, when the police department opened a community service office in South Memphis, Wine and the Invaders were among the first visitors, wearing what *The Commercial Appeal* described as "African costumes." They brought with them a man they said police had beaten and Maced for two hours.

But they were raising their concerns in the wrong place, said Detective Ed Redditt, a Black officer the department placed in charge of the community service office—the same Detective Redditt Mac had encountered months earlier in Assistant Chief Lux's conclave about spying on Clayborn Temple mass meetings. Redditt told them the community service office was for filing criminal complaints, asking questions, getting to know the officers. To lodge a complaint about police brutality, they'd need to visit the department's internal security bureau downtown.

By fall 1968, Mac had met many of the key players in the Memphis State-based groups he'd been charged with observing, the Black Student Association and Students for a Democratic Society. It hadn't been difficult, as Black students for the most part shared a sense of solidarity, and the hippies had a carefree manner that made them easy to get to know. As was his practice, he freely gave rides in his car, which now bore a new bumper sticker: DAMN THE ARMY, JOIN THE INVADERS.

He knew where to find his targets. While the Black students were more diffuse, many of the hippies hung out at the head shops near campus on Highland Avenue, as well as in the student center cafeteria at what people called the radical table. A few stood out. One, a hothead who worked for the IRS, didn't seem to fit with the rest of the group. With his paunch and thinning hair, he looked like he should've been a middle manager somewhere, not hanging around college kids.

And he acted suspicious, too. Once, he tried to persuade Mac to help him steal a hardwood mantelpiece from a grand old home slated for demolition. The place was in the path of a planned freeway that would soon cut through Overton Park.

"That stuff's just sitting there for the taking," he said, staring at Mac intently. "If we don't take it, somebody else will."

"Naw." Mac turned to walk away.

"It's just sitting there. We could get a lot of money for it."

Mac refused, and that was the end of it.

He found the episode unsettling. They weren't close friends by any stretch, plus the guy didn't strike Mac as the type to be involved in burglary. It smelled like a setup, but for what purpose?

And there was another guy, young and impeccably groomed with the kind of fancy sports car a typical student couldn't afford. Like the IRS man, things didn't quite add up with him. Mac wondered if they both might be working in roles similar to his. As the proverb goes, "A fisherman knows a fisherman from afar."

Mac befriended a white man named Ted Carter who, while not enrolled as a student, had a pad off campus where SDS-ers gathered. It was the flower child version of the crib, with a long dining table fashioned from cinderblocks and plywood and a few pieces of secondhand furniture. Like the Invaders, the SDS was a ragtag group that eschewed official meetings in favor of loosely arranged gatherings too casual even for word-of-mouth invitations. People just showed up, some with food or drink in hand, as folk music streamed from a small record player. If chairs ran out, people sat on the floor.

The BSA, on the other hand, advocated for specific measures aimed at Black students' inclusion in campus life, like the hiring of Black professors and the recruitment of Black football players. Leading their efforts was the studious and sincere David Acey, who brooked no radical talk from any quarter, whether the Invaders or SDS.

Though the Black Organizing Project counted the BSA as a subsidiary, Mac didn't see much connection between the two groups. There didn't seem to be much of an affinity, either. When Sweet Willie Wine gave a speech before a BSA forum in October—the same speech where he touted his support for Mayor Loeb and George Wallace—his words drew more consternation than anything else.

During the question-and-answer session that followed, BSA members peppered him with skeptical questions about his call for Black revolution. Where would he get guns? ("Russia," he answered.) Did he expect the Russians, who were white, to give him guns to kill other white people? ("All I have to do is show them my record as a Communist," he said.) What kind of government would he have? (He had no answer for that.) What would he do with all the whites after the revolution? ("The Germans killed 20,000 Jews in World War II," he claimed, citing a false figure that was obviously far below the actual count. "And that's what I intend to do.") The audience tore into him, and he was visibly furious.

Finally, one of the two Invaders accompanying him, Maurice Lewis, spoke up. "Y'all MSU students are crazy! We got a better reception from the SDS at Southwestern!"

Then Wine and his crew walked out.

Though the SDS was a racially mixed group, fraternizing with them as an Invader was something of a delicate operation. The SDS was integrated, but society wasn't. Mac hadn't given the issue much thought until an Invader he barely knew, Johnny Frierson, confronted him in the University Center one afternoon in early November.

"I see you hanging with all these crackers, but then you want to be an Invader when you get off campus."

Mac was sitting with SDS-er Ted Carter and his Black girlfriend, Muriel, who fell quiet as Frierson's words hung in the air.

"And now you got our Black sister running with 'em, too? So which is it—are you Black or are you white?"

Mac spat out a testy response, and Johnny replied in kind. Back and forth they went.

“Look, I beat up crackers every day,” Johnny said. “I put a white boy from this campus in the *hospital*.”

Mac stood. “Let’s go somewhere where we can talk about this.”

Frierson followed him into the stairwell, down a floor, and into a utility closet. Mac reached up and pulled the chain to turn on the ceiling light. Then he grabbed Johnny and shoved him against a wall. He pulled his .25 from his waistband and stuck it in Johnny’s face.

“Who I associate with is none of your business.” Mac kept his voice low, enunciating each word. “Say one more word about it, and I’ll blow your goddamn head off.”

“Okay, man! Okay! We cool!” Johnny sputtered, his eyes wide with terror.

Mac released him, and he took off down the hallway. Then Mac went upstairs and returned to the table like nothing happened.

Over the course of the fall, the BSA and SDS made gestures toward joining forces, though BSA president David Acey remained wary of anything that looked like radicalism. By the end of October, the BSA was talking about forming a committee to work with the SDS, but Mac didn’t see much happening on that front. For one thing, Black students tended to be suspicious of white people claiming to be allies, as demonstrated in an interaction Mac had later in the school year.

“What’s that SDS thing?” a Black student Mac knew only as Taylor asked one day in the cafeteria.

Mac and Taylor were sitting at a cafeteria table with several other Black students, including a guy who’d just been hanging out with Mac and the white SDS-ers at the radical table.

Taylor remarked that he didn’t see how the Black and white students at Memphis State had anything in common. How could they work toward a common cause? When the going got rough, he said, the white folks would bug out and leave the Black folks holding the bag.

There wasn’t much anyone could say in response.

For its part, the SDS formed a committee to explore cooperating with the BSA and other campus groups. They needed political alliances for a specific goal: to participate in student government, which they couldn't do currently because they lacked a charter. The word was that a charter could be granted only by the Student Government Association, and the dean of students had influenced the association to not grant them one. The SDS needed to win friends and influence people if they were going to have any say in how things were run on campus. They selected Mac to conduct outreach to the BSA.

But working with BSA, the Invaders, and other Black organizations wasn't always a given for the SDS. At a meeting in mid-November, a Southwestern University sociology professor said during a talk that the SDS should focus first on organizing the white community before combining efforts with Black groups. Noting people in the ghettos—both Black and white—were more interested in filling their bellies than engaging in political discussions, he said the SDS's work must begin with making poor and working-class *white* folks politically conscious and united in revolutionary aims.

As for the Invaders, "they know what they're doing," the professor said.

Meanwhile, the Invaders also had a favor to ask of the SDS: food and blankets for a planned sit-in in the administrative offices of historically Black LeMoyne College on the evening of Monday, November 25. With the Invaders' support, LeMoyne students were protesting a lack of action on a list of seven demands they'd presented to the administration, including a reduction in tuition, lower cafeteria food prices, and more Black history classes. Wine had spoken with Ted Carter about it, passing along the request for supplies.

This wouldn't be the LeMoyne students' first protest about this, as they'd held a brief sit-in the previous week. The president of the college, Dr. Hollis Price, blamed much of the trouble on outsiders.

"Non-students have been telling the students that with campus unrest elsewhere in the country they should be doing something," he told *The Commercial Appeal*. The school had a procedure "for orderly change" that the students should have followed rather than making demands the way they did, he said.

The afternoon of the sit-in, the SDS called a special meeting to discuss the matter. Sixteen people showed up.

"The SDS members shouldn't get too involved," Carter quoted Wine as telling him. "Just follow as the spirit leads you."

Around five in the evening, the SDS-ers headed over to LeMoyne in three cars, one driven by Mac.

Though the protestors were insistent—they proclaimed they weren't leaving until their demands were met—their numbers looked paltry to Wine. So an Invader named Don drove him and a couple of other guys around the neighborhood to scour the streets for recruits to the cause.

By a quarter to seven, twenty or so people were sitting on the floor in a circle inside the administration building, laughing and talking. There was a single point of entry and exit, a barred basement door where someone stood guard. Several faculty members tried to enter but were turned away.

Finally, Dr. Price showed up. He'd been on his way to a ceremony at Memphis State, where he was to be celebrated as Educator of the Year. He stood outside the administration building trying to talk to the protesters, but to no avail. Finally he left, only to return a couple of hours later to scold them and command them to leave. The faculty had met earlier that day and addressed all but one of their complaints, he said. His words got him nowhere.

At 10:30, Mac took three SDS-ers to various places to gather supplies—one to the Fred Montesi grocery store and two back to Memphis State. Then he returned to LeMoyne and took several others on a quick trip to get cigarettes, cigarette papers, and loose tobacco. Someone brought in a radio, and there was dancing and card playing. People came and went. By one in the morning, most of them had fallen asleep.

The protesters were still holding the administration building by sunrise and had expanded their occupation to two academic buildings. But that morning, they reached an accord with the administration: The aggrieved students would take part in committees alongside faculty and administrators to address their list of complaints, which had ballooned from seven to nineteen items. None of the protesters would face prosecution or disciplinary action.

"The quality of the education we receive is our primary concern," one of the students, who declined to be identified, told *The Commercial Appeal.*

By noon, protesters had retreated from the buildings, but the trouble on campus wasn't over. Around 3:25 p.m., a gunshot rang out. Two nearby workers called police, saying they saw "three young Negro men running from campus, followed by several other young Negroes armed with rifles and shotguns." According to police, the three men running were LeMoyne students who'd gotten into an argument with a group of Invaders after the students told the Invaders their involvement in the protest wasn't needed.

The Commercial Appeal noted that "a couple of Memphis State students" and Wine were among the outsiders involved in the demonstration. An unnamed student took issue with characterizing the Invaders as outsiders, noting, "This is a community college. They had as much right here as the newsmen."

In late fall 1968, the big issue animating the SDS was the Delano grape strike out of California. Rev. Dick Moon, a Presbyterian chaplain at MSU and close ally of the SDS, hosted a presentation by a representative from the United Farm Workers Organizing Committee, a young brown-skinned man from California named Venustiano Olguin Jr.

Olguin told the group of fifteen or so audience members, which included students, a nun, and a pipe-smoking Southwestern professor, that he'd organized a group at UCLA called the Brown Berets that was like a Mexican American version of the Black Panthers. He said he'd met with Memphis's Rev. Ezekiel Bell, a founding member of COME who'd just been elected president of the local chapter of the NAACP, and Bell had promised the NAACP's support for the grape strike. Olguin said this surprised him, as he'd found that most NAACP chapters around the country were made up of "Uncle Toms." If that remark offended any of the Black audience members, they didn't let it show.

He followed his remarks with a screening of a documentary about the grape strike, *Decision at Delano*, featuring United Automobile Workers of America leader Walter Reuther and the late Senator Bobby Kennedy. When the film concluded, he talked about the exploitative conditions underlying the grape strike, describing how growers kept wages low and hired undocumented workers, only to turn around and report those workers at the end of the season to avoid paying their wages. He ran down a list of actions people could take to support the strike: send letters to the stores that sold California grapes, set up picket lines in front of the stores, or damage the grapes by placing them under heavy items inside shopping carts and abandoning them at the checkout. Then he read off a list of the city's leading California grape buyers, which included all the big grocery stores—Pic-Pac, Kroger, Big Star, Fred Montesi.

The farm workers' grievances about low wages and lack of union recognition struck a familiar chord in the city, still anguished by the sanitation strike and now contending with a labor dispute between the city government and hospital workers. Their story hit Mac especially hard. He identified with these people scratching their living out of the soil yet remaining dirt poor, no matter how hard they worked. He'd lived it.

He made sure not to buy grapes, not that he would've before, but now he had an affirmative reason not to. He also demonstrated with the dozen or so people the SDS was able to amass. But he did his job all the while—watching, listening, reporting in.

When Mac agreed to infiltrate the Invaders, he probably hadn't envisioned himself in the ironic predicament he now faced: sitting in a South Memphis community meeting pretending to be an Invader pretending to be an authority figure. It was a community-building exercise organized by the Invaders, and all eyes were on him as he role-played a landlord.

From time to time, the Invaders hosted these gatherings in their new storefront office at 271 Vance Avenue, where they moved in December 1968 from their temporary digs at Clayborn Temple. Rev. Bell helped them scout out the new place, which was down the street and around the corner from

Clayborn Temple. The rent was $125 a month, and Rev. Bell agreed to cover it for six months.

The Invaders' needs were few, and they were able to provide for most of them from items they brought with them from Clayborn Temple: a file cabinet, three wooden chairs, and two tables. To that, they added a telephone, bookshelves, desks, a Xerox copier, and a Coca Cola machine.

Then they brought in an electric typewriter and mimeograph machine, giving them their very own printing press. They tapped out stencils on a typewriter, then rolled them through the mimeo machine, cranking out messages about Black power and community events as the space filled with the mimeo ink's sweet, phenolic odor.

The place had two rooms, one behind the other. Most of the office equipment was in the front room, while the bookshelves and mimeograph machine were in the back. The guys decorated the walls with portraits of Malcolm X, King, and Eldridge Cleaver, plus a couple of Black Power illustrations by one of their more artistic members. On one of the walls, someone scrawled in black marker, KILL THE PIGS. On the opposite wall, large black letters spelled out:

> HEY WHITEY, BLACK POWER IS GOING TO GET YOUR MOTHER
> HEY WHITEY, THE WORLD WILL BE SWELL IF YOU WILL LET US PULL YOUR TAIL DOWN INTO HELL

The community interest nights seemed to be Coby Smith's brainchild. He planned educational presentations, with someone giving a lecture or maybe playing a recording of a Malcolm X speech. Then there were role-playing sessions he called psychodramas, with someone pretending to be an authority figure—like an employer, teacher, or landlord—while someone else played the subordinate. They'd pretend to have a conflict, sometimes based on a real story from the community, then go back and forth about how they felt about things.

Coby didn't hang out with the guys much, but when he did, he talked business—issues in the community, unifying Black people, consciousness-raising, that sort of thing. He was sober-minded, one of the first two Black students at Southwestern, an elite liberal arts college. The community interest nights were important to him, and he asked the guys to invite people from the neighborhood. But more than once, they had to cancel because nobody from the community showed up. It infuriated him.

"You people are not doing your jobs," he'd say to the few Invaders standing around. "I know for a *fact* that each one of y'all can bring somebody down here with you. There ought to be a hundred people in here. I want you to get out on the streets tomorrow and recruit like you should!"

But most of the guys weren't as serious as he was.

Wine had a seriousness about himself, too, but where Coby waxed intellectual and didactic, Wine preached and inflamed, a seer and muse. Wine had star power, and even the stars seemed to recognize it. In mid-December, his connections at Stax records put famed singers and producers Isaac Hayes and David Porter together in the studio to listen to a song he wrote. A week later—on Christmas Eve—when Wine was locked up for something or other, Porter and blues star Albert King showed up at State Surety Underwriters and put up his bond.

In early April 1969 came the day Mac both dreaded and knew was inevitable. His phone rang. It was Arkin.

"Stay away from that Invaders meeting today," he said.

"Why?"

"We've got to get more information, but just stay away from there for now."

Mac knew what that almost certainly meant: The Invaders had found him out.

It had been a long time coming. Several weeks earlier, he'd had a close shave while out at a downtown nightclub with one of the Invaders, Melvin, when a guy confronted him.

"I know you," the guy said. "You're a police officer. You came in here last year."

Mac's mind raced to remember when he would've been there as an overt police officer. It would've had to have been just before the sanitation strike, but he couldn't remember.

Mac made sure he kept cool, like a guy who had nothing to worry about. "I don't know what you talking 'bout, brother. I ain't no police officer."

Then Melvin spoke up for him. "He ain't no police officer. He's been with us for over a year."

And there had been other run-ins, like the chicken joint incident and the strange phone call in the middle of the night—"We know what you're doing"—right after he went undercover. What was happening now could have been fallout from either of those incidents, or from something else entirely. After all, he'd been identified in the newspaper three times.

He knew it was just a matter of time before his identity was exposed. The entire enterprise of going undercover had been improvised. It *couldn't* have been planned in advance because of how it had evolved, beginning with him and Officer Richmond sitting in on a meeting at Clayborn Temple.

In fact, it was a minor miracle he'd gotten by so long without being discovered. He'd gone through sixteen weeks in the police academy, weeks of foot patrol in a popular shopping center during the busiest time of the year, and car patrols in two of Memphis's most populous Black neighborhoods. He was driving around in the same blue Fastback he had when he was a uniformed officer, and one of the Invaders was a brother-in-law's cousin.

The Invaders wouldn't have had to do much digging to learn the truth about him. He'd done what little he could to erase the evidence of his past, moving into a boardinghouse from his old apartment, where everyone on the street had seen him coming and going in uniform. But it wouldn't have taken much investigation to connect the dots. Of course, the group's casual attitude about vetting members was just more evidence that they weren't dangerous revolutionaries.

A few hours later, Arkin called back with more details. A woman named Tarlease Mathews had contacted several of the Invaders, saying she had evidence to prove Mac was a police officer. She arranged a meeting and passed them city payroll records showing he was a patrolman.

The department thought they'd taken care of that issue. Right after

Mac went undercover, the Intelligence Bureau had switched him from the regular police payroll to a different one that was supposed to be secure. He began getting his paychecks by direct deposit. Someone would've needed insider knowledge to understand that his salary was coming from the police budget. Just such an insider gave that information to Tarlease, who turned it over to the Invaders.

"Can you leave town for a little while?" Arkin asked.

"Yeah, I have folks up in Cleveland. But my wife teaches school."

"We can talk to them and get her some time off."

As soon as Mac got off the phone, he told Linda what was going on, then called his sister Pan and brother WT in Cleveland. He explained to them that his cover had been blown, and he needed somewhere to go until the police got a handle on things. Life as he knew it had been dangling by a delicate thread, and it was about to break.

After throwing a few days' clothes and toiletries into suitcases, Mac and Linda left for Cleveland that evening, taking I-40 east through Nashville, still a new highway only a couple of years old. They picked up I-65 through Kentucky, then I-71 into Ohio. The drive took about twelve hours, with a few brief stops.

They tried to fill the tense air with words. During the first part of the drive, they commiserated about how crazy everything was. It wasn't just their flight from Memphis that felt off kilter, but current events, too. James Earl Ray's murder trial had just gotten underway when the trial judge was found dead in his chambers. Though it looked like natural causes, it was still disturbing.

They were venting, but they were also trying to support each other, build each other up. About halfway through the drive, Linda was telling Mac her deep secrets, things that hurt to keep to herself. Mac listened quietly. This was one of the first times they'd sat together for a prolonged period and just talked. When their romance began, they were so caught up in mutual infatuation that they hadn't bothered getting to know each other.

He'd fallen in love with the *idea* of her, a beautiful, professional woman who'd chosen him. But between his various shifts at work and her job at the school, there wasn't much time for a deeper connection. One day, they were having dinner with Miss Elizabeth and going back to his place, and the next thing he knew, she was pregnant.

It seemed like the ideal Black middle class love story, the teacher and the police officer. But the reality was far different than either of them could have imagined, with Mac going undercover and talk of the baby ending without anyone acknowledging it ended. They had no friends in common, no social moorings.

Until recently, they didn't even have their own living space, but the previous fall, they moved out of the house they'd shared with Miss Elizabeth to an apartment on South Parkway East, not far from Memphis State. Living with Linda's mother had proven too much for the couple, or at least for Mac. Though she had a mild and quiet disposition, he'd never felt quite comfortable, like it was his house. He and Linda needed some space, some breathing room. The apartment represented a chance at a new beginning.

Now they were on a long drive to Cleveland, knowing little about what the other's life had been like for the last year, let alone before they met. Just as they'd run off to get married, they were running off again.

They needed each other now. Mac wasn't afraid for his life, but he was sure that at a minimum, there'd be a fight if they saw him on the street. For him, the scary part was the uncertainty, the sense of not knowing the next move. He had to lie low for a while.

For the first few days, they stayed with Mac's sister Pan and her husband in Wickliffe, a suburb in Cleveland's outskirts. It was a grand home with plenty of room for her ten children, though the oldest four were now living on their own. Each day, Mac and Linda visited WT in Shaker Heights, another fancy suburb. He ran a successful Exxon station, and Mac would spend the day with him there, just talking. Several evenings, Mac and Linda got dressed up and went out to elegant nightclubs with WT and his wife. Mac hadn't packed any dress clothes, so he had to borrow one of WT's suits, a single-breasted steel blue ensemble that he paired with a cream turtleneck. Though the sleeves and pant legs were about half an inch too short, he still managed to look debonair. Someone snapped a smiling photo of the brothers in WT's living room one night, Mac in the suit and turtleneck and WT sporting a double-breasted pinstripe suit and skinny black tie, the perfect sliver of white shirt cuff peeking from his sleeve.

Pan and WT joked with Mac that he'd finally been "run out of Memphis," but they never talked about his work or what it had entailed. No one went near the topic of Mac's presence at the scene of King's assassination, though the photo of him holding a towel to King's face had been in the press. They had to have seen it.

Every day, Mac checked in with the Intelligence Bureau, but there was no news, no information suggesting he was in danger. They were waiting to see what developed. Finally, after about a week, they said it was safe for him to return. Just like that, he'd be Officer McCollough again.

It felt like starting over, and in some ways it was. In April 1969, Mac began his education on how the Intelligence Bureau worked from the inside, a different enterprise from calling in reports as an undercover agent. He wouldn't be off on his own anymore. Now he'd have new colleagues, people he'd be working with every day. He was a rookie again, albeit an experienced one.

Housed in police headquarters on Adams Street, the bureau's main duties were to collect intelligence on and monitor "radical activities" in the city. What was considered radical? There was no official definition, but it could be anything that tended to upset the social order or cause disruptions. With their revolutionary talk, the Invaders fell in that category, as did anyone who entered their orbit. The bureau's padlocked file cabinets contained extensive files on the group, and when a new face showed up in their midst, they created a file on that person, too. They recorded the identities of anyone who showed up at an Invaders meeting or even just socialized with them. The preachers involved in Community on the Move for Equality, aka COME? The bureau documented their particulars down to where they lived, what cars they drove, and who their associates were. The bureau may not have acted on the information, but they kept it.

They didn't just monitor people and groups; they also kept files on events, particularly protests. That included the historic sanitation strike of the previous year, as well as the ongoing hospital strike. The bureau was collecting information about organizers' intentions, what gatherings were planned, expected crowd sizes, and any troublemakers who might promote disorder.

Some of their intelligence came from people calling in with tips. When someone called the police department switchboard with information that didn't rise to the level of an immediate criminal investigation or arrest, the operator usually sent it there. Often these were "I have information about radicalism" and "I want to talk about these militants" calls, though some reported upcoming protests, counterprotests, and threats. Most of the information turned out to be little more than rumors, tips that never panned out.

The officers filtered through the information, culling out valuable nuggets and tossing the rest. Anything associated with radicalism, they kept. If it had to do with an upcoming protest or other event, they held on to the information until the activity concluded, then got rid of it. They took reports and ran investigations, but they didn't make arrests.

Mac learned there was another guy embedded with the Invaders as he'd been. The bureau had given him the designation Agent 501. Mac, as it turned out, had been Agent 500.

Nearly every day, Mac met with FBI Special Agents Lawrence and Lowe, Lieutenant Arkin, and Detective Davis for lunch. Their usual place was an inexpensive steak restaurant, where they'd mix work talk with casual conversation.

Lawrence and Lowe maintained a keen interest in the Invaders. In fact, that was about all that interested them. They called the bureau often, asking everyone from the desk officers to the inspector for the latest Invaders updates: Who were the newest members? What were their plans? Was anyone coming to town to meet with them? After Agent 501 called in his reports, someone would call Lawrence and Lowe to relate their contents.

But the bureau didn't focus exclusively on Black militants. They also collected information on the Ku Klux Klan, though the group never got the continuous scrutiny and monitoring the Invaders did—despite being a dangerous organization with the body count to prove it. The bureau monitored the Klan through an informant rather than an embedded police mole. Mac never heard Lawrence or Lowe mention it.

These incongruities weren't necessarily the kind of thing you'd notice just starting out working there. Seeing the whole picture would take time and perspective, as opposed to the granular view of things that came with the day-to-day job. A veneer of normality, even equality, overlaid their activities. Anyone could call in with tips about anything pertaining to public safety, and plenty did. An office full of people supported the bureau's activities, and they all seemed to take for granted that they were advancing legitimate goals.

Why did they consider a simple demonstration to be potentially dangerous? Because they weren't viewing things through a First Amendment lens, but one of containment, as if they were preventing fires from spreading. The question wasn't whether something was a current threat, but whether it could grow into one.

Though Mac would later understand how flawed and absurd their work was, he nonetheless played the role he was given. "Just following orders," while never an acceptable excuse, was a big part of the job. The same had been true in the army. Policy drove the orders, and both policy and orders came from the highest ranks. His only discretion lay in how he executed the duties handed down to him. He took some comfort in believing he'd done so with as much honor as he could.

———

On Mac's first day in the office, he didn't wear a uniform as he had before he went undercover. The Intelligence Bureau dress code was civilian clothes—jackets and ties for the men, and smart dresses or outfits with skirts for women. Officers carried their badges in a holder inside a pocket.

The cast of characters had changed since Mac began working for them undercover during the sanitation strike. Inspector Tines was gone, and

Inspector John Smith was now in charge. Arkin and Davis were still there, and there was a Lieutenant Holcomb, as well as patrolman Al Embry, a linebacker-sized white guy who commuted in from Independence, Mississippi.

There were women officers there, too. Women hadn't been allowed to attend the police academy until recently, though they'd been permitted to become meter maids. But those were noncommissioned officer jobs with the power to do little more than write parking tickets. Eventually, some were commissioned as officers, including the stylish Detective Claudine Penn, hired as the department's first Black meter maid in 1963 and commissioned in 1968.

After meeting with Inspector Smith in his office and walking around the bullpen to say hello to his new coworkers, Mac went to see Davis, who took him up to visit Chief of Police Henry Lux—he'd moved up from his previous post as assistant chief. Lux welcomed him back, and it felt good.

Then Mac got his first assignment from Inspector Smith: Go through the files and pull those of people he saw committing crimes. He was to prepare synopses of those crimes—the who, what, when, where, and why. The bureau would take them to the city attorney, Joseph Canale, and seek indictments. Mac wasn't yet acquainted with Canale, who'd been an FBI special agent before his city attorney appointment.

Mac set about reviewing the files, reading over the reporting and seeking out criminal acts. They weren't hard to find, much less remember: numerous instances of buying and using drugs, plus the arsons. After a couple of weeks, when he was nearly ready to take his synopses to Canale's office, he heard from them first: They'd discussed the matter internally and decided it wasn't in the city's interest to bring charges.

Though Mac had put a lot of effort into the assignment, the decision made sense to him. Between the sanitation strike, the disastrous march, and the assassination, Memphis had already been through hell. Why reopen all those old wounds that were just beginning to heal for the sake of infractions that everyone had moved on from?

Now Mac could turn his attention to the Intelligence Bureau's routine work. But first, he needed to handle some personal business.

He walked over to Al Embry's desk—Big Al, as they called him. At a broad-shouldered six feet six or so, he stood a good seven inches taller than Mac. But not only was he friendly and mild-mannered, he could type as quickly and accurately as any secretary. While Mac had been writing out his reports longhand on yellow pads and giving them to the secretary to type, Al would get on an electric typewriter and bang out his own reports, his shirt sleeves rolled up and meaty hands flying across the keys.

"Al, come take a ride with me," Mac said.

With Mac driving, they went down to the Invaders' Vance Street storefront. A couple of guys Mac didn't know well were sitting up front when they walked in. Mac got right to the point.

"I know you guys don't plan to do anything towards me that's out of order, but if you put out pamphlets about me, you don't know what the average person on the street might do."

He was talking about the mimeographed sheets the Invaders printed and spread all over town to get their views in front of the public. He'd seen enough of their activities to know it was one of their possible next moves—putting out sheets calling him a traitor, a pig, an Uncle Tom. He had to do what he could to stop that from happening.

Al stood next to him, silent.

"So I don't expect and don't want to see any pamphlets like that," he continued.

"Naw mane, we cool," they said. They sounded sincere, if unperturbed.

"If you don't print those sheets, things will be fine, and I won't be back. But if you do, life could get bad for you. I'll be back here, and you'll pay for it."

What was he planning to do if they broke their word? He didn't have a plan, but he knew he'd find a way to back up what he said. He hoped it wouldn't come to that.

Judging by their reaction, they didn't seem like they'd pose a problem. Could it be that they thought Mac was on their side because none of them ever faced charges for the crimes he saw them commit? Maybe he'd benefitted from Canale's decision not to pursue them. In any case, it was in everyone's interest to leave the past in the past.

It didn't take Mac long to get the hang of his new role. When a call came into the bureau, any officer could answer on their desk phone, though callers sometimes had a specific officer they wanted to talk to. Whichever officer took the call was responsible for reporting what the caller said and following up as necessary. Say someone called on Monday with a report that the Klan was planning a rally on Beale Street Friday night. The officer who took that report would need to check it out, see if there were any other corroborating reports, keep Inspector Smith apprised of what was happening, and work with him to decide what to do next. The job was mostly fielding calls, drafting reports, and occasionally meeting with Lawrence and Lowe to discuss them—mostly when they pertained to the Invaders.

Being out from undercover and back to his real identity felt like trading an ill-fitting suit for a T-shirt and favorite pair of jeans. For the first time in over a year, he felt at ease, without the low buzz of danger droning in his ear. He could begin to repair the family ties he'd strained to the breaking point.

Before he'd gone undercover, he visited his sister Pirl and her husband Sonny most days, raiding their refrigerator and talking casually in the way that imperceptibly bonds relationships. But he couldn't do that once he infiltrated the Invaders, when the first order of business became protecting his cover. He didn't stop visiting altogether, but he cut it back to two or three times a month at the most. He'd try to make small talk with them like before, but it wasn't the same. How could it be? Still, they went through the motions. He'd ask what they had to eat, and they'd ask when the last time was he'd been down to see Walter and Miss Ethel. He couldn't tell them what he was doing, why he needed to keep his visits sparse. They seemed to sense not to ask.

His changed behavior must've seemed abrupt to them, much like his changing appearance. He never said, "I'm out of uniform now, working in intelligence to gather information on Black militants." But they knew he was still a police officer, so they must have intuited something was going on with his work. Plus, he'd mentioned early on that he was covering the sanitation strike. Leaving the details unsaid seemed like the safest way forward for everyone.

He did tell Walter he was working undercover, if only so his father wouldn't take one look at him and think he was destitute. He'd later hear that Walter was going around saying, "If you see Marrell out there in the streets, don't say nothing to him because he's deep into the underworld."

Walter had been righter than he knew. Mac *was* drifting in a sort of underworld, having left behind his family and dropped his friends. He'd made himself into a blank slate, and on it, he wrote another identity with a new appearance, new mannerisms, new movement patterns.

After it was all over and some time had passed, his younger brother Floyd would tell him how worried he'd been about Mac during those days because of how he withdrew from everyone. He said he couldn't tell where Mac was headed with his new persona. But Mac explained that it was all by necessity. He couldn't extend his world to his family without potentially exposing them to the Invaders. Staying away was the only realistic way to keep the two spheres apart. The only thing he could do now was try to pick up with people where he'd left off.

But some of the damage seemed beyond his ability to repair, like his unraveling marriage. Though he was out from undercover, he and Linda remained nearly strangers, the closeness they'd established during their brief trip to Cleveland having all but evaporated. Though they now had their own place, whenever Linda wasn't at work, she was with Miss Elizabeth at the house on Clementine. Step by inexorable step, they lapsed into their old routines of leading separate lives.

———

In the summer of 1969, Mac got an unexpected visit at home from a family friend from Mississippi bearing terrible news: Walter, his father, was dead.

Mac drove down to see Miss Ethel, who was beside herself with grief. From talking to her and other family members and friends, Mac pieced together what happened. Walter had been carrying on drinking and running to juke joints on the weekends, and one Sunday night, a woman he was out with cut him on the wrist. He went back out to his truck and bled to death.

Mac went down to the Tunica County sheriff's department and asked to see the police report. Because he was a police officer, they showed him the file, which wasn't a formal report but a clean sheet of paper half-filled with handwritten notes. It listed the woman's name, noting that she claimed Walter snatched her purse. She told police she'd slashed him to get it back.

That didn't sound like Walter at all. He could imagine the scene, two old folks who'd been drinking half the night getting into an argument. The woman pulls a knife, Walter holds up his hands, and the woman slashes, cutting him. Too drunk to get medical help, he stumbles to his truck and dies there.

It all hurt bad: that Walter was dead, that it happened the way it did, and that it was handled so casually by the sheriff's department.

The woman spent a night in jail but was never prosecuted. The injustice of that seared Mac. She'd gotten away with his father's murder. And though he was a police officer, there was nothing he could do about it.

In October, Agent 501 tipped off the Intelligence Bureau about a large demonstration that hospital strikers were planning to hold downtown. The Invaders had been showing up at strategy meetings and had pledged to provide unarmed security for them.

The police department sent riot control officers to the scene, and the Intelligence Bureau dispatched Mac and Detective Penn to observe. They were to identify who was involved and what was happening, and take photographs, too. The bureau issued them the standard kit of riot gear: a helmet, shield, and gas mask.

Mac enjoyed working with Penn, who exuded a warmth and wisdom that reminded him of family. She didn't affect toughness and swagger, as some officers tended to do. Her confidence was quiet.

They arrived at the protest in an unmarked car, which Mac drove. Uniformed officers were already there in force, fully outfitted in riot gear.

Mac turned to Penn.

"Claudine, you don't have your helmet on."

"No, I don't have it on, and I'm not going to put in on. And I wish you'd take yours off."

"What?"

"I said I wish you'd take yours off."

"Why?"

"You know what? We've got a job to do here, to check on things and do what intelligence folks do. But these white officers, when this is over, they're going to go back to their homes outside of town. You and I have to live with these folks. We don't want to be seen as occupiers with our helmets on. So I think you ought to just take it off."

Her words fell on him like weights. He knew she was right. If they got tear-gassed, would he stand there breathing through a gas mask in a sea of Black people coughing and crying? He knew what it felt like to face an occupying force, as he had the previous March, when the National Guard patrolled the neighborhoods with their bayoneted rifles. Would he now take up the tools of oppression amid his own people? He wasn't at war with them—why dress for battle?

They stepped out of the car, leaving the riot gear behind.

15.

Invader

As my flight landed in Memphis International Airport's Terminal B in December 2016, a nebulous sense of dread consumed me. I tried to comfort myself with the thought that I had very good reasons to travel there. I'd get to visit Ma, whom I hadn't seen in a year, plus other close family members I hadn't seen for even longer. And I had a lunch date with Invaders cofounder Coby Smith.

As trivial as it seemed, one source of my dread was the airport shuttle I'd have to take to the car rental agency. I hated the long and lonesome ride to the forbidding stretch of road some two miles from the airport where the car rental agencies were inexplicably located.

The terminal looked just like I remembered from childhood, its brick walls and glossy stone floor a study in browns and grays. The hallway was nearly empty. As I passed a security officer on my way to the escalator, I smiled and said hello, searching his face to see if I recognized him, but I didn't. He smiled and returned my greeting. I smiled again on the escalator when I saw the WELCOME TO MEMPHIS sign. I was home. My nostalgia turned to elation when I discovered that the car rental agencies were now located at the airport. Progress.

Soon, I was on the expressway in a sensible SUV with a new-car smell. The scenery had changed little from when I last lived in Memphis over twenty years ago, with one striking difference: The expressway was brand new. Its wide, smooth roads dominated the cityscape, ribbons of asphalt cutting black swaths through a wilderness of faceless buildings and gray streets. These were grand thoroughfares leading out of Memphis to exurbs in Mississippi or once-rural Tennessee.

Memphis has been dreaming of this for as long as I can remember, I thought.

During my childhood, the part of town where we lived—North Memphis—seemed to be dying before our eyes. It was a creeping, lingering death, as families moved away, businesses shuttered, buildings went vacant, weeds consumed empty lots. The process had begun long before I arrived. I remember looking through old high school yearbooks on my grandparents' bookshelves and seeing black-and-white advertisements for all kinds of shops and offices and services. As far as I could tell, most of those businesses were no more. Only faint markings remained of the neighborhood's former vibrancy—signs for shops that no longer existed or patrician accents on dilapidated houses. The aspirational Memphian sought the suburbs, where homes and schools were newer and bigger, shopping was better, and there was more in the way of entertainment and recreation. There was a growing hollowness as the streets slowly emptied out, the city's center fleeing toward its edges and beyond.

I sped along the gleaming expressway to one of these edges: Cordova, Tennessee, where Ma and my stepdad had moved from a less far-flung suburb when I was in college. Sprawling along a stretch of I-40 to the east of the city, Cordova was the home of Wolfchase Mall, the region's largest shopping complex, and the array of chain stores and restaurants found in most American suburbs.

By the time I reached their dark cul-de-sac, it was after 1:00 a.m. I'd called Ma when my flight landed, and again when I was a few minutes away so she could open the garage, but I was surprised to see my stepdad standing outside waving me into the driveway. I appreciated the help, without which I would've likely driven past the house.

I wondered if I'd been stood up. For close to an hour, I'd been waiting in a booth toward the back of the bustling Outback Steakhouse on Union Avenue in midtown Memphis. I'd set up my side of the table like a desk, with my pen, spiral-bound notebook, laptop, and phone spread before me alongside two large, splashy menus. A folder stuffed with articles about the Invaders peeked through the top of my computer bag slouching next to me on the bench. But where was Coby Smith?

Smith had chosen the restaurant, which was near his house, and I'd made the drive in from Cordova. Sipping my unsweetened iced tea, I scrolled through social media on my phone, occasionally glancing up at the restaurant's front door.

I ordered a cup of chicken tortilla soup. It was salty and opaque, just what I wanted. Moments after it arrived, I looked up and saw a woman and man standing together at the front of the restaurant. Recognizing the gray-haired, goateed man as Smith, I smiled and waved.

The woman introduced herself as Constance, Smith's wife. She had a regal bearing, and her plain knit cap had the effect of a fine turban. After we shook hands, Smith asked how Dad was doing. I told him Dad was doing fine and enjoying his retirement in South Carolina.

"Why the hell hasn't he contacted me all these years?" he said with a laugh. "You can tell him I said it just like that!"

He described how he, along with Charles Cabbage and John Burl Smith—no relation—created the Black Organizing Project in Memphis's Riverside neighborhood in 1967. They wanted to spark a grassroots movement among the city's youth to demand social and economic justice for the Black community.

Now his afro was gone, replaced by a low haircut. He looked professorial in his sweater and glasses.

"Your dad would eat at my house every morning. He was the only one with a car, so he did most of the work. Organizing when people would go and where people would go and how they would go—that sort of thing. So that was very important to us."

I later mentioned this to Dad, who told me that wasn't how he remembered it—including the breakfasts.

Smith described finding out that Dad was a police officer. "The police invited me down to headquarters and introduced me to Marrell as an undercover agent."

I asked him how he felt at that moment.

"Well, you have to understand the sixties. Everything was Black and white. So the fact that they gave me a Black undercover officer was fantastic."

We both laughed.

"But he was one of our best people, so that hurt."

I asked him what it was about Dad that made him one of their best people.

"He was a professional, efficient person."

As it turned out, the Invaders were riddled with informants. There were as many suspected infiltrators as there were known ones. "I'd like to know which ones of them *were* undercover," Smith said. "Marrell may know."

He talked about the turbulent environment in which the Invaders operated. "This was a very tough time. Riots were going on in almost every city. Are you familiar with the counterintelligence program?"

The server suddenly materialized next to the table to take our orders, breaking the flow of conversation. After ordering, Smith returned to the topic of Memphis's atmosphere in the late 1960s. "People would not recognize 1968 or earlier. Everything was segregated. Police would've come in here with *you* sitting at the table with us."

It took me a second to realize he was referring to my light complexion. "Now wait a minute!" I said, laughing.

"It was a very testy time."

He named people from the Invaders and the Memphis Police Department from the late 1960s he was still in contact with, people with pertinent information. Now and then, he had trouble remembering someone, and Constance would interject with suggested names until they settled on the right one.

"There's so much that's unknown. For example, on the day of the assassination, Charles Cabbage had a Mustang just like James Earl Ray's Mustang. Parked two cars behind where James Earl Ray's was parked with a 30-06 in the trunk. I've never had a reasonable explanation as to why."

I hadn't heard that before, and I wasn't able to confirm it afterward.

"Now, I'm not interested in everybody pointing the finger saying

Marrell did this or such-and-such did this, that, and the other. I want to know what John and Cab and all of them were doing."

I told him about how Dad couldn't find any of the Invaders' leaders in the assassination's aftermath.

"They *split*," he said. "Of course, I can't be upset with them for leaving." Coby said he knew that after King's march in support of the sanitation strike descended into disorder, the Invaders would be blamed. For that reason, he ordered its members off the streets.

Adding to the Invaders' difficulties was their adversarial relationship with the SCLC staff. Smith said the staffers didn't want the Invaders involved in the march, and they'd given King "bad information" about them.

Smith was well acquainted with King and his associates from his days in Atlanta, where he sold magazines after withdrawing from Southwestern at Memphis (now Rhodes College). He also got to know Stokely Carmichael, H. Rap Brown, and other Black activists—including his classmate Cabbage.

I asked him how he met Dad.

"He came to us—and infiltrated!"

We both laughed.

I told him how Dad's supervisors sent him down to Clayborn Temple to find out if the strikers were planning to intercept the sanitation trucks or interfere with trash collection in any way—something Dad didn't find any evidence for.

"Well, I wanted to stop the trucks." Smith wore a deadpan expression. "No need of me being too religious now—like, 'Oh, he's repented, and he's saved now, and he ain't gonna tell what happened.' My theory about the strike was, let's run it like a strike. Let's stop the trucks. So I was very much for stopping the trucks—however we had to do it."

"See, that's the kind of information Dad was looking for," I said.

"There are things that people misunderstand that have to do with issues like that. We sent John B. down to the Community on the Move for Equality to actually get them to radicalize their position. John went down there and told them to get their guns. Which—if you just say that, it sounds a lot different than the reality."

I asked him if the Invaders encouraged them to get guns for self-defense or some other purpose.

"Well, every day, after the sanitation workers get off work, they ride the bus home. Or walk. The police would harass them, stop them, do whatever they wanted to do. Arrest them. Beat them. That's why we started following the sanitation workers—to protect them. So in protecting them—you know, we're a bunch of guys sitting around. I never thought I'd get to be twenty-one, I'mma be honest with you. So we said, 'Man, we aren't making any progress like this. These people don't believe we mean business. So let's stop the trucks.'"

He paused. Then he named more former Invaders, including one he said he learned only last January was an infiltrator. "And here's a guy I talked to every year."

I could only grunt in mild surprise.

"He's a preacher now. They're all preachers. You know how you get religion? You turn around. 'That's in my past.'"

A couple of Invaders later went to prison for bank robbery, he said. My mind went back to the FBI-created ruse that Dad was wanted for bank robbery.

I asked him what misunderstandings people have about the Invaders.

"Well, one, that the Invaders started the riot after the first march," he said. He blamed a local pastor, Rev. Samuel "Billy" Kyles, in large part for that misperception.

Coby described himself as something of an outlier in the group. "A lot of the Invaders thought I was too conservative—kind of milquetoast a little. You needed to be picking pockets, pimping, or stealing for them."

"How does that help the cause?" I asked.

"We're talking about—most of the guys met in jail or met on the street."

Smith said Dad tried to warn him about the criminal element in their organization. "He said, 'Coby, some of these guys you're hanging with are criminals. Now you're all right. But I want you to know that a lot of these guys have records.' And I said, 'Okay, fine. Tell me something new. What Black folks you know could live and not have some kind of record?' I was the only one who hadn't been to jail."

Despite the Invaders' conflicts with the local clergy and the SCLC, Smith said they still made a significant contribution to the sanitation strike, invoking Ernest Withers, the famed civil rights movement photographer who turned out to be an FBI informant. "Ernest Withers said there wouldn't have been a sanitation workers' strike if it hadn't been for the Invaders. Here we were, kids. No utility bills, no mortgage, no nothing."

They threw their entire lives into kindling a grassroots movement.

Still, Smith said he thought some of his former cohorts were undercover. Which wasn't necessarily a bad thing. "Now, I'm not opposed to people having been undercover. What I'm opposed to is things people did that led to harm."

Returning to the topic of Withers, he laughed as he described how the photographer asked him and Charles Cabbage to pose for a photo in front of a building that he later learned was an FBI office. "But wait a minute. Ten years later, I met Dr. Pepper down at the Brownstone Hotel," he said, referring to the attorney who represented the King family in their wrongful death conspiracy case. "And before I could get home, Ernest called, what, twice? Two or three times? And when I finally got there, he said, 'What you doing there meeting with Dr. Pepper? You know he ain't no good!'"

Then there was another, even more unsettling incident. "I was with Withers and his wife. I said, 'Wouldn't you like to know who killed Dr. King?' He said, 'For what? That ain't gonna bring him back!'"

Constance spoke up. "That's exactly what he said. Coby discussed it with me, so I know it wasn't sitting well with him."

"And here's somebody I had known all my life," Smith said. "Grew up with his children."

What did Smith want people to understand about the Invaders?

"I felt that my role was to dispel the idea of exceptionality for our people. Sammy Davis was exceptional. How many people you know could do everything he could do? That's not real. Folks thought, 'Okay Coby, you're okay, you're intelligent, you have the same aspirations we have. You're one in a million.' No sir. We all have some kind of gift."

I asked him if he was talking about the Talented Tenth, the concept popularized by W. E. B. Du Bois that an elite class of capable Black people would lead the race to prosperity. He was.

"Of the Invaders, we have about three or four who went on to become doctors," he said. "Some of us had a good background. There were some who were straight-out thugs all the way through. But what you had was the incarnation of what we were trying to achieve when we started the desegregation movement."

He turned to the topic of Memphis's pioneers in the struggle for civil rights. "In this area, we all live in the shadow of Ida B. Wells. She was probably the first and greatest of the organizers we had. She organized the anti-lynching movement in the country at the same time she was with the suffragettes. And she scolded them for not wanting to get involved in the anti-lynching movement. And of course, they ran her out of Memphis."

He talked about Robert Church, the reputed Black millionaire of the small park near my grandparents' church. "They ran him out of town. In fact, they burned his house in a fire exhibition when I was a kid."

He'd left a mansion, but the city had burned it down.

Smith noted the losses the Black community suffered due not only to King's murder but also to the sidelining of activists like himself—and even police officers like Dad. "A lot of the guys in the Invaders have been in exile. Your daddy's been in exile; he wasn't even *in* jail. I've been in exile. They took us out of society just like they took Mandela out for doing the same thing."

The thought hadn't occurred to me before, but it made sense—Dad had been in a sort of exile.

He continued, "It seems like to me, somebody would've said, 'Marrell McCollough, will you come and lead our police department here? Will you come and redo the criminal justice system so that you don't have to choose between being undercover and being a criminal?' That, to me, is a question. How do we bridge the gap? We never get to use all of our resources."

16.

Narco-9

In fall 1969, Mac and Linda bought a new house in an integrated Southwest Memphis neighborhood called Westwood down Highway 61, close to the Mississippi line. This was the second time they'd moved in a year, not that the apartment on South Parkway East had been a bad place to live. The swimming pool was a big plus, and Mac's son Terry loved it when he came up from Mississippi to spend the summers with them. But they soon found they needed more room than that little apartment. They were ready for a house and yard again.

Westwood was one of a handful of neighborhoods in Memphis where Black people lived alongside white people. In East Memphis and other white enclaves, Black people still couldn't buy.

Westwood's developers built a community of mixed-income housing where homeowners' financial means helped determine the size of their mortgage payments. The homes were of comparable quality, with low-income households intermingled with the rest without apparent differences from home to home. Some of the poor households were Black, but not all.

At $17,000, the house stretched their budget but seemed like good value for what they got. It had three bedrooms and was all electric. That sounded like a great selling point, as electricity for heat felt like the way of the future. But then the electricity bills started coming in, and they were more than the mortgage payments.

Linda continued devoting her nonworking hours to caring for Miss Elizabeth, spending less and less time at home until she was gone altogether, back to living in the house on Clementine. Mac remained in the new house, and his sister Joyce and her two young sons moved in with him. Joyce had a good job at the Memphis Credit Bureau, and while she was working, a maternal aunt they called Babysister watched the boys.

Thanks to the neighborhood kids, Mac rediscovered his love of baseball. He noticed there were about a dozen of them hanging around, fifth or sixth graders with nothing to do. Remembering how baseball was a high point of his Saturdays growing up, despite Raymond's efforts to keep him from it, Mac took action, bringing the kids around to local stores to raise money for equipment and uniforms. Some of the stores contributed to the fund while others provided the equipment directly. He had T-shirts printed with their names, and soon they were a real neighborhood team playing games among themselves during the summer in the local park.

One day in the summer of 1970, after Mac had spent a little over a year in the Intelligence Bureau, Inspector Smith appeared at his desk with big news.

"Mac, you're reassigned to the Vice and Narcotics unit."

He had a week to have his desk cleared and reports submitted. Which was fine by him—he felt no particular excitement or disappointment. Reassignments were part of the job.

What did bother him was that when he arrived in Vice and Narcotics, he was the only officer there without a partner. He found himself with no one to ride with, just as instructors warned about in the academy, though he'd done everything right. Each day, he sat lonely and bored at his desk as the other officers went out with their partners. His new boss, Inspector Hutchinson, must have noticed how down he was about it, because he stopped by Mac's desk one day to offer words of encouragement.

"Hang on. I'm working on getting somebody for you."

In the meantime, a chance came along for him to get away from his desk and out on the streets to make an arrest. A call came in, and he was the only officer available to take it. When he got back to the office, he grabbed a big yellow notepad and set to work on the state report, the document the state's attorney's office would rely on to get an indictment. It would lay out the series of events surrounding the arrest, describing how the officer went to such-and-such place, saw the offense, made the arrest, read the accused their Miranda rights, transported them. It needed to include all the pertinent details—weather, lighting, everything the officer saw and did as it related to the arrest.

Knowing he had to get the details exactly right, he went through a mental checklist: *Did I read the guy his rights? Of course—better make sure to put that in there.*

He looked back at the arrest report he'd drafted on the scene, played the events back in his mind, added more information, writing longhand. After working on it for a couple of days, he put the finished product in the secretary's inbox for her to type up and send to prosecutors. Miss Kay was a stout little woman who wore a full face of makeup and styled her hair in a stiff helmet. When he submitted the report, she didn't even look up.

Hours passed, and he heard nothing about his report. He noticed her inbox growing taller as his colleagues piled papers in it—on top of his, he imagined. The next morning, her stack looked smaller, but he still hadn't gotten his back. What was going on? Should he say something?

Miss Kay appeared at his desk.

"Marrell," she said, her sharp voice splicing his name's two syllables into one that sounded like *Murl*. "All Miss Kay needs is the subject's name, the date and time of the arrest, and what the charges are. I'll take it from there."

It turned out that she was drafting the officers' state reports herself. With the bare minimum details, she was putting herself in the officers' shoes, writing their first-person accounts. She knew what they needed to say, and that's exactly what she wrote.

In fall 1970, after Mac had been in Vice and Narcotics for a couple of months, Inspector Hutchinson relayed the good news that Mac was getting a partner: William Payne. After a while, Mac took to calling him by a nickname, "Billy Jack."

A muscular, square-jawed man with dark brown skin, he was a little younger than Mac and slightly shorter. Like Mac, he'd served in the army, but his career was cut short after his parachute failed to fully open during a training exercise and he spiraled to the ground. He wound up with a metal pin in his right shoulder, but to look at him, you'd never know he'd been injured.

Hutchinson assigned the pair a call sign—Narco-9—and they hit the streets. They got the 3:00 to 11:00 p.m. shift, though it could run later, depending on what was happening.

The main drugs on the streets were marijuana, heroin, and legend drugs—prescription medications like the Robitussin AC and Dilaudid beloved by some of the Invaders. Less common was cocaine, though it was out there, too.

Among them, marijuana was the most popular by far, and dealers sold it in a couple of quantities: the nickel bag, about a quarter ounce in a small envelope like the ones used for the church offering plate, for $5; and the lid, a full ounce in a plastic baggie (an amount somebody might buy for a party) for $20. Then there was the kilo, 2.2 pounds, which you wouldn't find on a small-time street dealer but in a raid on a *real* dealer. The low-level dealers wouldn't have any more on them than a lid, though they'd probably have more hidden somewhere.

Another major source of arrests was forged prescriptions. Someone, often a housewife, would get hold of a doctor's prescription pad and try to pass a forged prescription to a pharmacist. The pharmacists often did much of the investigative work, tracking down the doctor and confirming the forgery. Mac and Billy Jack arrested many people of all stripes for that—Black, white, inner-city, and suburban. But they were never able to make a case against a doctor for prescription fraud, though they did have their suspicions.

Unlike Mac's car patrols three years earlier, when Black officers were assigned to Black neighborhoods only, Mac and Billy Jack had no such constraints. They decided to tackle two areas known for drug trafficking: the intersection of Mississippi Boulevard and Walker Avenue in South

Memphis and the Highland Avenue strip near Memphis State, a popular hangout for hippies.

Finding popular drug transaction venues was one thing, but intercepting deals was another. Mac and Billy Jack hatched a plan to sneak up on people and catch them before they could run. They did a trial run one evening at the Mississippi and Walker intersection, near the LeMoyne Gardens housing project with its forlorn brick buildings.

With Mac driving the unmarked car and Billy Jack in the passenger seat, they crept down Mississippi just after dark, heading south. After they crossed Walker, Mac cut the engine, turned off the lights, and put the car in neutral. When he took his foot off the brake, the car rolled down the gently sloping street without making a sound. They slouched down in their seats with an exaggerated lean to the side and their heads down, "riding slick," as folks called it. Mac brought the car to a stop next to the curb, where they could see all the happenings under the wan streetlights.

The first couple of times they tried it, they didn't see anything suspicious, so they used the same tactic on Highland Street. No results.

They returned to Mississippi and Walker and tried again, night after night. Finally, they saw something one evening. Two figures came into view. A small packet moved from one set of hands to another, and what looked like money passed the opposite way.

Mac and Billy Jack had found their quarry. They jumped out of the car, but as they approached the seller, he pulled a gun. Then he ran off, sprinting into LeMoyne Gardens. It was hopeless; he was gone.

Another night, a suspect ran into a dimly lit pool hall. Mac and Billy Jack chased him all the way through the place, catching him near the back. As they marched him to the front in handcuffs, the patrons fell silent, save for a few murmurs. Mac and Billy Jack put him in the back of their car, drove him to police headquarters, took him through the prisoners' entrance in the back. After hauling him up to the second floor for processing, they marked the drugs and money as evidence and placed it in the evidence locker. Now it was late, and their shift was over. They'd do it again the next day—and the days, weeks, and months to follow. Before long, they earned a reputation on the streets, and along with that came nicknames: Billy Jack and Dirty Mac, which was probably modeled on "Dirty Harry."

Down on the Highland strip, Mac and Billy Jack noticed a Black kid, a hippie, who was becoming a regular. That was unusual in Memphis, where the hippies were almost exclusively dope-smoking white kids.

Every time Mac saw him, he shook his head. *Doesn't this boy realize the difference between himself and these white kids?* he thought. *Once the white kids' rebellious days are over, they're going to cut their hair, take a bath, put on a suit, and get a job from their family or something, while he's going to be stuck.*

One evening, Mac and Billy Jack approached him and asked him where he was from.

Arkansas, he said, but he'd come across the bridge to hang out on the strip.

They asked him what he was doing with his life.

"Just coming down here."

"Tell you what," Mac said. "We're gonna take you back across the bridge to Arkansas where you come from, and we want you to go home. We don't ever want to see you back here in Memphis again. Do you understand that?"

"Yeah."

"Get in the car."

They drove downtown and picked up I-55, crossing the Memphis & Arkansas Bridge. When they reached the first turnoff, they let him out of the car.

"Now don't you come back across that bridge," they said.

Vice and Narcotics officers had to learn their way around the courtroom. The courts loomed large in the job, with its steady flow of warrants and arrests. The lessons came fast.

During one of Mac's early court appearances, a probable cause hearing, he had to testify about an arrest he and Billy Jack made at Mississippi and Walker. Under questioning by the prosecutor, he said they'd been watching the defendant from their car when they saw another man approach him, hand him a five-dollar bill, and take a nickel bag of marijuana in exchange. Then came the cross-examination.

"Now Officer McCollough, what did you *see*?" the defense attorney asked.

"I saw the transaction. I saw the bag being passed and the money being handed over to him."

The defense attorney turned on his heels and walked away from the witness stand until he reached midway between the front and back of the courtroom. Then he pulled something from his pocket.

"I have a denomination of money in my hand. What is it?"

Mac strained to see what it was. "I have no idea."

"No? But you're telling this court that at *night* on the street, under the streetlights—all the light you had—you saw my client pass five dollars and get a nickel bag?"

"Yeah, I saw that."

"How do you know that's what you saw?"

"Because when we arrested him, we got the nickel bag, and we got the five dollars."

"But you couldn't identify the five dollars from where you were."

"You are absolutely right." Mac was chagrined. "What I did see, though, was a transaction I've witnessed time and time again, of a nickel bag—a small church-like envelope—being passed from a seller to a buyer. And it's five dollars. And that's when I went and locked him up."

The judge wound up crediting Mac's testimony and binding the defendant over for trial. But it was close.

Though Mac didn't keep up with the outcomes of his cases, he knew they usually didn't go to trial. The defendants usually copped a plea and got their sentence of eleven twenty-nine—eleven months and twenty-nine days. Just one day shy of year, this sentence permitted a stint in the Shelby County penal farm rather than state prison. After that, they went back out on the street, many to be arrested again. Some became informants, but most remained on the merry-go-round of offending and jail time. *What's the point?* Mac would think as he locked up a familiar face.

Within a few months, Mac and Billy Jack were having pretty good success catching small-time dealers. It usually went down without much of a hassle, until one night when they saw two white guys buying dope at Mississippi and Walker. Mac and his partner sprang out of the car.

"Police! You're under arrest!"

But instead of surrendering, the men fought back. It turned into a real brawl, and though the guys could fight, they were no match for Mac and Billy Jack. When it was over, the suspects were bruised and bloody, and one had to be transported to the hospital. He ended up with white bandages wrapped around his head in what folks called a John Gaston turban, after the name of the public hospital where injured suspects were usually treated.

Mac and Billy Jack sought charges for not only the drugs but also resisting arrest. At the plea hearing, the men copped to the drugs but denied resisting arrest, claiming they thought the officers were robbers.

When it was Mac's turn to testify, he recapitulated everything that happened.

"Did you tell them you were a police officer?" the judge asked.

"Yes, but they didn't believe it."

"Did you show them your badge?"

"I showed them as soon as I could get to it, but the first thing I had to do was protect myself."

"Well, it's reasonable to believe that, not seeing a badge, they thought they were being robbed," the judge said.

Maybe so. Maybe they were a couple of scared hayseeds who didn't know what they were doing, and they thought the folks who sold them the drugs were trying to rob them. Or maybe it was hard for them to believe two Black men were empowered by law to arrest them. Whatever the truth was, the judge dismissed the charges for resisting arrest. Mac didn't feel too bad about it, though. He'd done his best, and the rest was out of his hands.

His candor on the stand about not showing his badge right away brought an unexpected benefit: One of the defendants decided to cooperate with police as an informant to reduce his sentence. He said his decision was based in part on Mac's truthful testimony.

That informant took Narco-9's operations to the next level, giving them valuable leads to make more arrests and develop additional informants, who in turn provided more tips. To verify the information they got, Mac and Billy Jack would set up surveillance, then send in an informant to make a buy using marked bills. They'd take the buy and run a rapid test to make sure they had the real deal.

Each drug had its own rapid test, which consisted of a chemical inside a vial. They'd remove the top of the vial, insert a bit of the suspected substance, then replace the top and shake the vial. The chemical's color would change if the drug being tested for was present, which was enough to establish probable cause for a search warrant, or to hold a defendant for trial. But for the trial itself, they'd have to send the substance off to the University of Tennessee medical center lab to get confirmation of the results.

With some buys and busts, they discovered the product being sold was just oregano or some other marijuana look-alike. But if it turned out to be an illegal drug—as it usually did—they'd take the evidence to court and get either a warrant to search the premises or an arrest warrant for the seller, depending on the circumstances. In the case of an arrest warrant, they wouldn't do it right away. They'd take their time, build a case, make multiple buys—a minimum of three.

It wasn't only informants making controlled buys; they had a couple of undercover officers making them, too. One, a sheriff's deputy, became legendary. Known as Candy Man, he developed information over the course of a year that led to dozens of arrests.

But the controlled buys were only one side of the coin when it came to drug busts. The other side was surveillance of suspected drug houses, which came into play when police were developing information to get a search warrant. Mac and Billy Jack would find a vantage point, anywhere they could observe well with the naked eye, or with the aid of binoculars if necessary. It was usually a car, but it could also be the home of a cooperating witness.

Then they'd watch the people going in and out, try to get a sense of what was going on. The idea was to see what kind of traffic entered and left, and at what hours of the day or night. Seeing known drug users—folks they'd already arrested—was a giveaway, as was seeing a bunch of people coming in and out who had no apparent family or friendship connection. Based on what they saw, they might send in snitches to make buys, which brought the controlled buys into play.

They'd pat down the snitch, give him—it was always a "him"—the money, take him to the neighborhood, let him go, and wait for him to come back. He'd come back with the drugs, which they'd take back and test. A positive test would form part of the basis for a search warrant.

Next came the drug raids, and there were two basic types: execution of a search warrant, where the police had developed evidence of drug sales based on surveillance and a buy, and execution of an arrest warrant, where police had made a series of buys. In either case, officers would show up at the residence in the early morning hours, four or five in the morning.

They'd put some time between the controlled buy and the execution of the search warrant, not wanting to bring too much attention to the snitch. Then when the time was right, the department would send over four Narco officers and a couple of officers from the neighborhood squad car. They had carte blanche for no-knock warrants, so they'd shout "Police!" while simultaneously breaking down the front door. This earned Mac an additional nickname, "Bigfoot," for his ability to kick down bolted doors.

They had no idea who or what they were going to find behind the door, so they divided up their tasks: The patrol officers maintained control of the occupants, making sure they weren't armed or destroying evidence, while the Narco officers conducted the search. If they turned up incriminating evidence—drugs, needles, syringes, and the like—they arrested the occupants on the spot.

With arrest warrants, police didn't generally anticipate the same kinds of threats posed by serving search warrants. These arrests involved individual suspects, often young and perhaps living with their parents or a spouse, rather than known drug houses. In these cases, two or three Narco officers would meet in the office and form a team with the goal of surprising the wanted person. They'd knock on the suspect's front door and arrest them when they answered.

A raid gone bad could easily cost lives. Mac and Billy Jack were involved in one that almost did. It happened at a two-story apartment building that had two front doors separated by a large picture window. A backup officer entered one door, while Mac and Billy Jack walked past the picture window and entered the other door. The people inside, who'd spotted them through that window, took off running in every direction. When Mac and Billy Jack burst in, they saw a suspect about ten yards away, running up a staircase. He got halfway up the stairs, then turned toward them. He had a pistol in his hand, which he raised above his head.

Mac trained his revolver on him. "Drop your weapon!"

The man didn't move.

"Drop your weapon!" Mac shouted again.

The man remained frozen. If he'd moved—except to drop the gun—Mac was prepared to shoot him.

From the corner of his eye, Mac saw Billy Jack on his belly, crawling toward the staircase. As the suspect stared at Mac, Billy Jack inched up the stairs. Then he sprang up, overtook the man, and grabbed the gun.

As they held the man, questions flooded Mac's mind. He wondered if he could've stopped the guy if he'd tried to shoot Billy Jack. Could Mac have gotten off a shot in time, and would it have been accurate? He'd made a split second decision not to shoot, which turned out to be the right call, but there was no way to know in the moment. They could have encountered death that day.

In the last weeks of 1970, the drug trade was getting more attention than it ever had, from federal to local authorities. The Nixon administration was crowing about a major offensive to stem the tide of heroin pouring into the

United States from overseas, and this martial attitude could be felt all the way in Memphis.

On December 14, Memphis and Shelby County announced that they would be pooling their resources to create a single unit, Metro Narcotics, to handle the area's drug enforcement efforts. The two jurisdictions' law enforcement agencies had been tripping all over one another, even unwittingly buying drugs from each other. Metro Narcotics' leadership came from both departments, with a sheriff's office inspector at the helm and a Memphis Police Department captain as second in command. No longer would the jurisdictional line separating the city from the county foil enforcement efforts. Its officers would have jurisdiction all over Shelby County.

From that partnership, Mac and Billy Jack gained a new partner, a Black sheriff's deputy named John. The three of them ran one car, but only two rode at a time while the third had the day off.

As a sergeant, John was senior to them in rank, but as time went on, they saw that that he lagged in experience and expertise. Mac couldn't make any good busts with him. But he seemed to enjoy riding around with them, even coming in on his day off from time to time. They didn't mind, even if some of his behaviors grated on them, like how he was always showing off a flashy watch he said Elvis Presley had given him. Then there was the time he invited them over to his place, but it was clear that he just wanted them to see his fancy house. He lived in Whitehaven, an upper-middle-class neighborhood in the early stages of integrating. As John was leading them on a tour of the plush home, Mac and Billy Jack noticed a coat of arms on his wall.

"Where did you get this?" they asked, barely containing their laughter.

"I ordered it." He looked irritated.

"John, don't you realize Black folks aren't supposed to have Irish coats of arms like this?" They were openly laughing now.

He never invited them back.

Mac and Billy Jack began hearing rumors of a major drug dealer in town, a shadowy figure known as Big Hand. He was reportedly the size of a football player and had enormous hands. His name kept coming up as a source among the lower level dealers, some of whom provided other relevant bits of information. Once the evidence began to accumulate, Mac and Billy Jack set up surveillance outside his house. They watched the traffic come and go and sent in informants, but it was all to no avail—Big Hand was too meticulous. If he didn't know someone personally, he wouldn't sell to them, and Mac and Billy Jack couldn't get anyone from his inner circle to attempt a controlled buy. Eventually somebody got him, because in 1972, a federal jury deliberated for only fifteen minutes before convicting him for heroin distribution.

Then there was another man, a successful restaurateur, whom Mac and Billy Jack suspected of running a lucrative trade in drugs from a sedate-looking suburb. They worked hard to try to make a case on him—surveilling, running informants, trying to make buys—but they never got anywhere.

There was a constant stream of chatter about various shipments coming through town, drugs being flown into Memphis International Airport and scheduled to be picked up there. None of it panned out, except one time when it halfway did. Mac and Billy Jack got a tip about an airport pickup that included a description of the pickup person, the car, the time, and the place—American Airlines arrivals. They went to check it out, and sure enough, a driver fitting the description showed up at the appointed time in a car that also fit the description. They stopped the man and searched the car, where they found $10,000 cash in a paper bag in the trunk. The driver admitted he had no job and couldn't explain where the money came from.

"I think you need to explain this to the IRS," they told him before seizing the cash.

But they couldn't lock him up because he hadn't broken any laws.

What had happened? It seemed clear that a transaction was about to take place, and either Mac and Billy Jack jumped the gun, or the deal just didn't materialize. But the man had the money.

Aside from drug investigations, Mac and Billy Jack provided drug education in junior and senior high schools across the city. They gave hour-long presentations, bringing with them a display kit containing photos of the most frequently abused drugs. It showed marijuana in its various forms, barbiturates, Dilaudid, cocaine, heroin being cooked, an arm with track marks, syringes. They told the teachers to call if they found something suspicious, and they'd come out and test it, but no call ever came.

From time to time, white parents would call Metro Narcotics to request that officers come speak with their teens. Mac and Billy Jack went out to the suburbs for that once, meeting with a boy suspected by his parents of abusing drugs. Afraid their neighbors might see the police car parked out front, the parents asked Mac and Billy Jack to call when they were on the way, and they'd leave the garage door open for the officers to pull inside.

"But we'll be driving an unmarked car," Mac said.

All the same, the parents wanted the visit to remain secret.

Mac also participated in a short anti-drug film produced by a local TV station, *A Day in the Death of Donnie B.* It chronicled a promising high school student's descent into drug abuse, which robbed him of his athletic ability, his desire to study, and finally his life. Mac played one of two arresting officers who finds him slumped over in a stupor. Seeing the officers, the boy springs to his feet and tries to run away, but Mac catches him. The boy throws down a syringe, and Mac picks it up. The officers find more drugs on him, put him in the back of a squad car, and drive away.

In May 1972, Mac completed his studies, graduating from Memphis State with a degree in police administration. But with this achievement came a painful realization: He had no future at the Memphis Police Department—not the kind he wanted, anyway. After five grueling years, he was still a patrolman, and there was no promotion in sight.

He'd been doing the job of a detective for the past couple of years, leading investigations, running informants, planning raids. He and Billy Jack were getting better at their jobs and making bigger drug busts—including the seizure of $39,000 in cash, an unheard-of sum in Memphis's drug trade. But none of it seemed to matter. He was stuck at the patrolman level for the foreseeable future. Meanwhile, there were folks making detective who'd never investigated anything in their lives.

There were no high-ranking Black officers he could look to as examples of what was possible. How high could a Black officer go? The most senior one to date was a major, and it had taken him his whole career to get there. Mac wasn't willing to waste the rest of his working life on scraps.

Overall, Memphis had been good to him. He'd been able to establish a burgeoning career and get a college degree. But now it looked like the opportunities were drying up. He didn't want to spend the next ten years stuck in some mid-level position, never getting a chance to ascend to the top ranks, no matter how much of himself he put into his work. Something had to change, and it wasn't going to be the police department.

What about a career at the FBI? Most police officers aspired to be FBI agents, he thought. It was a natural next step, like graduating and moving up. The department practically encouraged the move. And a career there paved the way for big things. Look at Fire and Police Director Holloman and City Attorney Joseph Canale—both former special agents. Holloman was said to be personal friends with J. Edgar Hoover. Plus, Special Agents Lawrence and Lowe knew Mac well; maybe they would put in a good word for him.

The next time he saw Lawrence and Lowe, he mentioned wanting to apply for a position with the FBI. One of them brought him an SF-86, the eighteen-or-so page standard personal history statement that was required for a professional job in the federal government. It demanded all his biographical information—where he'd lived and worked, financial information, foreign contacts, military service. As references, he listed Lawrence and Lowe, plus Davis, Arkin, Canale, and Holloman.

He put the completed form in the mail and waited.

Weeks turned into months, and he heard nothing. He wasn't sure what to think. Of course, he didn't know of any Black special agents. But on the other hand, if the Memphis Police Department had hired him practically off the street with next to no law enforcement experience, why would the FBI pass him over—especially now that he had a police administration degree and all this experience?

In late August, he heard from Lawrence. He wanted to meet at Mac's home to discuss the application.

"A question came in from Washington," Lawrence said. "Your application didn't list any dependents. Don't you have a son?'

"Yes, but I didn't list him because he doesn't live with me. So he wouldn't be coming with me to Quantico."

"I guess the question is, was this an intentional omission?"

Intentional omission? Mac thought.

As if he'd try to hide Terry, who'd spent the last four summers with him. Mac had even taken him to juvenile court, with Nellie's blessing, to have his last name changed to McCollough. The suggestion that he might be hiding the boy didn't make any sense.

Mac explained this to Lawrence, but that was the last he heard about his application.

All this was brewing in the background of Mac's thoughts one September day in 1972 as he sat in the car with Billy Jack and a ride-along guest, Dr. William J. Oswald. A tall, beefy medical doctor and reserve police officer, he'd joined them once a week for the past couple of months to gather information for a police department study he was conducting on officers' various roles in the department. Over the course of a shift, he observed their actions from the back seat, asking questions and engaging them in wide-ranging discussions. He looked to be in his early fifties and led a fascinating life, it seemed. From time to time, he'd disappear, then resurface saying he'd been to Latin America, South America, places like that.

"How's your application with the Bureau going?" he asked Mac during one of their conversational-style interviews. Earlier that summer, Mac had mentioned he was applying there.

"Haven't heard a word from 'em."

"Well, you should just forget them and apply with the CIA."

Mac turned around to look at him. "You've got to be kidding me. They aren't gonna hire me. They probably don't hire Black folks anyway."

"They have Black officers. You should apply."

Though he didn't realize it, Mac was having nearly the same conversation with Oswald as he'd had with his cousin Eugene five years earlier, when they'd heard the police recruiting commercial on the radio. "Even if I was interested, how would I go about applying?"

"Just write them a letter."

"What?"

"Write them a letter. Tell them who you are, what you're interested in, what you want to do."

"Okay, and *then* what?"

"Send it to CIA, Langley, Virginia."

It sounded almost like sending a letter to Santa Claus, North Pole.

Mac didn't know much about the CIA; in fact, it rarely crossed his mind. He imagined their work was paramilitary, with overseas operations doing things they wouldn't admit to, like the Bay of Pigs. It seemed like a far cry from the kind of law enforcement work he was looking to do. But on the other hand, he *did* have experience as a spy.

He didn't act on the suggestion right away. He sat on it for a few weeks, pushed it to the back of his mind. But he was sitting at home one weekend when Dr. Oswald's suggestion bubbled up in his thoughts.

Let me just try, he thought.

From his coursework at Memphis State, he knew how to write a solid query letter. He found a sheet of paper and started writing a letter longhand, addressing it to "Gentlemen." Referencing Oswald's referral, he noted his interest in advancing his career by working for the federal government. He described his qualifications: his work experience as a police officer, his degree in police administration, his military background. It occurred to him that the CIA would want to confirm his identity, that he was who he claimed to be. He listed his social security number and telephone number. Then he remembered he had a book or magazine with the photo from the Lorraine Motel printed in it. He found it and cut it out.

"To further establish my bona fides," he wrote, "I am enclosing a photograph you may be aware of that includes me."

He put the letter and photograph in an envelope, dropped it in a mailbox, and waited.

In early fall 1972, about two weeks after Mac sent his query letter to the CIA, he got a phone call from a recruiter out of Kansas City, Missouri. The man said he wanted to meet, and they set up a breakfast meeting at a Holiday Inn out in East Memphis.

The following week, over plates of chain hotel breakfast fare, they chatted about Mac's background and career aspirations. It went well enough that the man decided Mac should sit for the Agency's placement and assessment examination, the Professional Aptitude Test Battery. He gave Mac the contact information of a Memphis State professor who'd be administering it.

A couple of weeks later, he sat for the test. It was several hours of math, reading, logic, and reasoning questions. If Train A left the station at a certain hour traveling a certain speed, and Train B left a different station five miles away at a different hour traveling a different speed in the opposite direction, when would they meet? If you were lost in the woods, what techniques could you use to find your way out? Then there was a sequence about identifying the values of playing cards that bore no numbers, only symbols representing their suits. Mac knew he performed poorly on that part because he had little familiarity with cards and never learned any of the games.

About three weeks after he took the test, he got an employment application in the mail. It was an SF-86, the same document he'd completed for the FBI. He filled it out and sent it back.

A month or two passed. Finally, he got a letter from the Agency inviting him to come in for interviews in the spring.

Meanwhile, he *still* hadn't heard anything from the FBI and had all but written off the possibility of working there. It looked like the CIA might be a better opportunity, anyway.

He'd later learn that it had been a minor miracle his unsolicited letter got a response. The CIA got letters like that all the time and routinely disposed of them. Was it Dr. Oswald's referral that got his letter pulled from the pile? Did the man have some connection there? Or had circumstances lined up in a peculiar way that worked to Mac's advantage, independent of outside help? It was possible that someone in Langley got the letter and photo and said, "Hmm, maybe I should forward this to the recruiting office," and then someone in the recruiting office said, "Maybe I should send this to our folks in Kansas City."

It sounded far-fetched, but stranger things had happened. After all, none of this would've been possible if Mac and his cousin Eugene hadn't happened to hear a police recruiting ad on the radio—and on the last day to apply for the job.

Maybe something greater was playing out, a matter of destiny. It was impossible to say. But however this chain of events came to be, the practical reality was it *had* come to be.

By 1973, Mac and Billy Jack had achieved the highest arrest rate in Metro Narcotics, which Mac found especially satisfying because he came in knowing nothing and with nobody teaching him anything. He and Billy Jack figured it out for themselves—running informants, making controlled buys, putting it all together to make arrests. And they looked good doing it, too, in their jackets, bell-bottom slacks, and stack-heel shoes. More than once, they overheard somebody referring to them as the Mod Squad, after the stylish TV police drama.

The main thing detracting from their hip style was their assigned car, a Plymouth Sebring. It looked like a vehicle for shuttling a family around town, not busting drug dealers. And that's how it drove, too—no powerful engine or high-performance police package upgrades. All the Sebring driving units had was the flashing lights, which officers kept in the glovebox. Press the accelerator, and it would barely speed up, *put-put-put*. Mac hated it; his own personal car was faster. But the Sebring was the assigned car for all the Narco units, and homicide, too, because none of these officers were out doing car chases.

Just as the car wasn't glamorous, neither was the work. Their original informant, the white guy they got into the fight with, was dead. About a year after they'd started working with him, somebody found his body in a hotel room. He'd overdosed on brown heroin, which folks called Mexican

Mud. Then there were the cavity searches, which were unpleasant enough on their own but could occasionally be downright hellish. Normally, they were routine visual inspections for concealed drugs before a suspect went into the lockup, but one guy they'd arrested in a drug raid became combative.

"Search me! Search me!" he shouted.

Then he dropped his trousers to reveal masses of giant carbuncles, and Mac wished he were anywhere but in that room.

But it wasn't all misery, danger, and mediocre cars. Mac and Billy Jack had their fun nights out on the town, too, occasionally stopping by Hawaiian Isle, a popular South Memphis nightclub, when they finished their shift. The place looked nondescript on the outside, almost like an oversized convenience store. But inside, blues and soul music throbbed as the crowd chatted, drank, and danced under the low lights. After a long week of work, a night there was liberating.

The club's liquor license allowed it to sell beer by the bottle, but not liquor. A patron who wanted a hard drink had to bring their own bottle, which could be kept on the table inside a brown bag until midnight, at which point they had to move it to the floor—some kind of technical end-run around the liquor laws. The place sold what they called a setup, ice in a bucket and a mixer, as well as snacks like pork rinds.

Mac and Billy Jack were careful about how they handled themselves in their social lives, knowing that two off-duty police officers couldn't be out drunk and carousing. For one thing, it would look bad and potentially get back to the department. Plus, they never knew when they'd be drawn into some kind of predicament, like the night a terrified-looking man approached them at their table.

"I know you guys are police officers. There's a guy over here menacing us, and he's got a gun."

Tired from having just worked a full shift, the last thing they wanted to do was get involved. But they couldn't just sit there doing nothing. What if it ended in a shooting? They were sober and capable of handling the situation; the main thing was to avoid escalating it.

They approached the man alleged to have the gun.

"We're police officers," they said. "Come with us to the bathroom."

Once inside, they flanked him. They spotted the gun, a little Saturday night special, in his waistband. Then they noticed a patch of moisture on the front of his pants. He'd urinated on himself.

Every year, officers came up for review before a panel of six or so senior officers from the patrol division and detective bureaus. It was a meeting that decided an officer's trajectory in the department, whether their career was going anywhere. In 1973, Mac's day arrived on May 21, and the timing couldn't have been worse. That very afternoon, one of his colleagues was gunned down in South Memphis, along with four other victims and the murderer himself. The officer killed was David Clark, the younger brother of Mac's first partner, Tom.

No one knew what provoked the killing spree. Clark wouldn't have even been on the scene had the call not come in a mere ten minutes before his shift was to end. Now the entire department was grieving, Clark's murder the only topic on everyone's lips, including among Mac's review panel.

He could tell no one was engaged during the meeting. They asked his name, how long he'd been an officer, what his duties were, and that was it—meeting over. It was perfunctory at best, nothing like the more thorough discussions he'd had in previous reviews.

About a month later, the department released a list of officers eligible for promotion. After four and a half years of exceptional performance, Mac expected to be on it. He scanned the names and saw some of his contemporaries, and also officers junior to him, folks who'd never performed the kind of detective and undercover work he'd done. He read each name, from top to bottom and back up to the top. His was not there. A physical slap to the face wouldn't have felt more bracing.

In response, Mac did something he'd never done in his law enforcement career. He complained—not because he thought he had much of a future in the department, but because it wasn't right, and he wanted folks to know *he knew* it wasn't right. He decided to take his grievance to the highest level, even higher than the chief. He called Fire and Police Director Frank Holloman's office and made an appointment.

They met the following week, Holloman taking a seat in a chair next to Mac rather than remaining behind his desk. "What can I do for you?" he asked.

"Sir, I want to discuss the recent promotion process." Mac recounted the circumstances of his appearance before the review panel, and how he wasn't on the promotion eligibility list, though officers with less seniority and experience were.

Holloman looked at him with a blank expression. "What do you expect me to do about it?"

"I expect you to make it right."

"Look, this is what was decided, and I can't interfere with that."

"I'd still like for you to look at my career and what I've done and my qualifications. When I joined the department, I didn't have a college education, but since that time I got one. And I got it in police administration, not basket weaving." His tone, which had been measured until that point, took on a hard edge. "My name should've been on that list."

"There's nothing I can do, Mac."

"Well, I guess I'm going to have to move on from this department."

"Okay, if that's what you feel you need to do."

Though he felt defeated as he left Holloman's office, he'd gained something valuable: the grim confirmation that he'd been right about not having a future in the department.

17.

Flag

Could the Stars and Stripes be considered a hate symbol now? I wondered as I peered out the kitchen window at a pickup truck I didn't recognize with a U.S. flag bumper sticker. It was summer 2019, and the country was in the throes of the Trump administration's hateful antics. Everything and everyone seemed off kilter, reacting in some way to the daily pummeling of lies, graft, and grift—either with disgust and fatigue or smug support. People had become emboldened in their nastiness where they'd once been covert. Racist violence was on the rise, with the tacit, if not explicit, approval of the commander in chief, his cavalry of political toadies, and legions of fans across the country.

Using the American flag as a fasces of white nationalist fury, Trump had spent the past several years whipping up rage with his stated goal to "Make America Great Again." It felt like anything could happen, especially when that flag was on display. So I viewed the truck with the flag bumper sticker, parked on the road's dusty shoulder between my house and the neighbor's, with suspicion.

It might sound like an overreaction to some, but this is what white supremacy does—it keeps you off balance, questioning and second-guessing your own perceptions. It's the ultimate disinformation campaign. Perhaps I wasn't in any more danger than I'd ever been, and only my perceptions had changed. These were arguments I made in my head, even as my autonomic processes rebelled. My heart pounded, my breathing shallowed, my mouth became dry.

Surely I didn't think the driver of that pickup truck had singled out my kids and me for some kind of racist attack, just because we were one of the few Black families in this rural High Sierra town, which according to the most recent census figures was only 0.3 percent African American and 2.1 percent from two or more races. That sounded paranoid, and nobody wants to sound paranoid.

Sure, the tenor of the comments on the town's informal Facebook page, run by long-suffering volunteer moderators, had changed in small but disturbing ways over the past few years, but social media isn't real life, right? Anyway, it was little things—wink-and-nod, not-saying-just-saying things. What I sensed then, but didn't yet know, was that they would deteriorate over the next year to the point where I'd see allusions to slurs against Black people and support for vigilante violence. But this was before all that. This was back when I just had a feeling things were headed that way.

My gaze went from the window over the kitchen sink to the picture windows looking out over the deck, where the American flag mounted on the rail snapped and twisted in the breeze. It used to seem like a nice accent to the view, its crisp lines and bright colors set against the backdrop of blues and greens. We'd even replaced the one that faded, retiring it to a place of honor on the garage wall. I'd initially seen it as telegraphing the same message as the mountains, lake, and forest—freedom to roam, dance, *be*.

But that shimmying fabric didn't make me feel free anymore. With increasing frequency, those stars and stripes made my stomach clench, like I'd looked up to see someone brandishing a noose. And that's how some people intended it—much as they chanted "U-S-A! U-S-A!" while glorying in Trump's racist fusillades and calls for violence.

My first memory of the American flag was as a child of four, watching soldiers fold one with stiff precision into a tight triangle by my uncle Sammy's casket. Sitting off to the side with Ma and Grandma and the rest of the family, I was confused, but mostly sad because they were sad. The last time I saw Sammy, he was tall and strong and laughing at Grandma and Granddaddy's house. I once overheard Ma and one of her sisters talking about him having cancer. I asked Ma what cancer was, and she started crying, so I didn't ask again. I also kept hearing about something called Agent Orange. I didn't know then that this was used in Vietnam—but as far as I could glean, it was a chemical that gave people cancer, and then they died.

One of the soldiers played a long, slow song on a trumpet that put a knot in the base of my throat. It was the saddest song I'd ever heard, tailor-made for the background chorus of sobs and choked-down wails. The flag, still folded in its crisp triangle, went to Grandma and Granddaddy, and they kept it in the drawer of the dark, glossy buffet in their dining room. I knew it was a symbol of his service, which filled them with pride. I wondered if it made them sad, too.

In Tahoe, I was noticing more flags going up on houses around town. The Fourth of July was right around the corner, so it made sense, but I hadn't noticed so many flags in previous summers. In fact, I'd seen few around town when we'd put up ours a few years back, in 2014. I had no way to gauge this, of course, and there were too many variables that went into something like that. Plus, what if there *were* more flags? Why worry about an apparent surge in patriotism? The question seemed to whisper its own answer, also in the form of a question: Why would there *be* a sudden surge in patriotism?

I had clues. On the heels of the 2016 election, my husband and I joined three other couples at an isolated cabin in the woods, about fifteen miles from our house. We'd all gone in together on it at a charity gala and auction, and in addition to the night's accommodations, it included a multi-course dinner with wine pairings. The cabin lay off a narrow dirt road, and it had been a production to get there. By the time my husband and I arrived, it was pitch dark, and we had to use high-powered flashlights to navigate the way from our parked truck to the front door.

We entered to warm lighting and lively chatter as our fellow guests lounged on antique sofas. Curios and taxidermy spangled the walls, lending the place an eccentric feel. We knew two of the couples well, one of them from our children's school and another through mutual friends. The third couple, a woman and man I'd met at the gala, seemed to be good friends with the others.

We soon sat down to dinner at a long table in the kitchen, where the topic immediately turned to politics. That wasn't surprising, given Trump's ground-shaking election victory. I was still sickened by the outcome and in no mood to talk about it.

Somehow it came up that the couple I barely knew had voted for him. Normally, I kept my reactions subdued in these situations, as I was well accustomed to wearing a placid mask of cordiality to cover my mouth and conceal my expressions. But on this night, I felt the mask's rigid contours digging into my flesh. So I removed it and stared at them with my real face.

"How could you support a man like that?" I asked. The clinking of utensils stilled as a hush fell over the table. "What is it that you like about him?"

After a moment, the man answered. It was for financial reasons, he explained. He was a business owner and overregulation was an existential threat to his livelihood.

This was the "financial anxiety" justification, which hadn't yet been widely debunked and derided as the cover for the racist motives it was. Still, I was skeptical.

"Your shot at a better regulatory environment comes at a great cost," I said. "You seem to be overlooking his hate speech. Or does it not bother you?"

I knew all eyes were on us. I didn't care, because I didn't have anything to lose. Here I was, once again the lone Black face at the table, always making nice and keeping many of my thoughts to myself. But not anymore. I wasn't giving these people the benefit of the doubt. There would be no more benefits and plenty of doubts.

Who had I really been protecting, anyway? All this time, I thought I'd been keeping myself and my family safe, preventing us from becoming outcasts at school and work, among our neighbors. But my politeness hadn't protected us in the ways I thought. It hadn't spared us the nicks and bruises of disrespect. What it had done was render us palatable, inoffensive, safe. It bought us a cheap and superficial acceptance. I hadn't been protecting *us* so much as I'd been protecting white people from my authentic reactions. I'd been protecting their comfort, not ours. I was done with that now.

"I don't agree with that stuff," he said. "It's embarrassing. It's getting in the way of the good he could do."

"Let me tell you where *I'm* coming from." I talked about growing up in Memphis, where my first memory of the playground was two white girls telling me they weren't going to play with me because I was Black. I talked about my white friend who wore the confederate flag nightgown, and being student council minority vice president. I told him about what segregation had been like for my parents, and how it hadn't really ended. "So the things Trump says are personal for me."

More silence.

"I can't imagine what that must've been like. I didn't grow up in a place like that."

Looking back, I regret putting my wounds on display. But I was angry, and that was my visceral response. I also knew that wherever he grew up—I think he mentioned someplace out west—it *was* "like that," even if he didn't acknowledge it.

At the time, I was proud of myself for speaking up, though I later realized I'd let him off easy by allowing the conversation to center on my pain more than his accountability. But after watching the Trump administration cage migrant children, turn away refugees, promote violence, trounce civil liberties, and spew still more racism, bolstered by his supporters' increasingly lusty cheers, I told myself I'd never again try to reason with a Trump voter, or explain why they were wrong. Never again would I give them my energy, attention, or pain to feed on. Besides, there was nothing left to say.

From time to time, I thought about that evening and the man's seeming failure to connect both his life experience and his vote with white supremacy. Given the discomfort he'd expressed about Trump's rhetoric then, I wondered if watching the Trump administration in action had changed his mind. Probably not, I decided. If anything, Trump voters were more locked in than ever. How could they turn back now, after condoning his early transgressions? As the saying goes, he who says A must say B, too.

By now, I was getting the creeping feeling that I had more neighbors supporting Trump than I'd ever imagined. It was subtle in the way that the beginnings of horror films are subtle, though there was the occasional jump scare—as when one of the moms from school posted a photo of herself and her husband standing next to *him* and smiling broadly. Automatic unfriend.

And now there were American flags up and down the street. Was it patriotism or racist semiotics?

There was a quote from Dr. Maya Angelou that I tried to live by: "When people show you who they are, believe them the first time." In my experience, people inevitably revealed their true character—and their feelings about me—in small ways that eventually became unmistakable. Whenever someone transgressed against me in some way, with betrayal or disrespect, I could look back and see small signs I'd ignored or explained away. I was now wondering what I should make of the signs I was seeing in my community.

Until now, I thought I'd been navigating pretty well. The kids and I had made friends, gotten invited to parties—I was even the guest of honor at a couple—joined a church. I didn't feel the need to look behind things too much. I'd felt safe, but that was changing. It was time to pay more attention.

I couldn't have explained why in terms that would've held up to much scrutiny. There were no objective facts to which I could point, no incidents, no confrontations, no words or deeds that were menacing on their face. No one had personally threatened us. But that was one of the most insidious things about racism: it was nothing personal. It was often couched in language and behavior that could be explained away as innocuous. It was fine-grained as dust, blowing about in the air and settling just about everywhere, liable to being blown off as if it were nothing. It made you question the reality of what you saw, heard, and felt—whether you were safe or in danger. Yet your survival depended on knowing.

If pressed, I might've described it as an energy in the air. It would be several years before I could put words to what I found so disturbing: that most of the people around me either didn't care that we now had a president advocating racial hatred and violence, or they enjoyed it. It was as if I had a dangerous enemy who'd made known his feelings about me and my family, and the people around me were either indifferent or quietly supporting the enemy. How could I trust these people, or even eat with them? How could things ever be the same?

I thought about how I'd come to live in a place where I felt unsafe. For one thing, why was I living in a community where so few people looked like me and my family? The answer led all the way back to daycare, before I even entered school, when I became the first generation of my family to live in what was purported to be an integrated Memphis. Ending de jure segregation was momentous, of course, representing the hard-won gains of civil rights warriors and everyday folks who fought and sacrificed and, yes, *died* for children like me to get an equal education and be treated with the same dignity afforded to my white peers. But being thrust into those classrooms alongside white kids led me to expect equal treatment and mutual acceptance rather than marginalization. Perhaps that expectation hadn't served me well.

This kicked off a long chain of events from elementary school through law school and the workplace, and finally to the nearly all-white town in the High Sierra where I now sat, contemplating a racist American regime and my neighbors' seemingly newfound patriotism. In many ways, I hadn't been prepared—*couldn't* have been prepared—for what the white world held in store for me. I'd entered it mostly unguarded, open to the racist cuts, bruises, and body blows that greeted me, beginning with the girls on the preschool playground. I can still feel the shame and rejection, but also a sense of being in the wrong. I was outnumbered. If they agreed there was something wrong with me, they must have been right. This was my introduction to being in the minority.

It marked the first of many times I'd internalize these attacks, holding myself responsible for both open and hidden expressions of animus. How many of my scars now functioned as my inner architecture—the bones, ligaments, musculature of my psyche? So many times, I'd walked away from exchanges I now recognize as violence but saw then as natural consequences of some shortcoming or defect I had. When I was around ten and the Walt Disney World Jungle Cruise ride operator referred to my braids as "monkey ropes," I crumpled internally because I believed that perhaps my hair really did look like monkey ropes. Again and again, I contended with the idea that maybe my features were ugly, maybe I shouldn't be taken seriously, maybe I didn't matter, because that's what the majority—which happened to be white—seemed to think.

As I advanced from the playground to the college seminar to the office, the assaults grew more complex and difficult to discern. When I sat in a hall with around a hundred students and listened to a political science professor say that cultures that developed in hot climates had a lower work ethic than those that developed in colder environments (because the people didn't have to work as hard to feed themselves), I fumed. But as angry and humiliated as I felt, what could I do? He'd mentioned it as an aside, couched in an academic lecture about something or other—which I could no longer focus on—and maybe he was quoting someone else. But I didn't hear him refute it. Far from it; the words unfurled from his lips like a cocktail party bon mot. He wasn't saying, he was just saying.

But there were far more subtle and inscrutable insults, as in the case of the adjunct professor who seemed hostile and dismissive no matter what I said or did but tripped all over himself to flatter my white classmate from abroad, or the work-study job where everything I did seemed to invite criticism and derision. How much of the problem was theirs, and how much of it mine? They couldn't all be wrong, could they? I took on their scorn as a ship with a cracked hull takes on water. I worked harder. I tried to be better.

And now, after making it through college and law school, passing two bar exams and waiving into a third jurisdiction, successfully handling numerous cases, I was *still* unsure of whether I was now or had ever been good enough, smart enough, worthy. On some level, I knew I deserved my accomplishments by any objective measure. But knowing is one thing; feeling is another.

I'd still have experiences from time to time that took me back to that place of inferiority, of minority—a condescending interaction at a writers' conference, a knowing smirk at a charity brunch. I thought of myself as thick-skinned, but the arrows found their places in old wounds. I did the one thing I knew I was good at: I moved on.

But in doing so, I'd moved myself more squarely inside the problem, in that I again found myself in a place where I needed to be accepted, when I should have been in a place where I belonged. Between these two conditions lay all the difference in the world. If belonging is a rich, life-sustaining meal, acceptance is a thin gruel. You can survive on it, but that's about all you'll do.

18.

CIA, Langley, Virginia

In late spring 1973, shortly after his testy meeting with Fire and Police Director Holloman, Mac traveled to Northern Virginia for two days of interviews with the CIA. The first meetings on his schedule weren't at CIA Headquarters but another suburban building, where he was to take a municipal bus from his hotel. As he boarded the bus that morning, he asked the driver to let him know when they arrived at the designated building. He noticed that an older woman boarding ahead of him turned to look.

"Just follow me when I get off," she said.

It was a little strange, almost like something out of a spy novel.

A short ride later, she gave him a nod, and they disembarked. When they reached the building, she showed him where to check in. He wondered if the episode had been prearranged somehow, but it couldn't have been—could it?

No, she must've just been going to work, he thought.

His first interview was with a kindly man named John who was director of something called the Career Trainee Program, the Agency's main vehicle for recruiting management-track officers. The program fed talented recruits to various groups throughout the Agency, he explained, which selected the people they wanted. It was this program that had brought Mac in for interviews.

"With your law enforcement background, you're a perfect match for the Office of Security," John said.

Mac's presence at the scene of Dr. King's assassination intrigued John, and he wanted to know more—how Mac came to be there and what he was doing. Mac explained the circumstances as succinctly as he could, that he was a police officer infiltrating a Black militant group. That seemed to be enough of an explanation for the moment.

From there, Mac went to a couple more interviews with Career Trainee Program officers. They asked about the assassination, too.

Next, he went by shuttle bus to the CIA's massive Headquarters complex in Langley to meet with representatives from groups he was hearing about for the first time: the Office of Security, housed within the Directorate of Administration, and the Directorate of Operations. Not only was he interviewing, he was getting a crash course in the Agency's mission and organizational structure.

Established by the National Security Act of 1947, the CIA was the nation's premier civilian spy agency, charged with gathering, analyzing, and evaluating intelligence—and performing "other functions and duties related to intelligence affecting the national security." Much of its work came out of its four directorates: Operations, Administration, Intelligence, and Science & Technology.

The Office of Security was responsible for protecting CIA personnel, facilities, and information, as well as rooting out spies within the Agency. It was crucial work, though they didn't get much press compared to the mysterious and romanticized Directorate of Operations—perhaps better known as the Clandestine Service—which collected intelligence and handled covert activities around the globe. Operations' activities, which included everything from economic warfare to subversion of governments deemed hostile to the United States, was closer to most folks' idea of the CIA.

Mac spoke with high-level officers from several different divisions in Operations, all of whom wanted to know about the assassination. By now, he was used to retelling the story.

But things went differently in Security. Unlike the people from Operations, who had hiring power, the interviewer from Security was obviously less senior—and dismissive and disinterested, too. He didn't ask about the assassination, or much of anything else.

Soon after returning to Memphis, Mac got a call from John from the Career Trainee Program.

"What did you tell the people in Security?" he asked.

"What do you mean?"

"They aren't interested in your application. They said you didn't want to leave Memphis for a position there."

"I never told them anything like that." Mac wondered how in the world they could've gleaned that from anything he said. "I'm ready to move forward with a career there."

"I tell you what. If you're serious about working here, I'll find a job for you, but you'll have to go where I slot you." So Mac was in—provided he made it through the next steps in the hiring process.

Those steps arrived many months later, in early 1974, when he was scheduled to return for his medical examination and polygraph. But this was different from the long wait he had with his FBI application, where he heard nothing for so long that he could only presume his application was moribund. The Agency kept in touch with him, sending him a postcard every couple of weeks or so telling him his application was still in progress. And it included a name and phone number he could contact if he had any questions.

That wasn't the only thing that impressed Mac. Something John from the Career Trainee Program had said stuck with him. "There will be people in the program who have advanced degrees, who have more education than you have. But I'm convinced that the energy you put into your work and your desire to achieve will stand you in good stead."

Those words buoyed Mac. He believed them.

Now back for his medical exam and polygraph, he felt confident. He'd also developed a certain familiarity with some of the administrative staff, who remembered him from conversations he'd struck up during his previous visit. The day he was to visit medical, he made plans to meet a couple of women staffers for drinks in Georgetown. They spent the evening drinking margaritas from salt-rimmed glasses, and by the time he made it back to his hotel, it was after three in the morning.

At his medical exam, the doctor looked startled when he took Mac's blood pressure.

"This reading is awful. Why don't you go rest and see if we can get it down?"

He directed Mac to a cot and had him lie down for a few minutes. Then he took another reading. It was still sky high.

Sensing that the doctor was on the verge of disqualifying him, Mac tried to think of something to turn the situation around.

"I know it looks like I'm headed for a disqualification. But before you do that, will you at least talk to my doctor back in Memphis, Dr. Oswald? Because he knows my history, and he can tell you I don't normally have high blood pressure. If you let him explain, I'd be grateful."

Of course, Oswald, while a medical doctor, wasn't *his* doctor. But it was true that Mac didn't have a problem with high blood pressure, though it tended to be somewhat elevated. He been aware of that since his army days, but elevated blood pressure wasn't uncommon among Black people.

The Agency doctor gave him a business card with his name and P.O. box. "You tell your doctor to contact me, all right?"

As soon as Mac got back to Memphis, he went to see Oswald at his office. Handing him the Agency doctor's card, Mac explained what happened with his blood pressure.

Oswald rose from his chair, went to the refrigerator, and pulled out two beers.

He handed one to Mac. It was a Coors, and Mac was impressed. You couldn't get that brand just anywhere—it was sold only in eleven Western states.

"Let me take care of this," Oswald said.

He began dictating a letter into his Dictaphone, explaining that Mac's elevated blood pressure was understandable under the stressful circumstances of travel and a possible career change but was no cause for concern, given his history. Then he called for his secretary to type the letter and put it in the mail.

———

In spring 1974, Mac received a letter so life-changing, its bureaucratic tone couldn't conceal the possibility and promise of the news it contained. He'd completed processing, it read, and the CIA would like to offer him a position in the Career Trainee Program beginning June 17 at the level of GS-8, referring to the General Schedule pay scale for federal jobs. The higher the number, the higher the pay, and a GS-8 was consistent with a new hire who brought relevant work experience to the job.

The salary was somewhere upward of $10,000, and that figure was important. At the police department, he never managed to crack $10,000. He was currently hovering around the $8,000 range, with no prospect of a significant raise on the horizon. A $10,000 salary became something of a milestone to him, a marker that would signify that he was finally getting somewhere.

What he didn't know but would soon learn was that some of his fellow recruits with roughly equivalent experience, or arguably less, were being hired as GS-9s or 10s. It turned out that the offer had been negotiable, something that never occurred to him. He'd been so glad to have the opportunity that he hadn't considered negotiating, which to his mind might've put the job in jeopardy. But if he'd known that other recruits had done so, he would have, too.

When he raised it with the Career Trainee Program, they told him not to worry, he'd catch up before long. Once he finished his probationary period, he'd automatically be promoted to GS-9. Things would even out eventually.

Mac's first assignment in the CIA's Career Trainee Program was in a field office in the Office of Security in June 1974. It was an interim posting that lasted only about a month. Mindful that Security was where he'd hit a snag in the interview process, he threw himself into the work, determined to excel. And he did, earning the maximum grades possible in his interim report.

Next came a couple of months of Career Trainee Program classroom work, and then finally, the assignment that would set the course of his career: the Office of Security's training program. Despite rejecting him during the interview process, they couldn't very well say no after his stellar performance reviews.

It was in Security's training program that he met Billy, who came to be one of his closest friends in the Agency. A mustachioed white man from North Dakota, he was about Mac's age and, like Mac, had served in the army. He also grew up poor, raised by his mother and aunts. Once he and Mac got talking, they discovered deep commonalities.

After completing Security's training program in late 1974, he went back to the field office where he'd had his interim assignment. Soon after arriving, his new boss, a large-framed white man named Jack, called Mac into his office.

"I'm getting a lot of you new guys in," Jack said. "Let me tell you one thing: You'd better be good. Because you're replacing some of my friends who are gone now. Yeah, a lot of my friends have lost their jobs, and they're bringing you new guys in. So you'd better be good."

He was referring to officers who'd recently been forced into early retirement in a swirl of scandal following revelations about CIA misconduct. Mac knew little about it—something to do with burglaries known as black bag jobs and improper involvement with local law enforcement agencies—but within Security, the effect was seismic.

Mac listened without emotion. He'd been here before: the rookie who inspired no confidence.

Then he spoke. "Not only am I good, I'm *damn* good. If I wasn't, I wouldn't have gotten this job."

Jack's expression softened. "Welcome to the field office."

One of Mac's first jobs in the Office of Security was to help provide countersurveillance training for officers heading to overseas assignments, where they'd be subject to surveillance from foreign governments.

One day in 1975, when Mac was still new in his role, his team ended a long work week by stopping for beers at a Northern Virginia tavern. They sat around a table, drinking and trading stories, loosening up as the beers went down. After several rounds, a white guy named Tom began lamenting the changes to the office.

"It's not going to be the same anymore, because now they're hiring women and niggers."

Mac knew how to catch his anger, how to wrestle it down and subdue it before reacting. He'd had plenty of practice. "Tom, you know, I find this offensive."

Had the table fallen silent? Were all eyes on them? If so, Mac didn't notice. He continued, "I don't think you ought to be talking like that."

"Oh, well that's what it is," Tom said.

Now the others' silence was noticeable. They didn't say a word.

"I tell you what," Mac said. "If you continue talking like this, I'm gonna report you to the office."

"Well, that's what it is."

Mac rose from his chair. "I'm gonna report you, but I'm gonna leave."

He returned to the office and told their boss, Jack, what Tom said.

The following week, Jack called Tom in. Mac didn't know what Jack said to him, much less if he was disciplined, but he did apologize.

Mac didn't have any more trouble out of him after that. They didn't become friends, but they could work together.

Mac spent three years in the field office—from late 1974 through 1977—advancing a GS level each of those years, from GS 8 to 11. That was good progress, and with that came a new assignment to Headquarters in Security's Clearance Division. These were the folks who handled security clearances for all CIA employees, contractors, and anyone else with access to Agency facilities or information.

Management began giving him additional responsibilities, beginning with a position on the Office of Security's Management Advisory Group. Next, he was selected to join the Director of Central Intelligence's Management Advisory Group, where he was eventually chosen as its chairperson. Though there was no formal fast track in the Agency, there was one in practice—the officers everyone could see were performing well, getting the good assignments, progressing more quickly through the ranks. Mac was one of them.

The work was fascinating and challenging, and his supervisors were giving him great reviews. At the same time, he noticed that few in his office were people of color or women. That stood in contrast to the Agency's overall workforce, which seemed to reflect an effort to hire diverse employees. In fact, he'd been impressed by the number of people of color and women in his recruiting class. He wondered if the Office of Security's demographics were by design.

Did it have something to do with the fact that many of his colleagues were former FBI agents? As the Church Committee had shown the world in its recent revelations about COINTELPRO, the FBI had been far from the upstanding organization many people, including Mac, had thought. He was shocked when he heard about it. It was hard for him to square the terrible stories with his experiences working with Lawrence and Lowe, who seemed so forthright and aboveboard. But surely, they had to have been involved in some capacity. And to think that just a few years earlier, he'd wanted to work for them. Now it made more sense that they never gave him the time of day.

And maybe this had something to do with why the Office of Security told the Career Trainee Program director they weren't interested in his application. But the director placed him there anyway, and he was going to show them all what he could do.

Despite any recent efforts to hire diverse candidates, the Agency had few Black officers. Mac couldn't name any who'd progressed past GS-12 or 13 to what they called the supergrades—GS-16, 17, 18. And while there were a good number of women officers—outside Security, at least—he knew of only one who'd risen that high, a chief of station named Eloise.

Still, Mac was progressing through the grades on time, or even early. He never got what they called an in-grade promotion, where they just gave you a bump in pay if you didn't get promoted to a higher position within a certain time period. He was moving up, and he even began to believe there might not be a limit to how high he could go.

In the summer of 1977, Mac got a call from the CIA's Office of General Counsel. They told him investigators from the U.S. House of Representatives wanted to talk with him about King's assassination. The news caught him off guard, as the assassination had happened nine years prior, and he thought he'd put it behind him.

The House of Representatives had formed a Select Committee on Assassinations a year ago, he learned, to investigate the murders of King and President John F. Kennedy. It wasn't that Mac minded talking to them. The events were still fresh in his mind, even if he doubted he had any useful information for them. The problem was that no one was supposed to know he was a CIA officer.

An OGC attorney by his side, he met with select committee investigator Gerald Hamilton in a nondescript D.C. hotel room that had the air of a safe house. The meeting began with the OGC attorney explaining that the nature of Mac's work was classified, and they wanted to keep it that way.

"Oh yeah, that's not a problem," Hamilton said.

He was interested in Mac's tenure at the Memphis Police Department—when he'd begun working there and what his role was. He wanted to know what Mac was doing at the time of the assassination and the details of what he witnessed. Mac answered every question as carefully as he could, telling the whole story of infiltrating the Invaders, how he'd been dropping off James Orange and James Bevel when he heard the shot that killed King, how he'd run onto the balcony to try to save King's life. Before he knew it, a couple of hours had passed.

Soon after, OGC informed him that the select committee wanted to meet with him again to ask follow-up questions. At this second meeting, Hamilton clarified certain details about what Mac had previously told him—dates, times, and such.

"We were also wondering if we could have access to your personnel files," Hamilton said.

"Sure, but we'll need to get clearance," the OGC attorney said.

Not long after that, a group of investigators showed up at Headquarters to review Mac's records, including staff counsel William Webb, a Black man whose straightforward manner Mac liked. Unlike some of the other investigators, Webb didn't seem to sensationalize Mac's CIA employment. Mac grew increasingly frustrated with the ones who did. They seemed to act like it had some bearing on the investigation.

Finally, he had to say something. "If I'd left Memphis and gone to work somewhere like General Motors—in their security department—I don't think anybody would even be that interested in me," he said. "But it just so happens that I got a job at the CIA, and now that's all people see, like it's sinister or something. I just got a new job, okay? There's nothing there."

They all nodded.

Months passed, and Mac heard nothing more about the investigation. He had plenty of other matters to think about. He was working in a new job at Headquarters, Security Operations within the Office of Security. Known internally as the Green Berets of Security, they conducted special investigations, partnered with other agencies and law enforcement, investigated security violations, and more.

His marriage to Linda had ended in divorce, and he had a new wife, Peggy, plus a toddler and another baby on the way.

But the select committee's work proceeded apace, and in summer 1978, OGC called him again. The select committee's chairman, Congressman Louis Stokes of Ohio, wanted him to testify in a public hearing on King's assassination.

"But I already talked to them," Mac said. "I've told them everything I know."

"That's what the chairman wants."

"Okay, but what about my employment here? That can't be made public." Wouldn't that be one of the first things they asked him, where he worked? He'd have to tell the truth. And the career he was working so hard to build would be washed away like a sandcastle.

"If they ask you, you'll have to tell them. There's no way around that."

He couldn't believe the predicament he was in. They merely wanted to make an exhibit of him, he thought. They didn't care that it stood a serious chance of harming him personally—though it wouldn't do a single thing to further their investigation into King's murder.

Wasn't there some way he could get around blowing up his entire career over one question? What about the way they did things in court when he was in Vice and Narcotics, where an attorney would sometimes ask the judge if they could approach the bench to privately share information they didn't want to reveal to the entire courtroom? He couldn't picture in his mind how things would go in a hearing like that, but maybe the OGC lawyers would figure something out.

The hearing date was set for Monday, November 20, 1978, and as it approached, it took up more and more space in Mac's mind. He began to stew about it—especially when he learned from OGC in early November that Mark Lane, a pugnacious attorney who'd made a name for himself representing James Earl Ray, was planning to attend. They told Mac to be prepared for Lane to stand up and accuse him of assassinating King. They didn't know the basis of his claim, only that he was going to make it.

Mac could scarcely imagine that kind of foolishness unfolding in a congressional hearing. Surely no one would buy into what he was saying—would they? How do you prepare to be accused of murder in front of a room full of people? He imagined the ensuing commotion. In all the interviews he'd had with the investigators, no one ever asked him anything even hinting that he might've been involved in the assassination. They wanted to know what his role was at the scene, but they never implied they thought he was involved.

The whole thing was ridiculous, anyway, Mac thought. He'd already told the investigators everything he knew, and they'd been all through his personnel files, too. What was the point in dragging him out before the public when they already had the answers on record? He wasn't some kind of star witness; he'd just been a police officer doing a police officer's work. What was left to say?

The Friday before the hearing, Mac called OGC to discuss a few final details.

"Where should we meet?" he asked.

"I'll get back to you on that," the attorney said.

He called back soon afterward, sounding regretful. "We're not going to be able to go with you, Mac."

"What do you mean?"

"That would be like representing you, and we can't do that. We represent the agency only. We'll be there sitting in the back, but we can't be there *with* you."

Though they'd been by his side through all the meetings with investigators, they were parting ways with him on the eve of the big event.

"What good will it do for you to sit in the back? Who's going to help me handle the questions?"

"Just do the best you can."

Well, shit, Mac thought. The feeling of betrayal stung. All along, they seemed to stand by his side, but now that it really counted, they were making him go it alone.

That afternoon, Mac had one last meeting with the congressional investigators. With no one else to turn to, he found himself confiding in staff counsel Webb.

"Damn, Bill, I just started working here. If that gets publicized, I don't know what impact that's going to have."

"Don't worry about that," Webb said. "I tell you what we'll do. When you come in, just sit with our staff. That way, you won't stand out, and you won't have people coming up taking your picture."

"But what about answering the question about my employment?"

"Well, you've got to answer the question, but it doesn't have to be broadcast. Ask the chairman to hold the hearing in private. He'll have all the news outlets turn off their recording devices and everything. The media will have to go silent."

19.

Search for Meaning

In fall 2018, I crunched across the University of Memphis's leaf-strewn campus to the library, where I'd be paying an initial visit to its collection of sanitation strike documents and memorabilia. It felt like a pilgrimage. I'd first heard about the collection, part of the university's Mississippi Valley Collection, a few years prior. I found its existence intimidating, even overwhelming. Picturing a roiling sea of historical flotsam with crashing waves of people and events, I felt it might swallow me up if I were unprepared. Until then, I had not dared to approach it.

For more than three years, I readied myself, reading everything I could about the sanitation strike, watching documentaries, reviewing photographs. It had taken me months to feel like I had an adequate base of knowledge to discuss the sanitation strike with Dad, and even after hours of interviews with him, I felt just barely prepared to visit the collection.

I was visiting family for Thanksgiving, staying in an airy downtown loft in what was once a historic hotel, but this would be a working trip, too. The days slipped away from me. I'd arrived on Friday night, feeling run-down with congested nasal passages and a burning chest, thanks to wildfire smoke. On Sunday, I awakened to a sinus infection, and by the time I made it to the library on Monday, it was already mid-afternoon. I knew I wouldn't have time to do any in-depth research, and that comforted me. I'd just stop by for a quick visit, survey the coastline of information and take in its magnitude.

With Thanksgiving just three days away, the campus was nearly deserted, though I could hear strains of music from what must have been the marching band rehearsing. Blasts of cold wind blew leaves across the curved walkway to the library's front doors, biting the inside of my nose. The path felt appropriately long, turbulent, and indirect.

I waited as the cheerful woman at the information desk helped another patron, my stomach fluttering as I overheard her suggest that the patron meet with a research librarian for assistance. *That's what I need*, I thought. Now it was my turn. I told her I was researching the King assassination for a book about my father, who'd witnessed it due to his undercover work for the Memphis police. She directed me to Special Collections on the fourth floor.

Stepping off the elevator, I walked around the circular floor's perimeter until I found Special Collections behind a door that looked like it might have led to administrative offices; had it not been for the sign on the door, I would've assumed it was off-limits to the public. Opening the door, I walked down a short hallway and rounded the corner to the sprawling front desk with a woman standing behind it. I told her about my research.

"Sure, just a moment," she said, walking away. I surveyed the room. There were a couple of other patrons there, neither of them Black. One was using a scanner, and I made a mental note that I probably wouldn't need to bring the portable wand scanner I'd bought online and shipped to Mom's house.

She returned with a tall, gray-haired man.

"How can I help you?" he asked. I thought I detected a New Zealand accent.

Again, I explained.

"What's your angle?" he asked, lingering on the word "angle" as he peered at me.

What's my angle? I thought. The question rendered me speechless for a moment, and I felt my gut heat up. *Does everyone have to justify themselves like this when they come here?* I wondered.

"I'm telling the story of what happened," I said. "This is a father-daughter story, but it's also my father's account of what he experienced. I'm just looking for more details to add."

His face didn't change.

"Have you been to the website and looked at the finding aid?" he asked.

I hadn't. *Should I have done that first?* I thought. I steadied my thoughts, which by now were teetering on an emotional spiral staircase.

"You should begin with that. The finding aid alone is voluminous."

I nodded.

"Since I'm here, is there anything I should see?" I asked.

"You should start with the finding aid," he said.

As I sucked in a breath and held it, he ran through a list of the types of items in the collection—artifacts, audiotapes, films, and more. He mentioned the now defunct *Memphis Press-Scimitar* newspaper, and I grabbed hold of the reference.

"There's a local reporter, Kay Pittman-Black, who covered the Invaders. Do you have any of her articles?" I took another deep breath, ignoring the faint burning sensation that arose in the corners of my eyes.

"We don't keep newspapers here," he said, firing off the words rapidly. Those would be on a different floor.

"Got it," I said. "And I'm going to review the finding aid. I just figured it wouldn't hurt to show up, since I'm in town."

"Well, we're closing thirty minutes early today," he said.

I turned to an enormous card catalog pushed against a wall to my left, focusing my mind on its contents. The cards inside referenced photographs that the *Press-Scimitar* had published, and they were organized alphabetically by name. I pulled out a long skinny drawer labeled "I – Jackson, C" and searched for "Invaders." I found two cards—one for a militant group and another for a singing group.

Next, I looked for "Smith, Coby." I found one card, partially typed with the remainder handwritten in blue and black ink:

NEGRO SCIENCE FAIR ART 4-60
71639 PIX 9/64
7304 CLIP 8/67?
66579 CLIP 11/68
5446 [ILLEGIBLE] OF THE INVADERS

The room would be closing in a few minutes now.

Back outside, I tormented myself with questions. *Was going there a mistake? How could I have failed to do something as simple as look at the website? What the hell did I think I was doing, walking in there like that?* If nothing else, I'd exposed myself as an amateur. All that preparation, and I still wasn't ready.

As fast as the recriminations poured in, urgent rejoinders rose up to meet them. *How dare that guy ask me about my angle. Did I need his approval before I could view the collection? Here I am, the only Black person in the room, researching events involving my own father, and this white gatekeeper says I'm the one with the angle.* A hot tear scalded my cold cheek.

Along the sidewalk, blue and white banners rippled on poles:

U OF M

DRIVEN BY DOING

This is a message for me, I thought. *Focus on doing. Forget the rest.*

The man at the library hadn't been exaggerating when he noted the voluminous size of the collection's finding aid, a detailed directory that also described the collection's history and purposes. There was nothing left to do but plunge in. I did so on my tablet—an updated version of the same device I'd been using to scroll through British tabloids when I came across the article about Andrew Young that set me on the present course.

It began with a paper by the Memphis Search for Meaning Committee, the group that conceived the idea for the collection, describing itself as "an outgrowth of an April 11, 1968, meeting of Save Our City, a temporary (mostly white) citizens group, whose members believed the major newspaper coverage of the Memphis sanitation workers' strike was inadequate." One of Save Our City's objectives was to show there was "some support and sympathy in the white community for the 1,300 strikers who were, almost without exception, black."

Noting that the local newspapers "exhibited a perhaps unconscious bias" in their coverage of the strike, the group hatched a plan to document that coverage. That effort grew into a larger project to collect primary source materials and anecdotes, preserving stories the media had failed to cover.

The group sought to "achieve a fuller understanding of what had happened in our city and why it happened" from their "special on-the-scene vantage point at both the causes and effects of the events." From that vantage point, they set out to "understand them and, if possible, put them into perspective."

Self-described as "[d]iverse and always loosely organized," they were now a committee that included the following community members in its ranks:

> . . .the editor of a local magazine, a corporation lawyer, the office manager of a national food processing company, Memphis State University's Episcopal Chaplain and his wife, a medical student, the owner of a women's dress shop, a tax lawyer, an advertising woman, a jewelry sales representative, a retired department store executive, an insurance company executive, many housewives, a medical technician, a National Cotton Council public relations representative, a nurse, several secretaries, several free lance writers and former reporters, several Memphis City school teachers, private and parochial school teachers, a librarian, university faculty members and college students from Memphis State, Southwestern, LeMoyne, and Christian Brothers College.

Still raw from my visit to the collection, I raced through the finding aid on my tablet screen, slashing the highlighter tool across phrases that bobbed to its heaving surface:

"mostly white"

"[I]t has been our . . . contention from the beginning, that the story of what happened in Memphis in the spring of 1968 could best be told—honestly, effectively, uniquely, perhaps even profoundly—by those of us who were on the scene, body and soul."

"Do underlying racial attitudes control surface events, even when those attitudes are not consciously recognized?"

Underlying racial attitudes, I said to myself with a caustic laugh. I wondered if they considered their own attitudes, such as the position that their mostly white committee had been "on the scene, body and soul" with the sanitation workers and the Black community. Or that their "support and sympathy" gave them the right to decide what the sanitation strike's official record should look like—what would be included, and what would be excluded and potentially lost to history.

I detected underlying racial attitudes in the entire enterprise, elevating this committee's viewpoint to a "special on-the-scene vantage point" and granting it the singular privilege of putting the events into what it deemed their proper perspective.

But even as I seethed, I felt guilty. The collection owed its existence to the committee's efforts. These people were volunteers, and they came up with the idea on their own time and at their own expense. They assembled the materials and conducted the interviews, creating this invaluable resource that I was now grousing about. They wanted to help, and they did. Though I'd hit a rough patch at the library, was it right to let that color my view of the collection? Didn't I owe them some respect?

Then the counterarguments flooded in. What was *their* angle? Sure, they'd done a good thing in creating the collection, but what had they stood to gain from it? I thought I heard the faint rustling of cash as I turned the finding aid's pages:

> Memphis was swarming with authors, journalists, TV newsmen, and filmmakers that spring and summer of 1968, each trying to lay claim to a piece of the big King assassination–James Earl Ray story. Competition was keen; stakes were high; rewards promised to be astronomical. And the book contracts signed at that time were to provide the basis for several future lawsuits.

To their credit, the committee members had been transparent enough to acknowledge that their urgency in publicly releasing their findings was motivated, in part, by "a plain old-fashioned fear of being scooped," as they put it. I grunted under my breath when I got to that part, even as I appreciated their candor.

I later learned that my assessment of them was unfair, that the key people involved in the effort had done so unmotivated by profit and at personal cost. But at the time, I was so disgusted that I couldn't continue reading. I had to put it down.

For my family, the assassination was a lifelong wound, something we didn't touch for fear of aggravating it. I imagined the same was true for many. Somehow, it managed to become part of my lived experience, though I hadn't even been born when it happened. It had always been there, like the background of a bas-relief, maybe even encoded in my DNA alongside other trauma from generations past. It hurt.

Yet, after facing what felt like gatekeeping at the library, I thought I was confronting the prospect of people monetizing the pain, selling tickets to the pain show. Pain pornographers, speculators, colonizers. *Assholes*, I thought.

But then something else stopped me cold. What about me and my research? Was I doing the same thing? That question about my angle had hit a sore point, after all. And what was so bad about the question, anyway? I must have one; doesn't everyone?

I thought about how I'd jumped into Dad's story not knowing what I'd find and afraid of what I might uncover. At first, I thought the fear was driven by the conspiracy theories involving Dad, but I came to realize it went deeper, down to the heart of his identity, and by extension part of mine—what his story really was, who he'd hurt, and how much he'd been hurt. I was afraid of what I'd have to feel. If I had anything you could call an angle, it was to examine that, push through it, and come out on the other side, trembling, story in hand.

Which was why, I realized, I didn't like the question about my angle. Inanimate objects have angles, but I am a human being, a Black woman—which, after all, was part of the sentiment behind the sanitation strike's I AM A MAN signs. When it comes to my father, Black people, and American history, I have a *point of view*. Quite literally, I have skin in the game.

20.

A Very Cold Trail

Even though one of the biggest events of his life—testifying before the U.S. House Select Committee on Assassinations on Capitol Hill—was scheduled for the very next morning, November 20, 1978, Mac was determined to keep his normal Sunday routine. He drove his white Ford Pinto to 7-Eleven and picked up a copy of *The Washington Post*. When he glanced down at the paper as he stood at the checkout, the boldface headline leapt out at him:

> **REP. RYAN SLAIN**
> **AMBUSH AT GUYANA AIRPORT**
> **CONGRESSMAN, 3 OTHERS KILLED IN LATIN AMERICA**

His eyes raced across the article, taking in the shape and size of the horrific news. Mark Lane—the attorney who was reportedly planning to show up at Mac's hearing and accuse him of killing King—was among a party visiting a cult commune in Guyana called Jonestown. Part of the group had been struck by gunfire on an airstrip as they attempted to return to the United States, and while Lane wasn't with them, his condition and whereabouts were unknown.

Mac's heart sank when he got home and read the article more closely, learning of the sickening and bizarre events surrounding cult leader Jim Jones. A strange brew of emotions washed over him, waves of horror and relief. He felt awful for the victims—except Lane, who apparently had been down there helping Jones.

On Monday morning, Mac arrived early to the hearing venue, Room 345 of the Cannon House Office Building on Capitol Hill. Its imposing Beaux Arts façade and clean, formal lines would have captivated him on a normal day, but this was far from normal, and he barely noticed the building's sober grandeur. He scanned the ballroom-like chamber for familiar faces and noticed that a few Invaders were already there—Calvin Taylor, John Smith, and Charles Cabbage. They must've been slated to testify, too. He made eye contact with them as he made his way to the front of the room, where Webb and the rest of the investigators were sitting behind Chairman Stokes. The layout was almost ecclesiastical, with Stokes at his pulpit-like podium, backed by a choir of legislators and staffers. Viewers packed the chamber's remaining space like a devout congregation, the Invaders sitting on the front row next to the other witnesses while the press lined the walls.

Mac mentally reviewed what Webb had told him: to request that the hearing be held in private. Webb's advice and help put him somewhat at ease. He still had concerns about how it would go, whether the congressmen would extract his employment information and hoist it aloft like a severed head. This might be the day his hard work came to nothing and his aspirations died. He did his best to put it out of his mind.

At least he didn't have to worry about Lane showing up to make a spectacle. Aside from his concerns about disclosing his job, testifying would be easy. All he could tell them was what he knew.

Chairman Stokes called the committee to order and gave the floor to its chief counsel, G. Robert Blakey, for a brief preamble about King's involvement in the sanitation strike, from COME's request that King address a rally in support of the workers to the assassination to his disastrous march on March 28, 1968, the week before his death. Then Blakey turned to the FBI's dealings with King—that it sat on information warning that the March 28 march could become violent, failed to alert him to a bomb threat against him reported by American Airlines, even proposed news releases ridiculing him.

"Intelligence activities of the Memphis Police Department Intelligence Division in a conspiracy against Dr. King were considered by this committee," Blakey said. "Among the members of the division interviewed was Marrell McCollough."

Blakey described how Mac had moved to Memphis in 1967 after serving as a military policeman, attended the police academy that fall, and was commissioned as a patrolman three months later. He talked about Mac's first undercover assignment to attend a sanitation strike meeting, leading to his assignment to infiltrate the Invaders. Blakey pointed out that the police department shared his reports with the FBI.

"Mr. McCollough's presence at the scene of the assassination has been used by some to support a contention that government agencies, including the Memphis Police Department, were directly involved in the assassination."

He cited an article published in *Newsday* two years prior that quoted an anonymous Invaders leader as saying, "He had a 7.62 Russian automatic rifle and he was armed every time we were armed. He was always suggesting the action we should take; I never saw him physically attack anyone. But he was one of the most provocative members of the Invaders."

A 7.62 Russian automatic rifle? Mac had never so much as laid eyes on one the entire time he was undercover. In fact, that was one of the weapons linked to Charles Cabbage in the Invaders' ambush of the patrolman, Officer Waddell.

"One of the most provocative members"? Ridiculous. Never before had Mac heard about this *Newsday* article; what a bracing way to find out.

"Mr. Chairman," Blakey said, "it would be appropriate at this time to call Marrell McCollough."

"The committee calls Mr. McCollough," Stokes said.

Mac approached the podium. Speaking softly and leaning toward Stokes, Mac asked if he could give his testimony in private.

Stokes nodded. "At this time, I ask all members of the media to turn off their cameras and other recording devices."

Looking out at the gallery, Mac could see a constellation of cameras' red lights winking off.

Stokes swore Mac in, then recognized William Webb, who handled the initial questioning. Webb began with Mac's military background and early police career, then moved on to the Invaders' organization and structure. Next, he turned to Mac's undercover work, focusing on his actions and observations in the days surrounding King's failed march.

"Would you tell the committee what role the Invaders played during the pre-march hours?" Webb asked.

The committee was taking a hard look at the Invaders, it seemed.

"During the pre-march hours, as I said earlier, they were walking around making statements to the effect that the nonviolent aspects of the march wouldn't work and it was senseless," Mac answered.

"Mr. McCollough, can you describe for the committee how the march came to be interrupted?"

"The only word I can think of is 'spontaneously.'" Mac described how the march started peacefully but descended into chaos on Beale Street, with the sudden sound of windows being smashed.

Webb moved on to the days following the march, beginning with the Invaders' meeting with King the next day—which Mac knew nothing about. Webb asked if the Invaders bore any bitterness toward King because he stayed at a white hotel, the Rivermont, after the march.

"No, sir; there was no bitterness in the usual sense of the word felt toward Dr. King by the Invaders at all."

"Would that include areas besides the Rivermont? Is it fair to say that they were not bitter or hostile toward Dr. King at all during the period?"

"Yes, sir; that's fair to say."

Webb asked him about the day of the assassination—what he'd done that day and what he'd witnessed and done at the Lorraine—introducing as an exhibit the famous photo of Mac kneeling over King. Mac referenced it in describing how he'd run up the staircase to the balcony, as well as his conclusion that the fatal shot came from the boardinghouse across the street.

Next, Webb asked about the FBI report of his interview with Lawrence and Lowe about the assassination. Mac had never seen it before.

The report depicted him as the cover legend he created—an electric company warehouseman and "sympathetic supporter of the Memphis sanitation workers who had been on strike in Memphis." While it didn't explicitly mention his discussion with them about his conclusion that the bullet had exploded, it did note, "He also recalled seeing splotches of blood, possibly pinhead in size, in the immediate vicinity of the large wounded area, and his first impression was that these may have been minute pellet wounds, although he now feels they were probably mere blood splotches or spots." It also mentioned that "he was aware of an unusual odor which was similar to the odor which one smells when a firecracker is exploded."

"Does that fairly and accurately reflect your recollections at the time of the assassination?" Webb asked.

"Yes, sir; it does."

When Webb completed his questioning, Stokes recognized Rep. Robert Edgar of Pennsylvania.

"Let me begin by asking you, while you were in the army, did your duties include any intelligence activities?"

"No, sir; it didn't."

"Did you think of it as being a little bit unusual to be asked just a few months after assuming your duties as a Memphis police officer to be an undercover agent?"

"No, sir; I didn't think it was unusual at all." Mac explained that the undercover assignment developed organically from the police department's concerns about the sanitation strike's potential for disorder.

Congressman Edgar didn't try to hide his skepticism. "It is a little confusing to me how someone could walk in off the street and get an assignment to get to be an undercover agent with the Invaders and just go down to a building someplace and walk in and say, 'Hi, my name is Marrell McCollough. I am a student. I would like to get involved in your organization.'"

"Not quite that simple, sir." Mac explained that the upheaval of the sanitation strike gave him opportunities to engage with the Invaders, and it took time for him to gain their acceptance.

Noting that Mac was the first person to arrive at King's side after he was shot, Edgar asked him to describe what he did when he got there.

"He had a severe wound in his face and neck," Mac said. "And going through the police academy, I had been taught first aid, and the first thing came to my mind was to try to give him first aid."

"Could any of the actions have contributed to the death of Dr. King?"

Mac's heart dropped. He never imagined someone reaching that conclusion.

"To the contrary, it was designed to help save his life, but unfortunately it didn't. And to answer your question, no, sir; it couldn't have."

The next congressmen to question him—Richardson Preyer of North Carolina, Walter Fauntroy of D.C., Harold Ford of Tennessee, and Stokes—struck a similarly incredulous tone.

"You have given us a somewhat different picture than I, at least, had of the Invaders from general reading in the press," said Preyer, a former federal judge. "You were telling this committee the Invaders was a bona fide student movement that arose among students. It was not something set up by any governmental agency as a front for anything?"

"The Invader group was not a front for anything," Mac said. "It was just, as I said, grassroots young people in the community."

The implied charge against the Invaders took him aback. Not only was he under suspicion, but the Invaders were, too.

Congressman Fauntroy, a civil rights leader who'd been a friend to King, asked Mac if he knew the Invaders had approached the FBI for funds at one point.

"The Invaders? I am not even aware of that to this day, sir."

"I take it your answer would be to the negative to the claim that you were an agent provocateur and that you were running around encouraging them to engage in acts of violence?"

"That was totally against the police department's charter," Mac said. "It was totally against anything I would've done, so you are right, I definitely deny that."

Congressman Ford, whose district included Mac's old stomping ground of South Memphis, took an especially dim view of Mac's activities.

"You infiltrate the Invaders as an undercover agent for the Memphis Police Department, yet assured us that you did not participate in their activities," he said. "A young country boy from Tunica, Mississippi, walks into the big city, and the Invaders, a community-oriented group—and I don't think they were that radical, I think they were just concerned about the welfare and interest of the total Black community in Memphis—join with and participate with them, and they never questioned you. And they go to Carver High School and the other schools and turn the schools out, and you stand over by the tree and let it happen, and go back to the meeting the next night and say, 'Right on, brothers.'"

"Congressman, I have to admit that your characterization in all fairness is not one which I hope to have presented to this committee, so I will go back over what I have testified." He addressed Ford's statement point by point, noting the Invaders' loose organization and his use of his car to gain their confidence. "The other part, the innocence, being right out of the country, thank you for that, but again, I think I was resourceful, and I used what I had to the best of my ability, and I was able to get into the group and protect my integrity and the integrity of the police department and report fairly and report objectively about the group. I had a job to do, I was assigned to it, and I did it well, as far as I'm concerned."

Ford yielded back the balance of his time, and Chairman Stokes posed his own questions. "You are aware of the speculation that has grown up around Dr. King's having been in some way maneuvered out on the balcony," he said. "In light of the fact that it was known that James Earl Ray checked into the rooming house at around 3:00 p.m. that afternoon, there was speculation as to how he would know that Dr. King would be out on the balcony, and he would thereby be able to shoot him from the bathroom window. You have heard that, have you not?"

"This is the first time I have heard that he was maneuvered outside so that he could be assassinated," Mac said.

After a few more questions, from Stokes, then Fauntroy again, Chairman Stokes told Mac he was entitled to five minutes to explain or amplify his answers.

"Thank you very much," Mac said. "I hope that I have been helpful to the committee. I have been honest with you, and that is all I have to say."

Mac didn't remain to hear testimony from Calvin Taylor, John Smith, and Charles Cabbage, choosing instead to slip out of the chamber and head home. Relieved that he got through his testimony with his career and dignity intact, he couldn't put the episode behind him soon enough. His main worry, the disclosure of his CIA employment, never materialized; for that, he was thankful.

Had he remained, he would have heard testimony from these former Invaders that aligned with his in many respects—and was even vaguely appreciative of his presence in the group. Perhaps he would have found himself agreeing with Cabbage's closing remarks, which described in poignant terms the predicament in which Mac and these men now found themselves:

> When the federal government does not live up to its responsibility to protect the rights of all its citizens, it opens up a Pandora's box of subterfuge, innuendo, and outright distortion of the real truth. It is in this void that speculators are able to actually formulate and promote lies that tend to muddy the waters and create history based on nonexistent facts and honest, unsubstantiated theories, all stated to make the roads of truth more winding.

> A very cold trail now exists after ten years of inaction within these years. It is highly likely that the guilty will remain hidden and obscure while innocent victims are free game to misled seekers of truth, who in their zeal care not who they defame or libel.

If Mac had heard current and former FBI agents' testimony the previous week, he would have learned additional sickening details about the rampant racism and vitriol against King inside the bureau, with one agent admitting that he may have said either "We finally got the SOB!" or "They finally got the SOB!" when he heard that King had been murdered. Another agent's testimony that a high-level official consistently stymied efforts to recruit Black employees would have further confirmed his already devolving opinion of the Bureau.

Perhaps he would have read, in an exhibit to that testimony, the words of King himself regarding Black law enforcement officers, excerpted from an article he wrote for *The Nation* magazine:

> If, for instance, the law-enforcement personnel in the FBI were integrated, many persons who now defy federal law might come under restraints from which they are presently free. If other law-enforcement agencies under the Treasury Department, such as the Internal Revenue Service, the Bureau of Narcotics, the Alcohol Tax Unit, the Secret Service and Customs had an adequate number of field agents, investigators and administrators who were Negro, there would be a greater respect for Negroes as well as the assurance that prejudicial behavior in these agencies toward citizens would cease.

21.

Land

When I heard Dad and his wife, Patsy, were buying land in South Carolina in the early 2000s, I couldn't understand it. I'd spent much of my life either plotting to escape the South or vowing never to return. I would've thought he viewed things similarly, having grown up in Mississippi during the Jim Crow era. And it was in the South that he witnessed one of history's most devastating and pivotal acts of racial violence. To launch the kind of life he dreamed of, he had to leave. So why, when he could retire practically anywhere he chose, would he return?

"I'd originally planned to move back to Mississippi," he told me when I asked.

What?

"But it got too hot in the summer. It was hotter than I remembered it as a boy."

But what about discrimination, narrow-mindedness?

"I wouldn't want to raise kids here," he said. He described how voters in his newly adopted home shot down a local referendum for a small increase in property taxes to fund an education center. "Some folks just don't believe in the value of education."

"So what brought you back?"

"It reminds me of how I grew up." He enjoyed being close to the land, he said, planting a garden and watching it grow, taking care of animals. He decided on South Carolina after visiting with Patsy in the 1990s and falling in love with the scenery and the mild climate. They bought a parcel of land, and then more, and soon they had enough acreage for a small farm, complete with a barn, goats, and two ponds stocked with fish.

The first thing he did after closing was plant a garden. He bought a tractor and used it to clear a large plot, planting familiar vegetables from his childhood—tomatoes, potatoes, okra, collard greens.

After a few years, they built a large, handsome house with a tin roof. Dad said he chose the roof because he wanted to hear the raindrops drumming on it as he remembered from childhood.

After talking to Dad and considering the story of his early life, I began to understand why he moved back down South and reimagined his life there. I realized that though I thought I was running from the place, I'd wound up doing something similar.

Perhaps it's something most of us do on some level—try to recreate a place where we spent our formative years. For me, that's my maternal grandparents' white bungalow in Memphis's semi-industrial Douglass neighborhood.

Though their house sat on only a tenth of an acre of land, their place seemed as vast and varied as a country estate when I was a child. I spent more time there than I did at my own home a few miles away—nearly every weekday after school and over the summer.

Though close in proximity, Douglass and the neighborhood of Vollintine-Evergreen where I lived had completely different atmospheres. Douglass was historically Black, and the typical home was a neatly kept wooden bungalow on a small square of land. Every few blocks or so, you'd find a corner store where you could buy candy, chips, a cold drink, or hot pickles and pickled pig's feet from giant jars by the cash register. People sat on their porches, walked down the sidewalk, rode bicycles in the street. There were not one but two candy ladies on my grandparents' street selling penny candy and syrupy homemade freeze cups at bargain rates. By contrast, my neighborhood of Evergreen was historically white, though the white people had largely moved out as Black people moved in. The slightly larger homes sat on slightly larger lots, and while there may have been corner stores, I never went to any. Noticeably fewer people sat on porches, walked down the sidewalk, rode bikes in the street. If there was a candy lady—and there had to have been one—I didn't know her.

Grandma and Granddaddy moved to Douglass from the Mississippi Delta in the late 1940s, raising seven children in the same 1,100-square-foot house that became a second home to Micah and me. Ma told us stories of chasing and being chased around the yard by pet chickens and sitting in the living room with Granddaddy watching boxing as he pumped his fists and shifted his feet with the fighters on the screen. By the time Micah and I showed up with Mom in 1979, the chickens were gone, but Granddaddy still boxed along with the Friday night fights. Echoes of Ma and her siblings filled the air.

It was here I learned that a piece of land is a world. On a small parcel in North Memphis, Grandma and Grandaddy cultivated order, identity, and a measure of self-reliance every bit as much as they tended the trees, grass, and gardens.

The yard consisted of two kingdoms: the front, an outward-facing province of diplomacy and ornamental plants and neighborhood vistas, and the back, an insular region of industry, agriculture, and frontier. Connecting the two realms were narrow side yards that, for Micah and me, served as high-speed transit routes.

The front yard was the respectably dressed side, with the green and plush lawn, the rosebushes, the slender Japanese maple, the tall loblolly pine, the round holly bush with red berries. It was for games that you wanted other kids to join, like Red Light, Green Light and Duck, Duck, Goose. We'd play outside until the sun sank below the houses across the street, the streetlights came on, and a chorus of june bugs droned their languorous, buzzing refrain.

The front yard was also a watchtower, a place to look out for danger. From the porch, you could see who was walking or driving down the street. You knew who belonged and who didn't. Every once in a while, Grandma or Grandaddy would peer down the street with a furrowed brow. They'd spotted a white person, which they deemed inherently suspicious. The more I learned about Black history, the more I understood why.

The backyard, on the other hand, was the more intimate and interesting side, with its garden, patchy crabgrass, workbench, fishing boat, and green 1960s-era Ford pickup truck. The truck ran better than it looked like it would, at least on the rare occasions Granddaddy drove it. A couple of times, he let Micah and me sit in the truck bed for quick trips to the hardware store, our backs to the cab and the wind in our faces as he drove the minimum speed limit. It was almost as much fun as an amusement park ride. For her part, Grandma never learned to drive and was always a passenger, but only in the boxy blue Chevrolet Caprice parked in the driveway—never the truck.

Then there was the garden, which took up about a quarter of the backyard. The crops were always the same: tomatoes, cucumbers, okra, yellow squash, collard greens, cabbage, and eggplants. I was partial to the fragrant and bristled cucumbers, as well as the okra, but I wasn't a fan of the pungent greens.

Cornbread, Grandma and Granddaddy's staff of life, was a daily dish that figured into one of their most puzzling, least likeable (to me) snacks: cornbread crumbled into a glass of buttermilk and eaten with a spoon. Its combination of viscous tartness and gritty saltiness never made sense to me. I couldn't understand why they didn't at least add sugar. But Micah and I mostly ate as they did when we were there, which was how I imagine they'd eaten for much of their lives. My favorite meal there was breakfast—tender buttermilk biscuits made from scratch, plus rice and bacon or sausage, maybe with eggs. It wasn't until I left for college that I realized most Americans didn't eat rice for breakfast.

Grandma and Granddaddy's front door had three layers: the flimsy screen door on the inside, then the thick honey-oak door with a long window covered by a gauzy white curtain, and finally, the wrought-iron door rendered in whirling acanthus leaves. Directly behind these doors was the living room, with its variegated brown shag carpet and plush furniture covered in clear plastic. An imposing television console on the room's left side served as the focal point, next to a window mostly taken up by an air conditioning unit. Thin veneers of dark wood paneling shrouded the walls.

Directly across from the television, a three-foot longcase clock hung high on the wall over the gold velvet armchair where Grandma sat, its brass pendulum meting out the seconds in languid swoops. Installed in the wall nearby was a tall, rectangular heater; more often than not, you'd see a long, skinny switch lying across the top of it. Grandma and Granddaddy kept it there more for deterrence than actual disciplinary action, a heraldic symbol of jurisdiction.

On a quiet afternoon, you might find Grandaddy napping in his red velvet brocade armchair, the TV off so as not to "burn out the picture tube," as they sometimes warned, while Grandma worked in the kitchen. You'd hear the air conditioner's steady hum as it pumped out sweet, cold air, the quiet occasionally punctuated by the sound of dishes or Micah and me playing. The longcase clock *gong*-ed on the hour and half-hour.

The dining room, also wood paneled, was right off the living room. Grandma's crystal, china, and porcelain filled it, and a shimmering crystal chandelier hung over a glossy dining table spanning nearly the length of the room. Red brocade drapes hung at the windows.

Proceeding directly through the living room opposite the front door, you'd enter the kitchen with its red terrazzo floor and enameled steel countertops. At the back of the kitchen was a doorway into an addition, also wood paneled. The only giveaway that it was an add-on was a slight step down into its small vestibule, where there was a bookcase containing a full set of oxblood-colored 1954 World Book encyclopedias. The bookcase also held several thick photo albums and a mishmash of other books.

I'd turn the photo albums' clingy plastic pages and see snippets of graduations, weddings, and births, as well as casual and even silly moments, in crumbling sepia-toned portraits, sunny 1970s Polaroids, and muted drugstore prints. One photo in particular riveted me, a black-and-white image of Mom's siblings standing next to a sign reading COLORED DAY AT THE MEMPHIS ZOO. I studied it many times, searching for hints of sadness behind their eyes.

But most of all, I pored over the encyclopedias. I probably read the better part of that entire set. I'm not sure what prompted me to do it other than sheer boredom, especially during unstructured summer days that stretched out before us like dry pavement. When I later read how an imprisoned Malcolm Little—before he became Malcolm X—read the dictionary from cover to cover, I recognized the feeling of disappearing into a book to travel to all sorts of other worlds.

In the mid-1980s, when I was eleven or so, I interviewed Grandma and Granddaddy. For all the time I'd spent with them over the years, I realized I knew little about their early lives and the stories of their families. Occasionally, they'd let slip little anecdotes—some amusing, others bitterly revealing of the discrimination they endured in the Mississippi Delta during the early decades of the twentieth century. But much of their lives lay behind a heavy curtain that rarely opened. They didn't like talking about the past, and if their conversation touched on it, they didn't linger there.

As I slouched cross-legged on the living room's shag carpet, Grandma sat languid and elegant in her armchair, its plastic upholstery cover crinkling beneath her when she shifted. A few feet away, Granddaddy perched on his red armchair, also covered in plastic. They gazed at nothing in particular—nothing visible to me, anyway—while I formed my questions: What were the names of the towns where they were born? What were the names of their parents, grandparents, great-grandparents? What were the oldest tales they could recall?

They answered in turn, hesitantly at first, noting dates and surnames, mentioning towns, states, and even another country, Cuba, through which Granddaddy's ancestors passed before landing in the American South. I scribbled notes in pencil on a scrap of newspaper, the only paper I had handy.

This would be our only interview, extracting mostly biographical particulars. I took home the scrap of paper bearing my notes and put it in a desk drawer, where it lay for years among a jumble of trinkets and ephemera before disappearing in the whirlwind of packing for college. It never resurfaced, and I always regretted my failure to guard it more closely.

It later dawned on me that they *had* shared many of their stories with me, just not in an obvious way. I only had to pay attention to what they were saying with their house, their land, the way they lived. They may not have talked much about their upbringing, but their place did, with its rose bushes, vegetable garden, layered front doors, sumptuous chairs and couch under clear plastic, dining room chandelier, and cornbread with buttermilk. I wasn't only in a North Memphis bungalow; I was in a sliver of Mississippi that Grandma and Granddaddy had planted and cultivated.

While I had fond memories of Grandma and Granddaddy's lifestyle, I aspired to a completely different one, the exalted "deluxe apartment in the sky" lauded in *The Jeffersons'* theme song. Sitting in front of Grandma and Granddaddy's console television, taking in season after season of that show, plus nighttime soaps like *Dallas* and *Dynasty*, I set my sights on shimmering urban sophistication at an early age. I wanted a doorman and skyline views. I'd survey the industrial silhouettes behind the houses across the street and pretend they were skyscrapers.

The closest I ever got to that was a studio apartment in a mid-rise downtown D.C. building. Eventually, I wound up in a row house in the heart of the city's Northwest quadrant. It had no front yard, except for a couple of patches of dirt near the black metal staircase up to the front door. The backyard was so tiny that only an old-fashioned manual lawnmower could be used. Still, having a little bit of land awakened in me an interest in cultivating something and tending to it. I bought a few flowers and planted them by the front steps.

The next morning, I found only neatly dug circles where the flowers had been. Some pitiable soul had stolen them. I gave up after that.

My move a year later to an American Foursquare house in midtown Houston took me several steps away from my high-rise dreams and closer to my grandparents' way of life. Built in 1929 on just over a tenth of an acre, the place had the obligatory lush lawn in front and back. In fact, it was too pretty to tear up for a garden. Instead, we built a box for a "square foot garden," with tomatoes, cucumbers, okra, cabbage, and lettuce. I fried the baby okra pods and enjoyed the flavors I remembered from childhood.

I visited Grandma and Granddaddy's house in my dreams from time to time. Granddaddy died when I was in college, and Grandma joined him a few years later, but they were as alive as ever in my dream life. We were together again in the white bungalow, everything taking on a golden-hued glow as if lit by the rays of a low-hanging sun.

Less than a decade after the move to Houston came the overseas moves and several years of living in company-owned housing. I told myself it was freeing, that now we could see the world without the responsibility of real property hanging over our heads. In Kazakhstan, I planted lettuce and a few flowers in our townhouse's narrow plant beds, but they soon withered in the crackling clay soil.

Then we moved to Nigeria, a much better gardening environment with its tropical climate and rich soil. We had a detached home this time, with glistening grass kept perfectly thick and even by a gardener—a staff member every household seemed to have. But I ceded the turf to him from the beginning, a decision that was only reinforced when I saw a several-foot-long monitor lizard striding through the backyard.

Moving to Tahoe put me in the least hospitable gardening environment of them all. Though we were on slightly more than a third of an acre, the land was a dry, rocky hillside. With the stresses of getting settled there with the kids, growing plants was the last thing on my mind.

This was my horticultural nadir. I didn't bother planting anything in the yard because it couldn't even sustain grass. The potted basil plants from the grocery store that I sat near the kitchen window died within days, no matter what I did. I even managed to kill an air plant.

I continued in this manner for four years until 2018, when the kids and I finally joined my husband in the verdant East San Francisco Bay Area. It's a fantastic place for gardening, and just walking around neighborhoods looking at plants was inspiring. But what really got me interested was the coronavirus pandemic, which brought our regular lives to a halt in March 2020.

It felt like a strange bookend to the period in our family life that began with the Ebola epidemic. While the Ebola outbreak caused us to physically separate, the pandemic pushed us closer than we ever could have imagined. Amid lockdowns and supply chain disruptions, we found ourselves thinking about survival and sustenance, prompting us to consider how much food we could coax out of our townhouse backyard. We planted our old standby vegetables—tomatoes, cucumbers, and okra, plus yellow squash—thinking they'd flourish as they had in Houston, but the tomatoes languished, and the okra died before producing a single pod.

We sold the Tahoe house with ease, as a stampede of buyers, mostly from the Bay Area, poured into the area, snapping up homes in record time. A couple of months later, we traded our townhouse for another place in the East Bay on nearly an acre of land. It was about as far from a deluxe apartment in the sky as you could get—a modest bungalow with wood-paneled walls and a single air conditioning unit rather than central air. We added a china cabinet, chandelier, and long table to the dining room. Grandma would've been proud.

The front yard featured a grove of rosebushes, and the backyard had a terraced garden with raised beds. We set to work on the beds, pulling weeds, fertilizing, tilling. We planted our old familiar lineup of vegetables, minus the okra this time, and gave them our full attention, watering and watching. We parked our Ford pickup truck at the end of the long, narrow driveway, as close to the backyard as a vehicle could get.

I wondered what Grandma and Granddaddy would have thought of the place, imagining how they might survey the raised beds and irrigation system. Would they know their garden had inspired mine?

For so long, I couldn't understand why Dad had willingly moved back down South, why he cared so much about having land and a garden. But now I was beginning to see that it came down to one word: culture, derived from the Latin word *cultura*, meaning "cultivation" or "growing." It meant tending and growing, creating order, and resting, too. It meant making a world.

Grandma and Granddaddy made a whole world, which was what Dad was doing, too. Now my family was beginning to do the same. Such is the power of culture—which they knew, and I was learning.

22.

Work of a Nation

In 1987, Mac returned to the U.S. from Central Africa, his most recent assignment in nearly seven years of working for the Directorate of Operations. He'd begun training for the Clandestine Service in 1982, following his stint in the Office of Security's Security Operations group. Now he was returning to the office where he got his start, Security, to take on his first managerial assignment: Branch Chief, Africa Division, at Headquarters.

While the branch chief's duties varied depending on the branch in question, they generally involved managing people and work product. It meant ensuring that people followed procedures, checking that their work adhered to guidelines, and handling employee evaluations, too. It was big responsibility, and rarely dull.

The last time he'd repatriated from working abroad, in 1967, he'd been a newly discharged military policeman struggling to find his next job. Now he was scaling career heights once scarcely imaginable. Having been one of the first officers to go from Security to Operations, he was taking on his biggest job to date, becoming a boss in an office where he'd once been a rookie. He could feel himself getting closer to the glass ceiling fixed above him, a feature so barely perceptible that he could almost forget it was there, until the light hit it a certain way every so often.

But for now, he was ascending. Who would have believed that a manual laborer making minimum wage at Memphis Sash & Door could do it? Probably not too many people from where he grew up in Mississippi, where a lot of folks thought a Black person could get only so high. Even Mac thought that way at times, which was why he was initially convinced that neither the Memphis Police Department nor the Agency would hire him.

Eugene would've believed it possible, though, which was why he encouraged Mac to apply for the police department job in the first place. And surely the seeds of belief were germinating in Mac, or else he would have stopped trying to achieve anything before he left Mississippi. Now those seeds had sprouted, carrying him upward and outward.

Arriving at Headquarters, he noticed something right away—not a change, but a lack of it. Given all the years he was gone, he thought the Agency would've made major progress in hiring Black officers, but that hadn't happened. In the buildings' long hallways, he was seeing more or less the same small number of officers of color as he had seven years earlier. He had some idea of why this was.

Part of it, he believed, had to do with how the Agency was approaching its grueling security clearance process. They'd begun hiring people who were easiest to clear, those who were least likely to have a spot on their background check, whether financial or legal trouble, foreign contacts, or something else. That alone weeded out many Black folks and others from marginalized groups, particularly those who had some life experience and hadn't gone straight through from high school to college to a professional career.

But there was more to it than that. Over time, he saw that things weren't as equitable as they appeared, despite his early impressions and somewhat unique personal experience. While it was nice to have Black and brown colleagues starting alongside him, something funny began to happen around year three: the white officers began pulling ahead, getting promoted to higher levels of seniority, while officers of color didn't, moving laterally to positions at roughly the same level. On paper, it looked justifiable. The white officers had completed more challenging assignments and taken on more responsibility. Their experience had more richness and depth.

But there was a story the résumés didn't tell. The assignments that were considered preparatory for more senior positions typically went to white officers. In some ways, that shouldn't have been surprising, yet it still hurt. Mac had expected better from a place like this, a federal agency filled with educated professionals who said the right things and presented the right image. With one glaring exception, he didn't hear the kinds of overtly racist comments and crude language he'd heard at the Memphis police department. Walking around and watching people and listening to what they said, one wouldn't necessarily think there was a race problem. Everything had a veneer of fairness on it.

But the real story was between the lines. It wasn't so much what people said or did, but what they *didn't* say or do that was harmful. While he couldn't necessarily divine their intentions, it didn't matter—the real issue was the impact.

Overall, the Agency's culture was clubby—white, male, Ivy League, and to some extent, Catholic. Officers hired and promoted people who looked and behaved as they did, and if you didn't fit that mold, you had a harder time gaining trust and confidence. The situation played out more or less the same way every time: An officer of color and a white officer came up for promotion, and the white officer got the job based on a more impressive résumé. What could the officer of color say to that?

This was something Black officers discussed among themselves, but they had to be careful about how they did it. Gathering in the cafeteria was an impossibility, as they all knew, though no one explicitly told them. It was just understood that white people would view such a gathering with suspicion, as if they were planning something. Similarly, Black officers were careful not to be seen fraternizing much with a Black coworker whose work was held in low regard, knowing that, in the eyes of others, the penumbra of incompetence would extend to them.

So the Black officers got together on weekends, usually at someone's home or a restaurant. In these places, they could speak candidly about what was happening at work and piece things together. If one of them missed out on a job for which they seemed well-qualified, they'd discuss what happened. Working together, they discerned patterns.

An officer without seniority couldn't do much about the situation except watch in frustration and commiserate with friends, and even then, they had to watch who they confided in. As in any workplace, you couldn't trust everyone, including some of those who seemed friendly. There were people so focused on advancing their careers that they'd sacrifice yours to make it happen, and you didn't want to walk into that kind of trap. One Black officer had been a rising star, sailing through promotions and racking up valuable assignments, when he mysteriously lost out on a big job. He was shocked, as was his boss, who'd gone to bat for him before the Career Board. Neither of them could figure out what had happened. Then one day his boss came to him with the rest of the story: A white friend of the Black officer had gotten the job after complaining to higher-ups that the Black officer was advancing too quickly.

Few Black officers had the power or influence to change things, and even fewer were willing to speak up and risk limiting their careers or garnering the resentment of their white colleagues. But Mac couldn't stand by in silence, nor would he accept that things had to remain this way. One day, he decided to raise it with someone in management.

"Why don't we have more African American officers?"

The man shrugged. "We're trying, but we just can't find them."

That can't be right, Mac thought.

Before he'd left for his overseas assignments, he'd worked on minority recruitment, as they called it at the time, serving for several years on a minority advisory council to George H. W. Bush when he was Director of Central Intelligence. A sea change came in 1981 when Bill Casey, appointed by President Reagan, came on as director.

Casey was openly hostile to the Agency's diversity efforts. "Why do I need a minority advisory council when I've got an Equal Employment Opportunity advisor?" he asked during his first and last meeting with the council, which lasted no more than fifteen minutes.

They tried to explain that its function was different than that of an EEO officer, that the council was concerned with minority officers' experiences, observations, and suggestions. But it made no difference.

Given that Casey's tenure lasted until 1987, the year Mac returned to Headquarters, the Agency's lack of progress in hiring Black recruits wasn't altogether surprising, even if it still felt like a slap in the face. Even more galling was attending Friday management team meetings and watching the retired white officer charged with leading minority recruitment announce three times over a six-month period that some Black recruit he'd been "processing" had failed the polygraph. Mac couldn't understand why the Agency wasn't doing any better than this.

By early 1988, Mac had had enough. He brought it up to his buddy Billy, who'd been working with the Director of Security, Jim. Billy took Mac's concerns to Jim, who quickly arranged a meeting with Mac.

In the meeting, Mac told Jim he didn't buy the story that the Agency couldn't find suitable Black recruits.

"Would you be willing to go find them?" Jim asked.

"Yes, but I want to keep my branch chief job while I do that."

Jim agreed. From 1988 through 1990, Mac took the lead on minority recruiting in Security, bringing on board more than sixty Black officers and putting the lie to the claim that there were few suitable Black candidates. Some people questioned his results, intimating that he must have somehow lowered standards—a telling reaction. But what he did was what recruiters had been doing all along for white candidates: visiting schools in every region of the country and finding them. He took to calling these recruits his Little Macs.

He traveled to dozens of colleges and universities—Notre Dame, Florida International University, St. John's University, historically Black Winston-Salem State. He visited high schools—including Memphis's Central, East, and Hamilton high schools—to speak with guidance counselors about encouraging students to explore a career path at the CIA.

He was far from the only person at the Agency working on minority recruitment. There was a Black woman, Barbara, who was well known for her recruiting work, and she gave him a lot of good advice on how to go about it. The Agency also had an established program, the Minority Undergraduate Program, known informally as Muppies, though they later changed the name because folks found it unappealing.

While CIA recruiters weren't welcome everywhere they went, things had calmed down from the 1960s, when their presences drew protests on some campuses. But even in the late 1980s, there were stories about them being unwelcome at some schools. Mac and the other recruiters never knew how they'd be received.

Their solution was to come up with throwaway aliases to put some distance between their real identities and their recruiting personas. It had nothing to do with covert activities—these were just pseudonyms in case things got dicey. Mac chose the name Micah McCabe.

Little did he know the tactic would one day put him in an uncomfortable spot reminiscent of his near misses while infiltrating the Invaders. In 1992, he was visiting a school in Southwest Virginia, passing out literature with a fellow officer, when he heard someone halfway across the room shout his name: "Marrell McCollough!"

He turned and saw a face he hadn't seen since his Delta Center High days in Mississippi. It was Cottrell, a friend of one of his high school buddies, and he was barreling over to Mac's recruiting table. Mac's mind went to the name tag he was wearing on his lapel, which read HELLO, MY NAME IS MICAH MCCABE.

Mac covered it with his hand. Then he tried to unpin it—a struggle to do with just one hand.

"Cottrell!" Mac said as the man arrived at the recruiting table. "How in the world did you recognize me after all these years?"

"Because you haven't changed any! You look just like you did!"

By that time, Mac had managed to unpin the name tag, which he now held cupped in his right hand. Which meant he couldn't shake hands with Cottrell. There was only one decent alternative: he gave the man a big hug.

One of Mac's first hires was a young Black man from the South who'd been active in his local community but didn't have a background in intelligence. They met over lunch, where Mac questioned him closely, assessing the answers as they came. He needed to know if this candidate could meet the additional scrutiny he was sure to get. Supervisors often labeled Black officers as poor writers—and if you didn't write well, you wouldn't last long at the Agency, where most roles demanded clear, concise, error-free prose. This subjective assessment made its way into performance reviews, though it was sometimes removed when supporting evidence failed to materialize.

Not wanting to risk losing credibility by hiring Black officers that wouldn't pass muster in one way or another, Mac asked the candidate to compose a note right there at the table. The man dashed it off and handed it to Mac, who read it with pleasure. The job offer letter went out soon after.

Mac expected a backlash for his diversity hiring efforts, and he got one. His immediate supervisor, the division chief, noted in his annual fitness report that his frequent recruiting trips were impeding his job performance. Until this review, his reports had been stellar. After reading the comment, Mac decided not to sign it.

"But you do know that much of the time you spent recruiting could've been put into your branch," the division chief snapped when he met with him about the report.

Mac didn't budge. "I was recruiting at the behest of the director of security. If you're going to put that in my report, we need to talk this out with him. He'll confirm that he asked me to do this, and I did that *plus* my branch chief job."

To the security director they went.

"No way in hell we're putting this in the fitness report," the security director said to Mac and the chagrined division chief. "Mac has done an excellent job, both for recruiting and as branch chief."

The vindication felt deeply satisfying. Mac had been right, and now there'd be no more argument about it. He could think of other situations where he'd been just as right, but that hadn't mattered. Most of all, he was glad to be able to help the next generation of Black officers. He was under no illusions that he'd gotten where he was on his own, either in his youth or here at the Agency. And while there had been white officers who'd helped him, there was nothing like having Black role models to show you what to expect and how to navigate. He remembered with gratitude an older officer named Willis who'd advised him informally, and he wanted to be a support for others who were in the position he'd found himself in more than once over the years—that of a rookie.

There weren't many others who were willing to be vocal about minority recruitment and retention. It set him apart among his peers, and not necessarily in a good way, at least in the eyes of his supervisors. The safest, surest route to upper management for a Black person at the Agency was the same as it was in most workplaces: perform the job with near-unerring excellence, and don't make waves. The moment you started talking about changing this and that way of doing things, that's when the roadblocks sprang up. Was it worth it, sacrificing upward mobility for people who were below you in seniority and couldn't do a thing for you career-wise? Not if your primary focus was your own advancement—and that tended to be most people's primary focus. But living like that seemed empty to Mac. If there was no larger purpose, if he couldn't use his position to help someone else, what was the point?

He knew this day was coming, and in fact had been bracing for it for more than a decade. Still, it managed to surprise him in 1991 when he climbed smack into the Agency's glass ceiling. He'd expected something subtler, slicker, more oblique than the dull thud of the Director of Security's words: "I'm never going to promote you to SIS."

"Never"—it's a hard, heavy word.

SIS was the Senior Intelligence Service—the highest levels of seniority that replaced the old supergrades of GS-16 through 18.

The way it happened was uncannily like a situation Mac had faced more than fifteen years earlier at the police department, where he never got promoted past patrolman though he'd been doing the work of a detective. At this point in his career, he'd had many promotions, traveled the globe, and spoke nearly fluent French, but in some ways he'd come full circle. *Plus ça change, plus c'est la même chose.*

Frank, the Security director, didn't like Mac; that much was clear. Mac could never figure out why. Was he offended that his first day on the job, Mac's office happened to be having a going-away party for the outgoing director? Maybe it felt like a snub and hurt his feelings. Maybe that's why he told Mac he'd been sent to Security to "break up the old boys' network," which was why he was never going to promote Mac to SIS.

Mac, a member of an old boys' network at the Agency? The idea was almost laughable, though it would be a bitter laughter.

The trouble began when Security released a list of officers it was recommending for promotion to SIS. It would be sending the list up to the Directorate of Administration for a final decision. If someone had asked Mac if his name were going to be on that list, he'd have had no doubt about it. He was a GS-15, senior officer level, and he'd been fast-tracked almost the entire way. He'd gotten the right assignments, performed with excellence, worked in supervisory roles. The only time he hit a speed bump was in going from 14 to 15, and it wasn't much of one—just one in-step promotion before he progressed to the next level. There was no reason to believe he wouldn't be rewarded with the next promotion, too.

No reason except one: the ceiling. And when Mac saw that his name wasn't on the list, he knew he'd reached it.

He set up a meeting with Frank to discuss the matter. When he walked into Frank's office, Frank got up from his desk and invited Mac to join him in the office's seating area. They sat in comfortable swivel chairs across from each other, and Mac asked why his name wasn't on the list.

That's when Frank hit him with the line about never promoting him to SIS, slowly swiveling the chair as he spoke. By the time the conversation ended—and it didn't take long—the man's back was turned to him.

By 1995, Mac had climbed through a tangle of management and nonmanagement positions: a couple more chief jobs in Security, then a stint as an investigator in the Inspector General's office. True to his word, Frank never did promote him to SIS, so Mac remained at GS-15.

Now he was back on another tour in Security, this time as a subject matter expert. He knew it wouldn't be dull, but the excitement that soon developed wasn't the kind he'd bargained for.

He was sitting at his desk when the phone rang.

"Mac, you're not gonna believe this."

It was Bill, a polygrapher friend who'd just returned to the U.S. from an overseas post. He'd stopped by an airport newsstand to pick up something to read when he noticed a book about King's assassination.

"I've got this book here, *Orders to Kill*, by a guy named Pepper. And it's basically saying you were part of a military unit that was responsible for killing Dr. King."

"What?"

"Yeah, I'll give it to you. I bought it so I could show you."

A little while later, he brought it by Mac's office, saying he was as disgusted as Mac was. Mac brought it home that evening, and the more he read, the angrier he got. How could someone publish a book riddled with lies?

It claimed that in June 1967—three months before he entered the police academy—the army hired him as an "intelligence informant" and attached him to the 111th MIG, based in Augusta, Georgia. The book then turned Mac's congressional testimony on its head, stating that he admitted to being an agent provocateur when he had specifically said the opposite. It was like reading fiction, except it was being sold as the truth.

Then the author turned to Mac's career in national intelligence. "When I tried to locate McCollough later, I learned he had disappeared from Memphis; it was rumored that he had gone to work for the CIA."

The thought arose in Mac's mind that he should sue for libel, but he quickly dismissed it. First, he couldn't see how any rational person would believe the book's far-fetched version of events. Second, litigating it would only bring attention to its lies about him. The last thing he needed to do was make a big deal out it. Still, he did need to make sure the Agency was aware.

———

In early 1997, the switchboard rang Mac's desk phone to tell him he had a call on the line.

"Is this Marrell McCollough?" the caller asked.

"Yes. Who's speaking?"

"I'm a producer from ABC's *Primetime Live*, and I'd—"

Mac slammed down the receiver.

How did they let this guy through? Mac thought. Normally, they were careful about putting through calls; unsolicited callers weren't supposed to be able to give the operator a name and get that person on the phone. It did happen from time to time, though, like the time one of his cousins called like that, and they'd put it through. Around the time of his cousin's call, a *Philadelphia Inquirer* reporter reached him the same way. Similarly, he'd hung up before a conversation could begin.

Soon afterward, Mac learned that the producer's call had been featured briefly in an episode of *Primetime Live* with Sam Donaldson. The show painted him as knowing Loyd Jowers, a Memphis restaurateur who claimed to have hired police officer Earl Clark—the older brother of Mac's first partner, Tom—to kill King. Between this and the book, the lies seemed to be proliferating, if not gathering themselves into a writhing hydra.

As Mac had done before, he put the story out of his mind, focused on his work, went about his daily routines. Meanwhile, the monster of a story continued to grow in size and reach. In 1998, he heard there was a big proceeding in Memphis concerning King's assassination. He didn't keep up with the details, though it was covered in all the big newspapers. King's family had filed a wrongful death lawsuit against Jowers and unnamed coconspirators in state court, seeking $100 in nominal damages. And who had they hired to represent them? *Orders to Kill* author William Pepper.

It felt like things were coming full circle to the 1978 House Select Committee on Assassinations, right down to the call he got from the Office of General Counsel—but this time, they had news about a Justice Department investigation of King's assassination. The King family had requested an inquiry into Jowers's allegations that he was involved in the murder, including his claim that Mac and other law enforcement officers met inside his restaurant to plan the crime.

DOJ investigators had contacted OGC to arrange for Mac to come in for an interview and polygraph examination.

Mac swallowed his anger. "Sure."

—

In a downtown D.C. office building, Mac and an OGC lawyer met in a small room with a Justice Department investigator, a young Black man. The investigator began by asking Mac the same kinds of questions the congressional investigators had posed twenty years earlier: What did he see? What did he know?

The topic turned to a place called Jim's Grill, Loyd Jowers's restaurant. It occupied the ground floor of the rooming house from which James Earl Ray was convicted of firing the shot that killed King.

"What about it?" Mac asked.

"What can you tell me about it?"

"I can't tell you anything about it because I haven't been in there. The only thing I know is it was across the street from the Lorraine."

"But you know the place."

Mac knew *of* the place. It was a restaurant for whites. Black people didn't go in there and wouldn't have been welcomed if they did—as anybody who understood anything about 1968 Memphis would know.

"Yeah, but I wouldn't have gone in there."

"Why not?"

"It was for whites."

"Am I to believe that you weren't allowed in that restaurant?"

"You can believe what you want. I'm just telling you how it was."

Around they went, Mac's blood pressure rising as he tried to get this young Black investigator to understand how Black people were treated in Memphis during an era when the man was probably still in diapers. Though he was too young to remember those times, that was no excuse. This was the world he was supposed to be investigating, and he should've had a basic understanding of its racial dynamics.

"So you're saying you didn't meet anybody there?'

"No."

"Did you know Lieutenant Eli Arkin of the Memphis Police Department?"

"Yes."

"Did you know Special Agent William Lawrence of the FBI?"

"Yes."

"Did you ever go to Loyd Jowers's restaurant, Jim's Grill?"

"No."

"So you didn't meet with Lieutenant Arkin or Special Agent Lawrence in there?"

Anger rose in Mac's chest. "No."

"Were you involved in planning Dr. King's assassination?"

"No." Though outraged, Mac managed to maintain his composure.

"Okay, come with me for your polygraph examination."

"Sure."

Leaving his lawyer behind, Mac followed the investigator into an adjacent room, fuming as the man attached polygraph sensors to him. More than thirty years had passed since the assassination, during which time both the FBI and Congress had conducted two separate investigations. But despite Mac's years of honorable service in law enforcement and intelligence during those years, all it took was the word of this white man Jowers to put him in that polygraph chair.

The polygraph sensors now in place, the investigator again asked Mac if he knew Lieutenant Arkin and Special Agent Lawrence, if he ever went to Jim's Grill, and if he met Lieutenant Arkin and Special Agent Lawrence there. Mac gave the same answers as before, then the interviewer detached the polygraph sensors

"Please wait in the other room while I take a look at what we have."

Minutes after Mac had taken a seat next to the OGC lawyer in the adjoining room, the interviewer entered.

"There's an issue with your polygraph. The results are inconclusive."

Mac stared at him.

"I don't think you're being truthful."

"That's not my problem," Mac said. "I know I've been truthful with you."

"With what we have here, we can't determine that."

"About what?"

"Jim's Grill. About going in there."

With that, Mac hit the breaking point. "Do you know what Memphis was *like* in '68?"

The interviewer didn't answer.

"Do you know what the environment was like? Black folks were not *welcome* in Jim's Grill. It was a segregated, redneck bar where we weren't welcome. And if you *did* see any Black folks in there, they would've been washing dishes, not socializing and drinking and hanging out. Anybody who knew anything about Memphis at that time would know how totally ridiculous that question is."

"That's irrelevant. Are you just trying to cover for yourself?"

"What do you mean it's not relevant? It's relevant to the point that I didn't go there and wouldn't have gone there!"

"Mr. McCollough, I can see that something has you upset."

"I *told* you what's got me upset. Because the premise of these questions is ridiculous—that's what's got me upset!"

"Okay, let's just end here," the interviewer said.

As Mac and the OGC lawyer rose to leave, Mac was furious that he'd had to spend his time on interviews and polygraphs based on the lies of this Jowers character, that Jowers's word had been given equal weight to his—or perhaps more. It was the ultimate insult, as if his word and his life counted for nothing.

A short while later, DOJ invited Mac to take a second polygraph. He agreed. He went back to the same building with the same OGC lawyer, where he met the same investigator.

"Something had you upset the last time, so we're just trying to figure it out," the investigator said.

Mac just looked at him.

"We're not only looking at the assassination," he continued. "We also catch *spies*."

Mac said nothing. It was nonsense, an amateurish investigatory tactic. If he were some kind of double agent, wouldn't the CIA have figured that out during one of the reinvestigations he had to undergo every five years? But unlike the investigator, the folks at the CIA knew what they were doing.

The man went through the same questions as before, and Mac gave the same answers. The man said he could go.

This time, the polygraph results noted no deception.

Swallowing his anger and revulsion, he willed himself to carry on with life as normally as possible. The King family's litigation ended in December 1999, with the jury finding Jowers and unnamed coconspirators responsible for King's death and awarding the King family the $100 in nominal damages they sought. It wasn't until the following June that the Justice Department completed its investigation. In a detailed report, they concluded that Jowers's allegations weren't credible and that the evidence presented in the *King v. Jowers* case "was both contradictory and based on uncorroborated secondhand and thirdhand hearsay accounts." Due to a lack of reliable evidence of a conspiracy involving Jowers or anyone else to kill King, they decided there was no basis for further investigation.

When Mac learned about all this, his feelings were as jumbled as the news itself. He was glad the Justice Department's findings showed that conspiracy theories involving him lacked any sound basis. But he didn't think they should've been dignified with a federal investigation in the first place. He understood that the trial verdict would color some people's view of him, but it was out of his hands. He couldn't control what other people thought and did, only himself. That was the mindset that had seen him through every predicament he ever faced, and it would get him through this, too.

Nothing can prepare you for your retirement ceremony—the rush of emotions and the feeling of looking back while moving forward. It was 1999, and Mac's colleague and close friend Billy, now godfather to two of his children, made the presentation before the ceremony hall filled with people, including family and coworkers from every stage of his CIA career. Lauded by speaker after speaker, Mac received a bronze-colored medal "for honorable service," as its raised lettering read. On the medal's opposite side was the Agency's seal, with its compass rose, shield, and eagle.

Mac had reached the pinnacle of his career that year, at least on paper. He was a manager, but it was a desk job, an old man's job. His last *good* job was Chief of Africa Security, his post before this one. But then he got promoted to the one that would be his last, to work on policy. It might've looked good on a résumé, but it felt like a gentle way of being brought in from the field. It was just a preamble to retirement.

A swell of pride carried him through the event, a professional wake of sorts he could enjoy while alive and well. His work there, a pixel point in the country's national intelligence picture, had meant something, and as controversial as the Agency's image was, he had no doubt that he'd helped keep Americans safe.

At GS-15, he was retiring as one of the highest-ranking members of his recruiting class. Only one of his classmates had surpassed him, a guy who made it to SIS, but plenty of people retired at GS-12 or 13. When he joined the Agency in 1974, the highest-ranking Black officer he knew of was a GS-13, and if somebody got to 12, they'd say, "Oh, wow, I made it." Mac knew he had these folks to thank for paving the road he was able to travel.

Could he have journeyed a little further if he hadn't made so many waves about diversity? It was no secret that in 1996 he filed an EEOC complaint. But that wasn't about him, it was about equity for all officers and tearing down hidden barriers. He had no regrets about it because it achieved the results he wanted: more Black officers promoted to the SIS level, a Black Director of Security, an outside study done on the impact of office dynamics on officers of color. With both fists, he'd managed to knock a few jagged chunks out of the glass ceiling, even if he wound up slicing his knuckles. Some might have said he sacrificed himself, but that wasn't how he saw it. To him, it was a matter of doing what needed to be done. He'd never been one to take the safe route.

So while he had no way of knowing how much his internal activism had harmed his career, it didn't matter. His proudest achievement was his Little Macs, the Black officers he'd recruited and mentored over the years. This was an area where he *knew* he'd made a lasting impact. Not only that, but he'd also chaired a blue-sky committee that recommended best practices for recruiting and retaining Black officers—and held people accountable, too. His was more than a career; it was a legacy.

Now he was ready to move on, not only because the work wasn't as much fun as it used to be, but also because he'd always planned to retire at fifty-five. At that age, you still had a lot of time ahead of you. That's when you could get your *really* good government contract job and become one of those folks they called Beltway Bandits. You leave the government, taking with you the expertise you've gained over all those years of service, and take it to a contractor. They pay more.

Looking back over the life he'd led, and the one he was set to lead, he was satisfied. He'd had a varied career, working in Africa, Latin America, and the Middle East. He'd witnessed acute inflection points in the history of national intelligence—a hostage rescue that garnered the world's rapt attention and the ensnaring of traitor Aldrich Ames. Of the Agency's four main divisions—the Directorates of Intelligence, Operations, Administration, and Science & Technology—he'd worked in two, Operations and Administration, plus the Inspector General's office. His path hadn't been a straight line but meandering and circular, in the way that a trail up a steep hill encircles it as it advances.

That his labors took him from the army to menial odd jobs to the Memphis Police Department to the CIA may seem improbable, so much so that it's almost understandable to resort to labyrinthine conspiracy theories to try to make sense of what happened. The truth is far simpler, if more unfathomable. It was his life's circumstances that laid his path, based on his choices at each step.

What or who spun that web of circumstances, with all its synchronicities, horrors, and triumphs? It's a question with answers as numerous as a gemstone's scintillating facets, collecting light to reveal depth and fire.

Could these answers even be written in the stars? After all, the figure of a kneeling man illuminates the night sky as the constellation Hercules, the complicated ancient protagonist of many journeys and labors.

I'd return to this question countless times over the years as I considered the events that shaped my own life in ways reminiscent of his—due to either similarities or sharp differences. Economic circumstances hadn't compelled me to enlist in the army, thanks in part to my father's financial support and the employment opportunities his CIA career provided for me. In fact, I turned down the opportunity to apply for an Agency-sponsored program that would've paid for my college education in exchange for a commitment to work there when I graduated. I just didn't think it was for me. Looking back, the choice reflects breathtaking privilege. Not that I was anything close to wealthy. I just had enough economic and social resources at my disposal to have choices.

Still, when I arrived at my chosen university to pursue my chosen studies, I was broke—so broke that I fell into the trap that ensnares many a naïve and financially illiterate freshman as they walk down their campus's main drag: seductive credit card companies, with their slick sales pitches, easy applications, and cheap promotional loot. By the time I arrived at Langley as a sophomore for my first summer internship, I'd racked up a lot of debt, and I wasn't paying the bills on time because I didn't have the money. At orientation in a dome-shaped building folks called "the Bubble," a woman I didn't recognize approached me during one of the breaks. She told me I needed to clean up my credit, which was putting me on shaky ground.

And I did clean it up, fast. Then I went on to a career in law that paid enough that I'd never have to worry about my finances again. Not that I was rich, but the money gave me choices.

There were other points at which my life echoed Dad's in eerie ways, such as my becoming (briefly) an assistant federal public defender—the opposite side of the courtroom from the police—or the short time I lived in Africa, though under corporate rather than governmental auspices. If his path had been improbable, mine had followed a similar, if less momentous, course.

I sometimes wonder what my life would look like if I hadn't asked Dad about his story, or if I hadn't pushed through my tears to read past the third page of his notes. It scares me to think about that. It's like contemplating a brush with death—a near miss with unfathomable harm and loss. There had been many opportunities to drop the entire matter. Had it not been for the Ebola epidemic, who knows if I would have ever allowed myself the space and silence to be haunted by it. In Nigeria, there were always distractions, which I eagerly sought out: travel, tennis lessons, lunches. I didn't have nearly as many choices in Tahoe. I had to sit with my thoughts.

I suppose someone else might have tried to tell the story if I'd let it go—not that Dad would've cooperated. That prospect alone was a good reason to step in. Not only did I not want to see more lies, half-truths, and speculation about him, I didn't want him treated without care, handled as a curiosity and mined for content. So many Black figures' stories are exploited this way: "Look at this cool person/history/music I've discovered!" or "Look how this person helped *me* connect with *my* humanity!" It's like the storytelling version of colonialism. The documentation of a history creates authority—hence the word "author"—and in our society, authority isn't often allowed to Black people.

The Agency has two mottos, one official and the other unofficial. The official one is "The Work of a Nation. The Center of Intelligence." Dad knows something about the nation's work because he did it for decades, ever since he was duped into dropping out of school to enlist in the army. But he isn't bitter about that. The army gave him the kind of structure he had to fight for growing up, the structure he needed to launch his dreams. He values order in the truest and highest sense—the same rules, expectations, and considerations applied to everyone, every time—which is the only way to have the freedom to achieve, to grow, and simply to *be* in a world that constantly tears at your humanity. He'd spent his life telling himself that this kind of order was possible, that he could work within the current system while pushing toward something better. Wasn't that what the folks who blazed the trail for him had done? It sounded dangerously close to the proposition that you could uphold the status quo and change it at the same time—incrementalism, at best. But he hadn't seen progress made in any other way.

As for the CIA's unofficial motto, it's engraved on a white marble wall in the Headquarters lobby:

AND YE SHALL KNOW THE TRUTH

AND THE TRUTH SHALL MAKE YOU FREE.

All his life, freedom had been his lodestar, the goal of his strivings. It wasn't an abstract concept, but something real that could be felt and experienced, like lungs filled with air and vegetables sprouting from earth. It was patched clothes, going to school, and playing baseball on Saturdays. And it was also duties, being responsible to others. As simple as these things might appear, they hadn't been easy to attain and keep. It took community, order, and truth, which kept him alive, built him up, and gave him something to work for.

Now Dad is last of the twelve McCollough children still living, the patriarch of a network of McColloughs and related families spread throughout the country. He's located many of them himself over the years and welcomes them to yearly reunions he organizes. The guests are so numerous, some of them charter buses to attend. He devotes time to political and social causes, too, even joining an estimated 300,000 protesters at the 2018 Women's March in Washington.

He has community and order. And though truth had been trickier to get at, he has that, too. Because as he approached freedom—or something like it—he realized it was tethered to unspoken truths he'd kept inside himself, secret and heavy.

Acknowledgments

I would like to thank God. I also thank my father, Marrell McCollough, for sharing his story with me and the world. I thank my mother, Peggy McKenzie, for molding me. Thanks to my loving husband, Dimitri, for supporting and strengthening me in every respect, and to my children, Lee, Nelson, and Isaac, for bringing me joy.

Thanks to my siblings: Micah, for helping me remember everything and laugh at the same time; Kelly; Maya; Keenan; and Terry. To my stepfather, Kevin, for being an ever-present help with eagle eyes and keen journalistic instincts, and my stepmother, Patsy, for your steadfast loving-kindness. To Mary Hogan, for kindness. To Alexis, for telling me to just write the book. To Kamala Miller-Lester, for life-sustaining hilarity. To my aunts and uncles and cousins, my first community. To my entire family. And to my teachers. (There is some overlap here.)

Thanks to Jane Vandenburgh, whose friendship and wisdom I treasure. To Margaret Wilkerson Sexton, for deep and abiding sisterhood in writing. To Kathryn Goldberg, for shared joy in craft, ideas, aesthetics, and Friso. To Andrea Avery and Lauren Hough, for bonds of friendship that began at a writing workshop and grew as we did. To Janine Kovac and Julia Park Tracey, for solidarity from Section 10 onward. To June Sylvester Saraceno, for fellowship, fun, and inspiration. To Gayle Brandeis, for the creative nonfiction writing course that put me on this path, and also for the title of this book.

Thanks to everyone at Counterpoint Press who helped bring this book into the world, including my editor, Jack Shoemaker—whose vision, foresight, and faith have guided my work—and Dan Smetanka, Laura Berry, Katherine Kiger, Wah-Ming Chang, Megan Fishmann, Sarah Jean Grimm,

Lena Moses-Schmitt, Dustin Kurtz, Rachel Fershleiser, Selihah White, Lexi Earle, and Yukiko Tominaga.

To everyone at Hurst Publishers who helped bring this story to readers in the UK and beyond, including my insightful and discerning editor, Lara Weisweiller-Wu, and Kathleen May, Rubi Kumari, Raminta Uselytė, Lewis Russell, and Isobel Nutbrown.

To my agent, Michael Carlisle, whose hard work and wise counsel have been indispensable, and Michael Mungiello for his able assistance.

Thanks to the National Endowment for the Arts for my Creative Writing Fellowship, which helped make this work and more possible.

Thanks to the Community of Writers, the National Archives and Records Administration, the Central Intelligence Agency Office of Public Affairs, Memphis Public Libraries, the Mississippi Valley Collection at the University of Memphis, Ambassador Andrew Young, Coby Smith, Calvin Taylor, David Acey, Ron Stallworth, David Garrow, Jennifer Taub, Molly Jong-Fast, Kiese Laymon, W. Ralph Eubanks, Wesley Lowery, Hampton Sides, Dr. Gregg Michel, Flora Rodriguez-Mann, Dr. Hasan Jeffries, Deborah Douglas, Jason Roberts, Kate Crane, and Liz and John Sutton.

I am greatly indebted to the brilliant works of scholarship and literature that informed my understanding of this narrative's historical and social context. These sources include Shirletta Kinchen's *Black Power in the Bluff City: African American Youth and Student Activism in Memphis, 1965–1975* (2016); Wayne Dowdy's *Crusades for Freedom: Memphis and the Political Transformation of the American South* (2010) and *A Brief History of Memphis* (2011); Otis Sanford's *From Boss Crump to King Willie: How Race Changed Memphis Politics* (2017); Laurie Green's *Battling the Plantation Mentality: Memphis and the Black Freedom Struggle* (2007); Hampton Sides's *Hellhound on His Trail: The Stalking of Martin Luther King Jr. and the International Hunt for His Assassin* (2010); Gerald Posner's *Killing the Dream: James Earl Ray and the Assassination of Martin Luther King, Jr.* (1998); David Garrow's *The FBI and Martin Luther King, Jr.: From "Solo" to Memphis* (2015) and *Bearing the Cross: Martin Luther King, Jr. and the Southern Christian Leadership Conference* (2004); Tim Weiner's *Legacy of Ashes: The History of the CIA* (2008);

© Gretchen Adams

LETA McCOLLOUGH SELETZKY is a National Endowment for the Arts 2022 Creative Writing Fellow. A litigator turned essayist and memoirist, she has had work appear in *The Atlantic*; *The New York Times*; *TheGrio*; *The Washington Post*; *O, The Oprah Magazine*; and elsewhere. She holds a BA from Northwestern University and a JD from the George Washington University Law School. She grew up in Memphis, Tennessee, and now lives in Walnut Creek, California. Find out more at letaseletzky.com.

Andrew Young's *An Easy Burden: The Civil Rights Movement and the Transformation of America* (2008); Michael Honey's *Going Down Jericho Road: The Memphis Strike, Martin Luther King's Last Campaign* (2007); Kenneth Bolton Jr. and Joe Feagin's *Black in Blue: African-American Police Officers and Racism* (2004); and Loch Johnson's *A Season of Inquiry Revisited: The Church Committee Confronts America's Spy Agencies* (1985).

Additionally, I relied on numerous historical documents, including FBI reports obtained from the National Archives and Records Administration through the Freedom of Information Act and the King assassination appendix volumes to the House Select Committee on Assassinations Final Report. I also drew on personal interviews, chief among them those with my father.

To Memphis.